D0185095

PATHS
TO PROFICIENCY

HELEN NAYLOR ▶ STUART HAGGER

Longman

ESHER COLLEGE
WESTON GREEN ROAD
THAMES DITTON SURREY

Longman Group UK Limited
Longman House, Burnt Mill, Harlow,
Essex, CM20 2JE,England
and Associated Companies throughout the world

© Longman Group UK Limited 1992

All rights reserved ; no part of this publication may be
reproduced, stored in a retrieval system, or transmitted in any
form or by any means, electronic, mechanical, photocopying,
recording or otherwise, without the prior written permission of
the Publishers.

First published 1992

Set in Garamond Light 10/11.5 pt

Printed and bound in Italy
by Tipolitografia G. Canale & C. S.p.A.– Turin

ISBN 0 582 067577X

Authors' acknowledgements

The authors would like to thank:
Howard Middle (Publisher) for his enthusiasm for the project at
its early stages, Thérèse Tobin (Editor) for her encouragement,
efficiency and good humour, and the staff (particularly Fern
Judet) and students of the Swan School, Oxford.

CONTENTS

General Introduction

Dear Student

Paths to Proficiency *teaches and practises the language and skills that you need in order to reach the level required by the Cambridge Certificate of Proficiency in English. It can also enable you to reach an equivalent standard of English even if you are not attempting the Proficiency Examination itself. It is suitable for you if your general level of English is above 'pass' standard in the Cambridge First Certificate Examination .*

We have designed **Paths to Proficiency** *to help you whether you are working in a group with a teacher or studying alone.*

The course is very clearly organised in six distinct sections, so that you always know which aspect of your English you are working to improve. The six sections concentrate respectively on:

- *Reading* • *Writing* • *Listening* • *Speaking* • *Grammar*
- *Examination practice.*

Every chapter in the first four sections contains important vocabulary enrichment exercises (see Vocabulary Introduction on page viii).

Paths to Proficiency *allows for the possibility that different elements of your English are stronger or weaker than others – perhaps you speak quite fluently, but have problems in writing, for example. If you are studying alone, this means that you can choose your priorities, and concentrate most on those sections where you feel you need most help and practice. If you are working in a group, your teacher will identify communal and individual needs, decide how much work to do on the different skills, and plan the best order to approach them in.*

The clarity and flexibility of the course means that the material can be used in different sequences, and with different intensities, by different people. The only exception to this is that the chapters of the Reading and Listening sections should be worked through in order from beginning to end, since they build up step by step, systematically, from simple to complex problems.

The aim of this course is to make it possible for you to follow your own best route to your destination – an advanced standard in English and success in the Cambridge Proficiency Exam.

There are many paths to proficiency in English: it all depends where you start from, and who you travel with!

Good luck in the exam if and when you take it.

Stuart Hall   Helen Naylor

SPEAKING

GRAMMAR

EXAMINATION PRACTICE

KEY

TV = Topic Vocabulary
VC = Verb Combinations
I/M = Idiom/metaphor
S/V = Special Vocabulary
DV = Descriptive Verbs

Vocabulary Introduction

A good knowledge and use of vocabulary, or lexis, (concrete, abstract and metaphorical) makes the difference between a good intermediate and an advanced learner of English. In all sections of the Proficiency exam, but particularly in the reading and writing sections, the range of vocabulary required is extensive.
The aim of this book is to present and teach lexical items in such a way that you will see/feel a systematic improvement in all areas of your *active* vocabulary.

The vocabulary is woven into the four main skills sections – *Reading*, *Writing*, *Listening* and *Speaking*. It covers the following areas:
- 20 groups of **Topic vocabulary** related to themes: politics, relationships, etc.
- 20 groups of **Verb combinations** organised thematically and by 'preposition': *up*, *through*, etc. (*see below for explanation)
- 20 groups of **Idiomatic expressions** grouped systematically: colour idioms, idioms connected with number, etc.
- 10 groups of **Special vocabulary**: abbreviations, paired nouns, etc.
- 10 groups of **Descriptive verbs**: verbs of walking, holding, etc.

*Throughout the book, the term 'verb combination' is used to cover both phrasal verbs and prepositional verbs – in other words, verbs followed by what look like prepositions, e.g. *come **across**, feel **up to***.
Recognition of the distinction between phrasal and prepositional verbs or of 'adverb particles' does not make them any easier to learn, which is why the term 'verb combination' is used to cover all.
It *is* important to know whether a verb combination is transitive and needs an object, (e.g. *he put off getting a job*), or intransitive and very often followed by an adverb, (e.g. *he turned up late*); and whether the combination can be separated or not (e.g. *she turned off the light*; *she turned the light off*).
The only way to get a complete understanding of any verb combination is to consult a good English–English dictionary; but be careful to check the right definition of the verb combination (some combinations have more than one meaning!).
As you are working through the verb combination exercises, you will notice the words *s'thg* (something) or *s'one* (someone) in places where the position is important for the accurate learning of the phrase.

Vocabulary

Topic vocabulary

Verb combinations

Idiom/metaphor

Special vocabulary

Descriptive verbs

Reading

> Reading is to
> the mind
> what exercise
> is to the body.
> Sir Richard Steele

INTRODUCTION

Reasons for reading

People read, in their own language or a foreign one, because
a) they want to
b) they need to, or
c) they are made to

a) If your aim in reading is pleasure, or instruction, you yourself choose what to read from all the material available; you know in advance what the subject-matter is, and expect to enjoy it or learn from it.
b) If you hope to achieve something as a result of reading (for example an instruction booklet, a textbook, a report, a timetable), you again know the subject-matter, and have a clear and authentic reason for choosing it.
c) If you are *required* to read something and show your understanding of it, as in an examination, many problems arise which do not occur in the 'real' situations described under a) and b). You do not know the subject-matter, or the context, before you start to read. The text may not be one that you would normally choose to read outside the classroom or examination room; and material is always more difficult to understand if it is outside your personal taste, experience or interest. You may not even be allowed the use of a dictionary to help you with words you do not know.

In this section we suggest a systematic approach to solving the problems presented by an 'unseen' text which you are required to read without access to a dictionary.

Approaching the problems systematically

1 Read a paragraph, page or passage in full, preferably more than once, before looking at parts of it that you do not understand.
2 Satisfy yourself that you have a clear idea of what it *is* – a part of a story, a humorous essay, a serious discussion of a topical issue, etc.
3 If there are individual words, word combinations or sentences which you do not understand, use the methods suggested in the following chapters to deduce possible meanings.
4 Always read the whole passage through again before trying to answer questions about it.

CHAPTER 1   Words 1

Unknown words

What to look out for

1   The grammatical function of the word in its sentence.
2   Clues in the word itself (negative prefixes such as **un-** or **dis-**, other prefixes or suffixes such as **re-** or **-ness**). If you know other European languages, do you recognise a possible Latin, Greek or other derivation?
3   Clues in the context of the sentence or paragraph. Does the word seem 'negative' or 'positive'? Does it involve movement? Is it referred to elsewhere by a different name? Could it be a thing, a substance, an emotion?
4   If you replace the word in your mind with a blank space, remembering its 'function', are there *any* words in English or your own language which you could put into this space, which would give a reasonable meaning to the sentence?
5   If there is still something illogical or strange about what you have read, is it possible that the writer may ironically be saying the opposite of what he or she means? (see Chapter 9)
6   Does the general meaning which you have deduced for the 'unknown' word make sense in the context of the whole paragraph or passage, when you re-read it?

1.1 Awareness exercise

Look at the following extract about a man who confuses all his friends by changing the way he uses words. Although the result looks nonsensical, it is easy to deduce all the objects in the last paragraph from the context, and from clues like **at** or **on**.

What's in a name?

'Always the same table,' said the man, 'the same chairs, the bed, the picture. And the table I call table, the picture I call picture, the bed is called bed, and the chair is called chair. Why? The French call a bed 'lee', a table
5 'tahbl', they call a picture 'tahblow' and a chair 'shaze', and they understand each other. And the Chinese understand each other too.'

'Why isn't the bed called picture?' thought the man, and smiled, then he laughed. 'Now things are going to
10 change,' he cried out, and from now on he called the bed 'picture'.

'I'm tired, I want to go to picture,' he said, and often in the morning he would lie in picture for a long time, wondering what he would now call the chair, and he

15 called the chair 'alarm clock'.

So he got up, dressed, sat down on his alarm clock and rested his arms on the table. But the table was no longer called table, it was now called carpet. So in the morning the man left his picture, got dressed, sat down
20 at the carpet on the alarm clock and wondered what to call that.

So the next morning the man lay in picture for a long time, at nine the photograph album rang, the man got up and stood on the wardrobe, so that his feet wouldn't
25 feel cold, then he took his clothes out of the newspaper, dressed, looked into the chair on the wall, then sat down on the alarm clock at the carpet and turned the pages of the mirror until he found his mother's table.

Now, together with a partner if possible, look at the last paragraph of the above text and agree on the meanings of the following:

picture	newspaper	carpet
photograph album	chair	mirror
wardrobe	alarm clock	table

1.2 Awareness exercise

Write a paragraph describing what you did yesterday, replacing some of the verbs with completely different English verbs, or with verbs in your own language (if you are working in a multi-national group). Exchange texts with your friend, and try to deduce what he or she originally wrote.

1.3 Awareness exercise

Read the following sentence and answer the questions which follow.

Her dissertation on the breeding habits of the spur-winged plover was couched in such abstruse terms that nobody could understand it – except possibly a plover, as her professor jocularly suggested.

1   What is the grammatical function of 'couched'?
2   Is 'abstruse' negative or positive in general meaning?
3   If someone handed you a 'dissertation', would you
     a) sit on it?
     b) write it?
     c) read it?
4   Which word(s) give a clue as to what a spur-winged plover is?
5   Which word is the best definition of 'jocularly'?
     a) angrily
     b) humorously
     c) sadly

1.4 Practice exercise

Dervla Murphy is an Irish woman who travels to remote parts of the world on a bicycle. In this extract she is describing the unwanted passionate attentions of a Kurd on the Turkish–Iranian border in 1963.

Read the text below: there are fourteen nonsense words in the text which have been put there in place of fourteen difficult items of vocabulary. As you are reading, see if you can identify these words and at the same time think what real word could be used instead. Look closely at the word endings, which should help you to find alternatives with the same grammatical function.

Fighting back

At Dogubayzit, the last little town en route to the Persian frontier-post, I stayed in the local clong, where my bedroom was a tiny box leading off the wide donk which
5 accommodated the majority of the patrons. This room had a blapy door, without any lecking, and there was no movable piece of furniture which could have been placed against it as a security
10 measure. The scrofous bedding was inhabited by a host of energetic birks, but their attentions were wasted on me and, within minutes of swissing, I was sound asleep.
15   Some hours later I awoke to find myself faltic of bedding and to see a six-foot, nagily-stidded Kurd bending over me in the moonlight. My gun was beneath the pillow and one shot fired at the ceiling
20 concluded the matter. I felt afterwards that my Kurdish tactor had been shown up rather badly; a more shavive admirer, with his physique, could probably have disarmed me without much difficulty.
25   As a result of the loud flashion and my visitor's rapid retreat, there was a minning of many bodies on the floor outside my room and a few sleepy puttings – then quiet.

Vocabulary

Topic vocabulary: fights and violence

Check your understanding of the phrases in the vocabulary bank before doing the exercise that follows.

aggression; aggressive	the armed forces	to invade; an invasion
a threat	troops, rebels, guerillas	to evacuate
a strategy	a professional army	to annex
an outbreak (of violence etc.)	a conscientious objector	to overcome
a dispute	diplomacy	to flee
an incident	conventional, chemical,	to surrender
a fight	nuclear weapons	to dominate; to be dominant
a riot		
	to bully; a bully	
a treaty	to attack	to enlist (in)
a ceasefire (to honour or to break)	to break out	to be conscripted or drafted
a truce	to advance	to do military service
a compromise; to compromise	to deter; a deterrent	to negotiate; negotiations
	to declare war on	to mediate between
	to defend	to struggle for or against
	to retreat	

1.5 Exercise

Complete the following sentences, using the vocabulary from above.

1 In my class at junior school, there was a boy who was very *a* .... He used to *b* ...... the weaker kids and steal their money.
2 *T* ...... loyal to the government *a* ...... the armed *r* ...... who were *d* ...... the northern territories.
3 As the dog *a* ...... , the postman *r* ....
4 The government has decided to *d* ...... *w* ...... on litter louts. They hope the *t* ...... of a heavy fine will *d* ...... people from dropping their rubbish.
5 Residents in Main Street were *e* ...... from their homes last night when a gas leak caused serious problems. Many people were *o* ...... by fumes.
6 In the United States, there is no compulsory *m* ...... *s* .... Young people can choose to *e* ...... in the *a* ...... *f* .... However, during the Vietnam War, many young people were *d* ...... and sent to fight for their country. As in every war, there were some who objected to fighting for moral reasons. These *c* ...... *o* ...... very often had to *f* ...... the country.
7 There was deadlock in the *d* ...... between management and workers over pay, so the conciliation service was brought in to *m* ...... *b* ...... the two sides. Eventually a *c* ...... was reached.
8 Rover the dog was planning his *s* .... Tiddles the cat was lying in her usual place in front of the warm fire, oblivious to what was about to happen. Rover sprang into action and *i* ...... her territory, but Tiddles refused to *s* .... War *b* ...... *o* ...... in front of the fire, and only the skilful *d* ...... of Mrs Smith prevented a sticky end. Rover was placed on the left and Tiddles on the right and, for the moment at least, there was a *t* ...... in the never-ending *s* ...... for supremacy of the fireside.

Current questions

1 Might is more important than right.
2 The United Nations is a toothless organisation.
3 Is it possible to stop the increase of violence?

Verb combinations: 'over'   *Theme: war*

1.6 Exercise

Look at the underlined verb combinations in the text and work out their approximate meanings from the context.

The Funrovian Government at first hoped that the trouble in Azaba would <u>blow over</u> but they soon realised that, unless something was done quickly, civil war would develop. The army minister wanted to send in the troops and this request was <u>thought over</u> very carefully before being agreed to by the central committee. General Gunn <u>took over</u> the leadership of the force from General Cruise who was considered to be too 'soft'.

The troops arrived in Azaba and prepared to fight their fellow countrymen. Although they were professional soldiers, some of the troops were from the region itself and were unhappy about the forthcoming attack. They were keen to <u>get it over with</u> and then they could go back to the capital. General Gunn <u>went over</u> the plan of attack with his commanders and the troops went into battle. The tanks rolled down the main street <u>knocking over</u> the barricades that had been put there by the citizens. Owing to their superior power, the government troops were able to overcome the rebellion and a settlement was reached. Prisoners were <u>handed over</u> to the respective armies and the people were left to clear up and <u>get over</u> the loss of some of their menfolk.

Check with your teacher, or with an English–English dictionary, that you have 'guessed' correctly, then write down the agreed definitions and an example sentence for each one.

1   to blow over ....
    to become less important, to stop being a problem.
2   to think s'thg over ....
3   to take over ....
4   to get (it) over with ....
5   to go over ....
6   to knock over ....
7   to hand over ....
8   to get over s'thg ....

Note also: a takeover, turnover

End of vocabulary

CHAPTER 2 Words 2

Hidden difficulties

> ### What to look out for
>
> You may apparently 'know' all the words, but still find it difficult to understand a sentence. There can be various reasons for this:
>
> 1 You may have misunderstood the grammatical function. Newspaper headlines present particular problems of this kind (see page 119 for more work on headlines) but **-s**, **-ed** and **-ing** can always be misleading, e.g. *This building houses valued items from the last century.*
> 2 Simple words often have more than one meaning (e.g. *purely, pretty, till*) e.g. *I found the way in which he had designed the building pretty ugly.*
> 3 Proper names at the beginning of a sentence cannot be identified by their capital letter.
> 4 Words may be used literally or figuratively. (see Chapter 4)
> 5 Words may have to be understood as combinations, not as individual words. (see Chapters 3 and 4)

2.1 Awareness exercise

Discuss with your partner what grammatical functions the following words can have. Where the word is used in a less common way, think of an illustrative sentence.

e.g. *commercial*: adjective, noun (= a TV advertisement)
Michael Jackson appears in Pepsi-Cola commercials.

short	searching	stroke	reading
past	work	living	lounge
set	talks	record	match

Now look at the following sentences and say what functions the underlined words have. Look back to the points in 'What to look out for' to remind yourself of the possibilities.

1 <u>Support</u> programmes for the unemployed should be introduced.
2 There is one <u>outing</u> to the Eastern Isles weekly, when people <u>view</u> <u>seals</u> and seabirds.
3 No barrister will <u>further</u> her legal career by consistently refusing <u>briefs</u> simply because she does not approve of those she would be required to defend.
4 Murders expose the surroundings in which they happen, and <u>present</u> intimate portraits of stressed human beings which the most <u>searching</u> profiles of the <u>living</u> can never <u>match</u>.
5 Drive, Hackforth! Have you lost yours? We're not the kind of organisation that discards its executives after <u>forty</u>, but we need to be sure that our top people still have all their energies.
6 Reading next stop! He closed his book.
7 <u>Penguins</u> first brought classics of fiction within the price range of ordinary people.
8 Imports <u>Fuel</u> Trade Deficit.
9 £600,000 Health <u>Cuts</u> Spark Row.
10 Many <u>wanted</u> men from high security prisons <u>found</u> hiding in Black Basil's Surbiton <u>retreat</u> were rounded up by the police.
11 Few old parliamentary <u>hands</u> remembered anything like it.

2.2 Awareness exercise

Look at these extracts and answer the questions.

1
KEEP REFRIGERATED
Once pack is opened, eat within two days.
Do not exceed the use by date.

2
No use by unauthorised personnel.

3
This platform for Cambridge.
Over crossing for Royston and Kings Cross.

- In 1, what does 'once' mean?
  a) one time
  b) when
  c) before
- In 1, which words must be understood together?
  a) the use
  b) by date
  c) use by
- In 2, which words must be understood together?
  a) no use
  b) use by
  c) by unauthorised
- In 3, 'crossing' is:
  a) a noun
  b) a participle
  c) a gerund

2.3 Practice exercise

Read the following text and do the exercise which follows.

Are you a lark or an owl?

If you are reading this article over your breakfast table, then you may well be a 'lark' or morning type of person. 'Owls', or evening types, tend not to spend much time over breakfast. They have little appetite then and, as 5 they are usually late risers, they are probably running short of time anyway. The time of day at which one is most alert and mentally at one's best has been studied by those interested in the circadian rhythms.

Around half of the adult population are morning or 10 evening types, the rest fall somewhere in the middle. There can be up to a twelve-hour difference in the time of day when the two types are at their peak. Larks tend to reach this point in the late morning, owls reach it at around 10.00 p.m.

15 Such contrasting times are due to more than just a difference in sleep habits. Larks and owls take similar amounts of sleep, although, as one might expect, larks tend to be 'early to bed early to rise', and owls the opposite. But there is seldom more than a three-hour 20 lag in sleeping times between the two, especially for those who go out to work.

Although the time of peak alertness differs considerably from lark to owl, the circadian rhythms of other body functions, especially that of body 25 temperature, do not differ by more than an hour or so between the two types. In both larks and owls, body temperature reaches its daily peak around 7.00–9.00 p.m. and a trough at about 4.00 a.m.

This is interesting, as it is commonly thought that the 30 circadian rhythm of alertness is closely linked to that of body temperature – more specifically, to brain temperature. That is, the warmer the brain (within limits), the greater the alertness.

Whereas the evidence from evening types tends to

support this hypothesis, with both alertness and brain
temperature rising over the day, morning types tend to
disprove it. Alertness falls from around lunchtime
onwards, with body temperature still rising steadily.

In the 1930s it was thought (wrongly) that the
predisposing factor for being one or other of the types
was a dominance of either the sympathetic or
parasympathetic nervous system. In the 1940s,
Professor William Sheldon, renowned for his
classification of body build, turned his attention to
temperaments. His 'somatotonic' persons (active,
assertive and aggressive people) were claimed to be
clear cut morning types, whereas 'cerebrotonics'
(restrained, inhibited and withdrawn from social

contact) were evening types.

More recently, psychologists have considered owls to
be mainly extroverts and larks introverts. One
explanation for this seeming contradiction is that
extroverts are more inclined to enjoy socialising and
nightlife, and therefore they are more likely to be owls.
But our work at Loughborough has shown that this is
not the case: there is no correlation between
introversion–extroversion and morningness–
eveningness. One can easily find the extroverted
morning type who is the life and soul of the breakfast
table, and the introverted evening type who reads well
into the night. There is, in fact, little by way of obvious
personality differences between the two types.

WHAT'S WRONG WITH YOU? I'VE ALREADY DONE TEN MILES!

Decide which alternative best describes the meaning or function of the words in the passage.

1 *over* (line 1)
   a) above b) at c) on
2 *or* (line 2)
   a) or, in other words b) or, in contrast c) or
3 *risers* (line 5)
   a) verb b) noun c) adjective
4 *running* (line 5)
   a) becoming b) moving quickly c) going
5 *circadian* (line 8)
   a) worldly b) musical c) bodily
6 *fall* (line 10)
   a) descend b) are c) stumble
7 *peak* (line 12)
   a) end b) best c) top
8 *lag* (line 20)
   a) change b) difference c) lack

9 *trough* (line 28)
   a) first point b) worst point c) lowest point
10 *types* (line 34)
   a) verb b) noun c) adjective
11 *onwards* (line 38)
   a) verb b) noun c) adverb
12 Which is the correct combination? (line 47)
   a) clear morning b) cut morning c) clear cut
13 *seeming* (line 52)
   a) verb b) noun c) adjective
14 *life and soul* (line 59)
   a) inspiration b) food and drink c) worst aspect
15 *well* (line 60)
   a) quickly b) late c) clearly

2.4 Summary exercise	Which sentence best summarises the theme of the passage?
	a) If you are reading this article . . . (line 1)
	b) There can be up to a twelve-hour difference . . . (line 11)
	c) The time of day at which one is . . . (line 6)

For discussion

Which is your best time of day? Do you fit into either category above? Should awareness of your 'peaks' and 'troughs' affect how you plan your day, or what work you do?

Vocabulary

Idiom/metaphor: animals (1)

2.5 Exercise

Complete the two-line conversations with one of the 'animal' idioms below, making any necessary changes.

to be a guinea pig
as the crow flies
to have butterflies (in your stomach)
I could eat a horse
to have a bird's eye view of

a dogsbody
to have a frog in your throat
to be a scapegoat
to flog a dead horse
to make head or tail of s'thg

1 A: How far is it from London to Edinburgh?
   B: About 400 miles . . . . . .
2 A: Are you hungry?
   B: Yes, ...
3 A: Why is it always me that gets landed with the boring jobs at work?
   B: You mustn't let yourself be used as . . . . . .
4 A: Can you understand these instructions?
   B: No, I can't . . . . . .
5 A: Why do you keep coughing?
   B: . . . . . .
6 A: This dish is an experiment, I've never made it before. Try some.
   B: No thanks, I don't want . . . . . .
7 A: Did you enjoy your flight over the mountains?
   B: Yes, we had . . . . . .
8 A: Why was I blamed for the wrong information being sent to the newspapers? It really wasn't anything to do with me.
   B: I'm afraid the management needed . . . . . , and you were it!
9 A: Are you nervous about getting married tomorrow?
   B: Yes, I've got . . . . . .
10 A: I've told him many times about his behaviour but he doesn't pay any attention.
   B: I should give up if I were you. You're . . . . . .

Use your artistic talent and draw the correct animal opposite the relevant sentence. It might help you remember the idiom!

Special vocabulary: paired words (nouns)

e.g. 'the <u>life and soul</u> of the breakfast table' (*Larks and owls* text)

2.6 Exercise

First, match the words in Column A to their partners in Column B. Then find the correct definition of the phrase in Column C.

e.g.

Column A	Column B	Column C
aches and	outs	= a person who lives on the streets
down and	pains	= all the details of a situation
ins and	out	= several minor health problems

Answers: aches and pains = several minor health problems
down and out = a person who lives on the streets
ins and outs = all the details of a situation

Column A	Column B	Column C
odds and	goings	= exact data
pros and	downs	= various activities or topics
give and	ends	= advantages and disadvantages
peace and	parcel	= a tingling feeling in your limbs
this and	take	= tranquillity
ups and	figures	= the busy activity at a scene
pins and	cons	= good times and bad times
part and	that	= a variety of different items
comings and	quiet	= an essential component (of a problem)
facts and	needles	= concessions on both sides

Now, with the aid of your dictionary, write ten sentences using the above phrases.
e.g. *It's very difficult to explain the various <u>ins and outs</u> of the leadership struggle.*

End of vocabulary

CHAPTER 3
Word combinations I

> **What to look out for**
>
> 1 Words which may belong together, even though at first sight this is not obvious.
> 2 Verb and preposition combinations (see Vocabulary Introduction page viii).
> 3 'Difficult' looking words which may not be a problem if understood as part of a phrase.

3.1 Awareness exercise

Read the following sentences and, together with a partner, underline/circle the word combinations that have to be understood as a single unit. Then, re-express them in simple language.

e.g. If you're out of sorts, you may have to take time off work.
If you're not feeling very well, you may have to be absent from work.

1 It was touch and go as to which one of them would reach the end first.
2 When you see him in the flesh, he's disappointingly ordinary–looking.
3 Nobody has been granted paid leave before.
4 Our horses were none the worse for their long journey.
5 She felt resentful about always being at his beck and call.
6 There was a time in the Sixties when mini-skirts were all the rage.
7 She was at her wits end after the theft of her credit cards.
8 The old man had kept his wits about him even though he was confined to a wheelchair.
9 He was very hard-working and well-meaning, but prone to errors of judgement.
10 He reached his present position only by dint of hard work.
11 Many people are all too prepared to criticise what they do not understand.

3.2 Awareness exercise

Rewrite the following paragraph, replacing the underlined phrases with the simple definitions given after the text.

'I'll just run through your statement, sir, before we type it up for you to sign,' the desk sergeant told Howard. ' "When my girlfriend chucked me up and turned me out, I was really cut up about it. I think I'd always taken it for granted that she'd put up with me even when I was messing her about. I hit a bit of a low then, and I'll grant you that doing over that shop was out of order – but if you'll let me off this time, I'm determined to go straight." '

tolerate   become depressed   not punish   repeat   assume
behave badly towards   reject   very upset   behave well   eject
wrong   copy   admit   rob

3.3 Practice exercise

Robbery with violence: passage 1

While walking alone in the small hours of the morning in the unfrequented locality of the Great Western Canal, a young man, Mr Peter Baker, observed the body of an
5 individual in difficulties in the water, on the verge of unconsciousness. At great personal risk and totally unaided, he effected a timely rescue. The person having been recovered from the water, it
10 became apparent to Mr Baker that the individual concerned had been the victim of a criminal assault before being unceremoniously pushed into the canal. His attackers had robbed him of all his
15 valuables and had left him to his predicament. Two cars passed by and could scarcely have failed to be aware of the man in the water, but they failed to stop. He was taken, in a critical condition,
20 by Mr Baker to a local inn, where the police were called to interview the victim.

In one simple sentence, say what happened.

Now read a second version of the same incident.

Robbery with violence: passage 2

Right, you ask me what happened last night. Here's the whole story. I'll tell you straight. I missed the last perishing bus and had to walk home along past the canal. It
5 was creepy and dead lonely. Suddenly I saw a hand flapping in the water. I thought that's a stupid place for a midnight swim, then I realised. I dashed down to the edge and there was this bloke half in and half
10 out of the water. Just about had it. I dragged him out and pumped some water out of him and after a long time he came to. Didn't know who he was or how he got there. I sat him up and threw my
15 jacket over him. No wonder he wouldn't talk. He'd been knocked about something awful. Anyway I got some sense out of him and he reckoned he'd been set upon by some thugs who mugged him and
20 shoved him in the canal after they'd nicked all his money. While he was struggling to get out of the water, a couple of cars passed with their headlights full on him; but did they stop? He yelled out but they
25 took no notice. One slowed down but when they saw he was alive they'd left him to make the best of it. Anyway, to cut it short, I carted him off to the King's Arms and told them to clean him up a bit. They
30 called the fuzz and that's that really.

1 Where do you think the two passages might have come from?
2 Which is harder to read/understand, and why?
3 By using Passage 1 to help, can you work out the meanings of the underlined word combinations in Passage 2?

3.4 Practice exercise

Stephen Fry, the journalist and actor, and his father Alan Fry talk about each other. (If possible, Student A should read Alan Fry's story and Student B should read Stephen Fry's version).

Relative values: Alan Fry

I don't think Stephen and I have ever agreed about anything. We've always had a turbulent relationship. I was conscious in his early years of getting in his way because I've always had a big spread of interests;
5 everywhere Stephen looked, there was father telling him how to do it.

When Stephen was small he did virtually nothing except glue himself to the television set while our other children were out and about, doing things. On a fine
10 summer's day he'd draw the curtains and frowst away six inches in front of the black and white screen. As a result he has an encyclopaedic knowledge of films and television from the Sixties.

We were always trying to cajole him into doing things
15 ordinary little boys did, blissfully unaware that ordinary little boy he was not. When he was about 13 he announced that he wasn't going to marry because it was silly, that he was going to be a writer, and that he'd always have plenty of money. As I was struggling to pay
20 his school fees at the time, I was very cross indeed.

For a variety of reasons he left most of the schools he ever set foot in, which was distressing for his mother

and me because we very much wanted him to fulfil whatever it was he had in him. Although we're very
25 different, we both find it difficult to conform; I was never any good at <u>working under people</u>. Stephen found at school that he didn't like being <u>forced into this mould</u> of schoolboy. His mother always <u>had a simple faith in him</u>, that he'd <u>turn out all right in the end</u>; I suppose I didn't
30 really.

In the times when he'd come home from school, we were virtually running a mini-school, in which I taught him maths and physics and a bit of French, and his mother, who is a historian, taught him that.

35 He has a phenomenal memory, just staggering. Also, everything he does is highly original and unexpected. After we'd had one <u>almighty row</u> about something terribly important, like the state of his room, I noticed the house seemed <u>oddly silent</u> and it soon became
40 apparent that Stephen was no longer there. At about ten o'clock that evening, we had a call from the Norfolk and Norwich Hospital saying they had a young man they believed was my son, suffering from loss of memory. He'd walked to Norwich, about ten miles, spent the
45 afternoon watching colour television in the Royal Hotel, and then at about six o'clock, wandered into the casualty department of this hospital, holding his head and saying:

'I don't know who I am.' I arrived there to find this huge form on a trolley, overlapping at either end, moaning
50 gently, and claiming not to know who I was.

It's a big and complex mind, and it would diminish my son to say that I understood him. He's not secretive exactly, but he is strangely private. One sees that paradox in a lot of people who <u>tramp the boards</u>; <u>out of</u>
55 <u>the limelight</u> they tend to be private and shy. We don't agree about alternative comedy; I like my comedy to be bland and untroubling, just to sit there and chuckle. But we both adore John Cleese. I <u>roll about</u> at *Fawlty Towers* and Michael Frayn's play *Noises Off* <u>made my ribs ache</u>.
60 I sometimes feel like saying to him, 'Stop doing this pappy and ephemeral stuff on <u>the box</u> and <u>get down to</u> some serious writing', but it's not really any of my business. It's just that I feel he spends a lot of energy doing things that aren't worthy of him.
65 At an early age one <u>puts one's father on a pedestal</u>; it's not until much later on that one discovers what <u>feet of clay</u> the old fellow really has. Stephen was perhaps a little slower in his disillusionment than he ought to have been. I'm sure if I were attacked he'd be <u>a tiger</u>
70 <u>unleashed in my defence</u> and vice versa. Basically, he's very generous and kind. Everybody likes him.

Relative values: Stephen Fry

I lived in fear of my father until I was about eighteen, fear of the eyebrow and the sniff. In public I had to swallow twice, then cough, and the voice would come out all croaky whenever I tried to speak in his presence. It was
5 very hard to prove myself because he did tend to frown at anything I did with any degree of competence, like learning the entire *Guinness Book of Records* by heart.

The television used to be in my father's study, so I'd have to sneak in when he wasn't there. I think he found
10 my addiction annoying because, as a child, he'd had a phenomenal range of interests, like building speedboats and stripping down motorbikes. Although I was an indiscriminate viewer, I did always want to be part of television. I was an insomniac as an adolescent and I
15 spent a lot of time listening to the BBC World Service. I'm sure that's how I came by my rather strange voice.

My father is a great problem-solver. Just before I was about to sit my maths O-level he found out I could barely add up; I simply hadn't grasped the principles. So
20 he set out to solve the problem of my number blindness, and within a week we were doing things that would have been part of the A-level syllabus.

He balled me out for the minor things, like watching too much television and my messy bedroom, but the big
25 things were always a matter for serious talks. To their eternal credit my parents were much more concerned about my happiness and state of mind than whether or not I was embarrassing their friends.

After I'd left my last school, I pinched a wallet full of
30 credit cards and went ape-shit in about five different counties. The police eventually caught up with me in Swindon. I was given two years' probation, and served a couple of months at a prison called Pucklechurch in Avon. After public school, it was a breeze. Prison turned
35 a corner for me. I enrolled at a sixth form college in Norwich, and went on to sit the Cambridge entrance exam. I won a scholarship.

We do talk and argue all the time when we're together, but now we have quite civilised arguments
40 about the art of science and the science of art.

I do hope he derives some enjoyment from my work. Our relationship is still spiky enough for me not to get many signs that he does. He has always worked phenomenally hard, sometimes even on Christmas Day.
45 While he's not poor, I do feel guilty that the rewards for what I do are so much greater than his, and I'm aware of the absurdity of the recognition for flinging your face around.

It's a splendid marriage, they adore each other, and
50 I've never known them have a cross word. I'd never had to deal with people openly rowing in public. I think sex is terribly stupid, but I now think marriage is actually rather a good idea.

He's rarely given me advice, it's mostly been by
55 example. He is always polite to people, giving them his full attention. Both my parents have a gentleness and fundamental decency which I'm proud of.

When you have read your passage, answer the following questions and then get together with someone who has read the other passage and exchange answers. In this way you can build up a more complete picture of the two people and their relationship.

1 What do they admire in each other?
2 How did TV figure in Stephen's early life?
3 In what ways was Stephen's education unusual?
4 What is/was Stephen's attitude towards marriage?
5 What examples are there of any eccentric/anti-social behaviour?
6 What are their feelings about Stephen's work?
7 In what way has their relationship changed over the years?
8 How does either the father or the son come across to you?

3.5 Practice
Exercise: word combinations

Look at the underlined word combinations; together with your partner, rephrase them.

e.g. glue himself to = *constantly watch*

3.6 Summary exercise	Choose two or three key words from each passage to summarise each writer's view of the other.

For discussion	Do you feel your parent(s) really understand/understood you? Did they ever do something which took you completely by surprise?

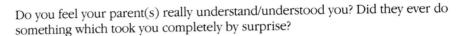

Vocabulary

Topic vocabulary: relationships

Mums and dads, brothers and sisters – these words are no problem; but in the following sentences, can you name either the people or the family situations that are described?

3.7 Exercise

1   Your father marries again. His new wife has two children, a boy and a girl. How are you and the new wife related? And how are you and the two children related?
2   Your sister's son is your ......
3   When you are married, your spouse's parents are your ....
4   If your spouse dies, you are described as a ...... (woman) or a ...... (man).
5   Your grandfather's mother is your ....
6   When a child is baptized in the Christian church, a man or a woman agrees to take responsibility for their religious/moral upbringing. These people are the child's ......
7   A child whose family dies for whatever reason is an ....
8   In some countries it is the custom for only the mother, father and children to live together. This is called a .... family. In other countries, the grandparents, aunts, uncles and cousins also share the same house. This is a(n) .... family.
9   People in your family who lived a long time ago are called your ....
10 For official documents you are often asked to name the person who is your closest living relative. This person is described as your ......

3.8 Exercise

to be close to someone
to get on (well, badly) with someone
to be on good terms with someone (*more businesslike*)
to have a lot in common with someone
to have (great) respect for someone
to have a good or bad relationship with someone
to have a close friendship with someone
to be tolerant of someone
to be jealous or envious of someone
to drift apart (from someone)
to hate the sight of someone

Use the phrases above to talk about/describe your relationship with:
your brother/sister
your mother/father
a childhood friend

Current questions

1   Is it better to have brothers and sisters or to be an only child?
2   Do you think marriage is a better institution for men or for women?
3   Friends or family – which is more important in your life?

Verb combinations: 'out'   *Theme: education*

3.9 Exercise   Work out the approximate meanings of the underlined verb combinations below.

1 Teachers have to <u>carry out</u> many duties apart from just teaching, so it's not surprising that, by the end of a term, most feel the job has <u>worn them out</u> and they need a rest.
2 'Janet, I'd like you to <u>hand out</u> these books to the class and then, children, I want you to <u>work out</u> the answers to exercise 9 on page 20.'
3 In a mixed ability class, some pupils will <u>stand out</u> as above average in intelligence, whereas others who are more shy will need to <u>be drawn out</u> before the teacher can assess their level.
4 When supervising children in the playground, teachers have to <u>look out</u> for troublemakers. It is also necessary sometimes to stop fighting <u>breaking out</u> among the boys.
5 During exams, pupils have been known to <u>pass out</u> owing to stress and anxiety. Others sit there watching the clock, knowing that time is <u>running out</u>.

Check with your teacher, or an English–English dictionary, that you have 'guessed' correctly.

- to carry out ....
- to wear s'one out ....
- to hand out/give out ....
- to work out ....
- to stand out ....
- to draw out/bring out ....
- to look out (for) ....
- to break out ....
- to pass out ....
- to run out ....

Now choose six of the above phrases and write sentences of your own.

Note also: a handout; a lookout; an outbreak; a breakout; an outlook

End of vocabulary

CHAPTER 4
Word combinations 2

Figurative use of language

What to look out for

1   Words used singly or in combinations, whose literal meanings you may know, but which are being used more 'colourfully': often these will be well-established 'idioms', whose meaning can be found in a dictionary.
2   Metaphorical use of words – describing something more vividly by using language from a different context.
3   Similes – comparing something colourfully with something unexpected – introduced by **like** or **as**.

4.1 Awareness exercise

In each of the following sentences, underline the words which do *not* have their normal, literal meanings; if possible, rewrite the sentence replacing the words with non-figurative language

e.g. He came <u>thundering</u> into my office like a <u>herd of wild bulls</u>.

He came into my office very noisily, (and angrily?)

1   Although I had no reason to believe the police were waiting for me, I walked straight past the restaurant without going in: I suppose something just smelled fishy.
2   The snow lay in a thin covering on the hillsides, like long torn bedsheets, the earth showing through in black streaks.
3   Vodka is said to bequeath no headache to its victims, only a painless anaesthesia, but my head throbbed and filled my eyes with lead.
4   I was deeply wounded by what she said.
5   You'll recognise her by her flaming red hair.
6   What a pig he is! Look at the way he shovels food into his mouth!
7   After the wedding, well-wishers launched our raft with champagne; lashed together, not far out, we sank.
8   They stared out of the train windows at the houses, and the houses returned the stares.
9   Like triffids on the march, politicians have surged out of their normal habitats – Newsnight, Any Questions, Question Time, Today in Parliament, World at One, People and Politics, party political broadcasts and every news programme – and are intent on colonising hitherto politician-free zones, popping up in situation-comedies, in plays, on videos, on panel games, in pulpits.
10 The Fitness Action Research Trust is a rubber-stamp organisation set up by the beer trade to investigate everything but the effects of alcohol. When the Government's own Commission for Research into Alcohol Problems crossed swords with it recently over the extent of alcohol addiction among young drinkers, it was the latter, not the former, who were carpeted by Whitehall.
11 Steering a perilous course through icy, uncharted political waters, Captain Jacques-Yves Cousteau was in dangerous mood launching his campaign to save the Antarctic in Britain this week.

4.2 Awareness exercise

In the following short passage, the writer describes her reactions to being married: underline any examples of figurative language, metaphor or simile.

Growing out of marriage

For a few years I was satisfied enough, the drama of my life absorbed me, it was a stage and I was the star. First a house to play with and later, in case the audience began to cough and fidget, a pregnancy to hold them riveted.
5 Later, like Alice in Wonderland, I came across the cake labelled 'eat me' and whenever my husband was away at work, I ate and I grew. My legs stuck out of the windows, my arms snaked round the doors, my head above an endless neck loomed through the chimney and
10 my heartbeat rocked the room. Each day, just before 5 p.m., I nibbled the other side of Alice's cake and, in the nick of time, shrank to being a little woman again. Hullo, darling, how was your day? Me? Oh, nothing happened. Terrified, I knew that one day I wouldn't make it down
15 again and my husband, returning from work, would fall back in horror at the monster who had taken over his home and push me out into the big wide world.

4.3 Awareness exercise

In the following passage, the writer is describing tourists at Ephesus in Turkey, but using language normally associated with the description of a military invasion. Read carefully, and answer the questions which follow.

Tourist invasion

But at Ephesus, in September temperatures that had leapt into the 90s, I was truly in the combat zone, with St Paul's Ephesus the prime object of attack. Here, quite apart from the lowly infantry disgorged from all the
5 bellies of all the coaches, I had to contend with a regiment of crack tourist troops, old stagers in these campaigns, an elite army from the cruise liners, who had taken the beach head at Izmir the previous day and were now advancing inland. Hordes of hefty vintage
10 Americans in Pierre Cardin slacks and baseball caps, with their camp following of dripping rich women in silk trouser suits, jangling bangles, orange lipstick. The lower ground at Ephesus was stormed at once, the bastions of the city overwhelmed half an hour later with only a few
15 casualties – an American dame of the blue rinse brigade fainted on the steps of Hadrian's temple, another in quite unsuitable Gucci sandals cut down with a sprained ankle while attempting to force a passage up the Arcadian Way. The sun was at its height as the
20 marauding army took a final victory, completely engulfing the city, gorging on the spoils of victory, not with eyes or minds but only through the lenses of a thousand Pentaxes and camcorders, so that the air was filled with a cicada-like clicking and whirring.

1 Underline all the words or phrases involving 'military' vocabulary.
2 Substitute alternative words or phrases of a non-military nature

e.g. in the combat zone = *in an area with a large number of tourists*

the prime object of attack = *their principal destination*

3 Why do you think the writer chooses to write in this way, and do you think it is effective?

4.4 Practice exercise: two stories of childhood

Work in pairs. One of you read Text A on the next page and the other Text B on page 240. Tell your partner the story using non-figurative language.
Use the following questions to help you focus your thoughts.
1 What's the paragraph about (1 sentence answer)?
2 What does it show of the author's feelings?
3 Describe what happened either on that day (Text A) or in general (Text B).

Text A: Concert for two

Smirking with misery I walked to the stage. Eileen's face was as white as a minim. She sat at the piano, placed the music crooked, I straightened it, it fell to the ground. I groped to retrieve it; we looked at one another with
5 hatred; the audience was as still as death. Eileen tried to give me an A, but struck a B instead, and I tuned up like an ape threading needles. At last we were ready, I raised my fiddle; and Eileen was off like a bolting horse. I caught her up in the middle of the piece – which I believe was a
10 lullaby – and after playing the repeats, only twice as fast, we just stopped, frozen, motionless, spent.

Now read each other's texts, identify the examples of figurative language, and discuss which parts you find particularly successful.

Vocabulary

Idiom/metaphor: adjective intensifiers

4.5 Exercise   Match the intensifiers with their adjectives.

e.g. squeaky   sober
        filthy   clean
        stone-cold   rich
   Answers:
        squeaky clean
        filthy rich
        stone-cold sober

Intensifiers	**Adjectives**
crystal	drunk
razor	upright
freezing	new
boiling	wet
soaking	black
rock	dry
bone	broke
filthy	asleep
pitch	awake
brand	thin
stark	dirty
fast	sharp
blind	clear
flat	cold
bolt	hard
wide	hot
wafer	naked

Now describe
a)   yourself after a 25 km. walk in the rain!
b)   a cowboy asleep in the desert.
c)   the scene at the party following Elizabeth Taylor's most recent wedding.

Special vocabulary: similes

As in most languages, there are many recognised similes in English, that is descriptive phrases made up of **as** . . . **as** (*as quick as a flash*) and **like** . . . (*like greased lightning*).

4.6 Exercise

Re-express each sentence on the left by using one of the similes on the right. The beginning of the new sentence has been underlined.

e.g. She *spends money like water*.

1	She is very forgetful.	–money like water
2	She ran very fast.	–like a bomb
3	She slept very deeply.	–like a sieve
4	She didn't 'fit' with the others.	–like a bull in a china shop
5	She is very wasteful with money.	–like a log
6	Her car goes fast, despite its age.	–like a fish out of water
7	She's always knocking things over.	–like a bat out of hell
8	She only weighs 45kgs.	–as dead as a dodo
9	The village has no 'life' after 8.00 p.m.	–as light as a feather

4.7 Exercise

Now create your own! Similes make language colourful and they can be used very creatively to express your feelings.

For the following, think of a colourful way to finish these sentences by using a simile. Think of the qualities that you associate with your simile, then say or read your sentence to your neighbour and see if he or she can imagine what you were trying to convey.

e.g. He had eyes like …

> *stones* (cold and hard)
> *or*
> *velvet* (soft and warm)

1	She had hair like …	4	Her car made a noise like …
2	The grass was as … as …	5	The desert was as … as …
3	The bed was as soft as …	6	She moved like …

End of vocabulary

CHAPTER 5   Sentences I

> **What to look out for**
>
> 1 Words may have been omitted, because they are grammatically unnecessary if the sentence can be understood without them.
> 2 Punctuation may convey meaning (especially commas).

5.1 Awareness exercise

Add **which**, **who(m)**, **that**, **when**, or a phrase introduced by one of these words, to each of the following sentences to make them easier to understand.

e.g. It can be embarrassing to be in the company of someone you are not acquainted with and not to speak to them.

Answer: ... someone ***who(m)*** you are ...

1 There is little doubt the teenager the police have arrested is completely innocent.
2 Unfortunately the train I jumped onto was going in the wrong direction.
3 Those friends we had disappeared from sight, just like that.
4 The time I was out of work was very difficult for me and my family.
5 It's extremely dangerous to reheat meat already cooked and left unrefrigerated.
6 You'll probably be horrified at the amount drinks bills work out at here, I'm afraid.
7 Earthquakes are most commonly caused by the jar given the earth's surface when a fault occurs.
8 The sweet little kitten I had started to show me who was going to be boss.

5.2 Awareness exercise

Although the sentences below are correct, it is possible to add words which may make the meaning easier to understand. Supply the 'missing' words. The first five sentences are marked * to show where the word(s) should be inserted. In the last five sentences, you have to decide where and what to add.

1 In the winters, the cattle were herded in from the fields and the sheep * from the hills.
   (* ....)
2 Although it doesn't state in your contract that you must arrive at school before 9.20, I really think you should * . After all, your salary is high, and your holidays * generous.
   (* ....) (* ....)
3 As far as food was concerned, we were assured that plenty * would arrive; but somehow, it never seemed to * .
   (* ....) (* ....)
4 Bill brought the brushes, Lenny * the ladder, and Peter * the paint.
   (* ....) (* ....)
5 I was delighted to hear from Sue again and, despite the opposition of my wife, * agreed to meet her.
   (* ....)
6 The reaction is irrational, and therefore ineffectual as a means of defence.
   (..........)

7   Dogs and cats are capable of calming and reassuring people, particularly when ill, lonely or afraid.
    (. . . . .)

8   Journalists may well feel angry if asked to rewrite articles they had thought acceptable.
    (. . . . .) (. . . . .) (. . . . .)

9   Disowned by her family, cut off from everything she knew and loved, she found her will to fight on was quickly eroded, and her spirit broken.
    (. . . . .) (. . . . .) (. . . . .)

10 The manager saw John's success as a fluke, and his popularity with the workers in terms of weakness.
    (. . . . .)

5.3 Awareness exercise

Notice the use or omission of commas in these sentences, and answer the questions.

1   Every year, he sent a Christmas present to the headmaster who had advised him not to become a teacher, at any cost.

    Had he received advice from more than one headmaster, or only one?
    (see Grammar: Chapters 14 and 15 for further work on relative clauses.)

2   **A:** Which island would you prefer to spend the weekend on?
    B: Lindisfarne, or Holy Island.
    A: And the summer holidays?
    B: Oh, definitely Alderney or St Agnes.

    How many islands are referred to, two, three or four?

3   She chose the least expensive package holiday, which offered a week in Hull.

    Was there more than one Hull holiday?
    (see Grammar: Chapters 14 and 15 for further work on relative clauses.)

4   It was a pretty old house.
    It was a pretty, old house.

    What is the difference?

5.4 Practice exercise

Read the text on the next page and do the exercise which follows.

London

There is a Third World feel to many parts of London: people queueing outside post offices and benefit offices; beggars; plastic bags full of rubbish everywhere; tatty goods in the shops. In a city with tens of thousands of
5 homeless people, and as many brand new cars, the contrast between private wealth and public poverty has become almost intolerable over the last ten years, and now healthcare is set to go the same way.

There have also been changes for the better. When I
10 first moved here, London was a culinary desert with no decent cup of coffee to be found. The word 'café' was synonymous, not with coffee and cake but with greasy food, and wine with overpriced sugarwater. During my first few years, all visitors from Germany had to bring
15 enormous food parcels full of real bread, real coffee, real chocolate, etc. Maybe I felt insecure. Now every supermarket sells ground coffee, and I can buy *Lebkuchen* from my local garage. Thanks to those deplorable yuppies, off-licences now have affordable as
20 well as drinkable wines, and I can swill champagne in wine bars instead of going to a pub – the only British intitution I have never learned to love.

London is, of course, different from other big cities in Britain. No other city is so much like a whole country in
25 itself, a whole continent; it is hard to think of leaving, once established. Life in London is anonymous, certainly, and many people are isolated. But isn't this also why they came to live here? If you want to know all your neighbours and all the gossip, you live in the villages.
30 London is a city of privacy, but a place where you can also say hello to the greengrocer or the garage cashier. It is exciting, full of things no one needs, full of useless discoveries, cinemas you will never go to, bands you will never hear, restaurants you might one day go to. The
35 only really negative factor is provided by its size – visiting a friend in another part of town can be a day trip.

I also enjoy the feeling of living in a city I still don't quite know. After twelve years here I still discover new walks by the river or along the canals, parks I have never
40 walked in, or some old bridge or railway station. There are dozens of galleries and museums I still haven't seen, and I can shop at any time of day or night. In Munich, I hated the deadness that descends on the city at the weekend. Life there stops by noon on Saturday, and if
45 you don't do your shopping by then, you eat out or not at all. No sweat in London.

Based on the text, write questions to produce the following answers. When you have finished, work with a partner and take it in turns to speak the questions and answers. Decide which are the best questions, yours or your partner's.

e.g. Answer: They reminded me of a Third World city.
    Question: *What impression did the contrasts that you saw in London between poverty and wealth make on you?*

1 Answer: At the moment, by the large numbers of homeless, and the large numbers of new cars.
2 Answer: The same thing will probably happen – it'll become divided between the rich and the poor.
3 Answer: Overpriced sugar water.
4 Answer: Because I knew those things would be difficult, or impossible, to find.
5 Answer: Because the yuppies demanded it.
6 Answer: It's hard, especially when you've been here a while.
7 Answer: Because they enjoy leading anonymous lives.
8 Answer: No, not at all. I'm still discovering things.
9 Answer: Two things, pubs and the size of the place.
10 Answer: London is alive at weekends whereas Munich is dead from Saturday afternoon onwards.

5.5 Summary exercise

Which of the following titles do you feel is most appropriate as a summary of the whole passage?
a) London in decline
b) Absence is such sweet sorrow
c) I am not a tourist, I live here
d) London times are changing

For discussion

Can one ever feel truly at home living in a foreign country?

Vocabulary

Topic vocabulary: travel and tourism

5.6 Exercise   Read the text 'Travel: no thanks' on the next page, paying particular attention to the underlined words and phrases.

Travel: no thanks

Travel is said to broaden the mind. But does it really do this for the majority of people who go abroad? Imagine a typical tourist who goes to another country on a package holiday. He probably travels at peak time when the airports are crowded and unpleasant. If he's lucky, his charter flight will only be delayed a few hours. When he arrives at his destination, he may well find that the facilities promised in the holiday brochure are not up to expectations. What looked like unspoilt countryside (in the brochure) will probably turn out to be an over-commercialised area where tourists have no chance at all of meeting any of the local people – they, very wisely, have escaped before the annual invasion. The only local people he will meet are the over-worked waiters and hotel staff who will be only too happy to 'perform' for the tourist and thus confirm his stereotyped idea of a Greek or Spaniard. The tourist will go home with little or no new insights into another culture and with most of his prejudices reinforced. Why travel?

Agree definitions for the underlined words and phrases.
e.g. brochure = a publicity booklet, with pictures

Current questions

1 What is the cartoon on page 25 saying about air travel today?
2 Tourism brings more advantages than disadvantages to the host country.
3 Holidays abroad are just another kind of status symbol.

Verb combinations: 'through'   *Theme: travel and transport*

5.7 Exercise

Match the verb combinations on the left with their definitions on the right.

- to fall through =   to connect two people on the 'phone
- to see through s'thg =   to complete s'thg despite problems
- to get through (to s'one) =   to experience/suffer
- to put s'one through =   to pass/succeed
- to go through s'thg =   to make contact with
- to break through =   to fail (particularly a plan)
- to see s'thg through =   to make an important advance
- to get through s'thg =   to be able to see the reality behind the story

Now complete the following sentences using the correct forms of the verb combinations from the left-hand column above.

1 Scientists claim to have .... in the race to launch a manned flight to Uranus.
2 His plan to travel round the world .... In the end, he only got as far as India.
3 My car broke down on the ring road and I spent the next two hours trying to .... to the emergency breakdown service.
4 I .... agony every time I travel by air. It makes going on holiday a torture.
5 Now that we've made all the plans for the expedition, we'll have to .... to the end even though we don't want to.
6 It's much more difficult to .... a driving test in Japan than it is in England.
7 When he rang to ask about the arrival of Pan Am flight 324, he was .... to immigration control by mistake.
8 The information desk official said the flight was full. It didn't take a mind reader to .... that excuse. I knew she was just feeling too lazy to try and help me.

Note also: a breakthrough (it is more commonly used as a noun than in verb form)

End of vocabulary

CHAPTER 6   Sentences 2

> **What to look out for**
>
> Words such as **it**, **this**, **that**, **such**, **one**, **his**, **they**, **the former**, and many others, which refer to people, facts, ideas etc. elsewhere in the sentence or text. It will be impossible to understand the sentence unless you identify exactly what these words represent.

6.1 Awareness exercise

Read each of the following short texts carefully, noticing how certain words refer back to earlier subject matter, and then say what each of the underlined words or phrases describes.

e.g.   Let me have men about me that are fat;
Sleek-headed men, and <u>such</u> as [=who] sleep o' nights:
Yond Cassius has a lean and hungry look;
He thinks too much: <u>such men</u> are dangerous.
such = *the kind of men*
such men = *men who, like Cassius, look lean & hungry and think too much*

1   What on earth do children gain from being at school? If we dismiss the need to acquire social skills – they pick <u>these</u> up <u>outside</u> anyway – we are left with the idea that they're <u>there</u> for <u>their</u> own protection.
these ....   there ....
outside ....   their ....

2   I am cheered – although also ashamed – that the US public appears to be putting more pressure on its government to avoid war in the Gulf than we are putting on <u>ours</u>. A major reason for <u>this</u> must be that the Americans' recent experience of war is of a long drawn out struggle which was ultimately lost, whereas <u>ours</u> was of <u>one</u> that was short and victorious.
As any Gulf war seems more likely to resemble <u>the former</u>, I hope that our lack of experience of <u>such</u> a war does not mislead us into acquiring <u>it</u>.
ours ....   the former ....
this ....   such ....
ours ....   it ....
one ....

3   He must, therefore, be able to justify the choices he makes, and <u>this</u> obviously limits his subjectivity.
this ....

4   The Conservatives are in turmoil because the economy is in recession; but <u>that</u> is a party issue. <u>So</u>, too, is the Prime Minister's personality.
that ....   So ....

5   The language of amateur writers is generally rather less well-constructed than <u>that</u> used by professional writers. <u>This</u> often leads to a less readable style.
that ....   This ....

6 School is for work. It is an institution. Why put children in an institution? The real reason is that <u>it</u> gets the brats out from under the parents' feet. The purported reason is that <u>this</u> is the best way to get useful information into the skulls of the little darlings.

it ....   this ....

7 Eighty per cent of lower back problems are the result of too little movement rather than <u>too much</u>. Prolonged sitting, for example, leads to inflexibility, and adaptive shortening of the hip flexor and hip rotator muscles. <u>This</u>, in turn, leads to skeletal imbalance and subsequent back pain.

too much ....   This ....

8 Reduction in the support available to the voluntary sector is likely to result in a rise in the demands made directly to the Social Services Department, and <u>thus</u> in the cost of providing services.

thus ....

9 I spend too much of the time when I should be asleep agonising over the problem of mind versus body, as psychiatrists would describe <u>it</u>. <u>That</u>, for me, is what is of most concern during <u>those</u> long, anxious, open-eyed hours.

it ....   those ....

That ....

10 In the sixteenth century most meat was cooked by heating it over a fire. The effectiveness of <u>this</u> depended on what you were cooking, how hot the fire was, and how long the cooking lasted. Too much smoke probably meant that the bacteria-ridden meat was not cooking thoroughly. <u>This</u> could seriously increase the danger of disease, <u>as</u> is still the case with some methods of cooking today.

this ....   as ....

This ....

6.2 Practice exercise

Fill in the gaps in the following text using words that refer back to something that has already been mentioned. The first two have been done for you. Examples: 'Neolithic Britons' indicates that gap (1) must be filled by something which refers back to them, and which fits grammatically into the space – *their* is the best answer; 'first gods' is the phrase to which gap (2) refers, so the best answer is *them*.

Early Britons

Long before the pyramids were planned, <u>Neolithic Britons</u> raised stone circles on sites sacred to (1) .... gods. Who those <u>first gods</u> of Britain were we do not know, all that remains of (2) .... are the
5 enigmatic monuments. Perhaps a trace of them lingers in a ring of dancers whirling on a village green, or in some folk ritual whose origins passed out of memory centuries ago.

The people who worshipped the forgotten gods
10 began to drift into Britain 5,500 years ago when (3) .... had become separated from the Continent. When (4) .... settled to become agriculturists, their awareness of the seasons must have been the most important factor in (5) .... communal lives. They had
15 to be in harmony with nature, and if the gods who personified (6) .... could be influenced, so much the better.

It was most likely to this end that prehistoric man left his signature on our landscape – amazingly, hundreds of
20 stone circles still stand in the British Isles apart from monoliths, cromlechs and barrows.

The calendar by which (7) .... lived has blended into the religions which followed and today – when nature is at last under threat from man – festivals which
25 once marked the winter solstice or the arrival of summer are still the landmarks of our year.

The polished flint of the Neolithic people gave way before the bronze of the Beaker people, who in turn retreated from the iron-wielding Celts 2,500 years ago.
30 And it is with (8) .... that British mythology begins, confused though (9) .... is.

Although much of Europe was once the home of the Celtic people, most of the information about (10) .... mythology comes from the British Isles, particularly

35 Wales and Ireland, where stories and sagas were preserved. (11) .... tell us enough for it to be realised that Celtic mythology has an Indo-European background.

What makes (12) .... difficult when trying to get a 40 picture of their beliefs is that more than 400 names of Celtic gods are known. It would seem that every tribe had (13) .... own tutelary deity, and (14) .... is endorsed by the Irish sagas when it was usual for a person taking an oath to say 'I swear this by the god by 45 whom my tribe swears'. (15) .... also suggests a taboo against speaking the name of the tribal god, or at least taking (16) .... in vain.

6.3 Practice exercise

With reference to the passage, make the questions for the following answers.

1 Answer: Only the monuments.
2 Answer: About 5,500 years ago.
3 Answer: In order to influence the gods of nature.
4 Answer: No, not with the Beaker people but the Celts.
5 Answer: By examining the stories and sagas of the Celtic people.
6 Answer: Because there were so many Celtic gods.
7 Answer: It seems that it was taboo.

6.4 Summary exercise

What is the main theme of the text?
a) early British gods
b) early religion
c) the importance of the Celts
d) the beginnings of British mythology
e) ancient monuments and stone circles

Which sentence(s) in the text support(s) your opinion?

Vocabulary

Idiom/metaphor: time

6.5 Exercise

The text on *Early Britons* talked about a time long past; now look at the following expressions related to time. Match each one with one of the definitions.

• Let's call it a day.	= well before the deadline
• He left on the dot of 6.00.	= a disastrous day
• You can stay here for the time being.	= spontaneously
• She goes to bed in the early hours.	= give pleasure
• We decided on the spur of the moment.	= at 3 a.m. or 4 a.m.
• Some good news can make my day.	= just before it's too late
• I like to arrive at the airport in good time.	= at exactly that time
• It was just one of those days.	= very quickly / soon
• He'll be here in no time (at all).	= finish what we're doing
• She left the building in the nick of time.	= temporarily

Complete the following sentences using one of the above 'time' expressions.

1 It's impossible to make such a big decision ...... ; I need to think about it first.
2 The photocopier has broken down, and now the car won't start – I guess it's just going to be ......
3 Don't worry, the ambulance is on its way. It'll be here ......

4 He's a very precise sort of person. If his meeting is at 9.30 a.m. then he will arrive at 9.30 ......

5 This solution may not be perfect, but we have to make a quick decision: I believe that .... we should leave things the way they are.

6 Last night I was frying some steak when the telephone rang. I started talking and forgot the steak. Suddenly I smelt something burning so I rushed into the kitchen and turned off the gas .....!

Now write your own sentences with the four remaining expressions.

Verb combinations: miscellaneous   *Theme: faith*

6.6 Exercise   Fill the following sentences with any word or phrase that makes sense.

1 He was a fanatical supporter of Liverpool United football club, which explains why his children have such curious names: they were all .... players in the team.

2 When she attended a revivalist meeting at the village hall, she was .... the amount of energy that was put into the singing.

3 Some evangelists, like Billy Graham, are very skilful at .... their message to large audiences.

4 I know many people don't believe in astrology as a guide to the future, but the astrologist I went to see last week .... a genuine and sincere person.

5 I know you have faith in your invention, but don't .... just yet or you may be disappointed – we've got to find someone to finance and develop it.

6 Towards the end of his life, a devout Buddhist may .... all his possessions to the poor and become a beggar himself.

7 My father really believed I would .... him in every way, including the way I looked. Naturally, I made every effort to do the opposite.

8 The family was .... by the different loyalties of the brothers – one supported the Catholic cause and the other the Protestant cause.

9 Although you haven't seen your cousin for years, she always .... you. She has always supported you through thick and thin.

The following verb combinations are in the same order as the sentences above. Together with a partner, discuss the best definitions, after looking back at the ideas you have already had.

- to be named after ....
- to be taken aback (by) ....
- to put across ....
- to come across (as) ....
- to get carried away ....
- to give away ....
- to take after s'one ....
- to be pulled/torn apart ....
- to ask after s'one ....

For further practice choose six of the above phrases and use them in your own sentences.

End of vocabulary

CHAPTER 7 Sentences 3

What to look out for

1   The underlying basic subject–verb–object structure in long or complex sentences.
2   Inversion of the normal word order.
3   Multiple or confusing negatives, including inherently negative words such as **lack, deny, neglect, ignore, hardly, few**.

7.1 Awareness exercise

Answer the questions that follow these short passages. Also discuss which of the three points above are the causes of the confusion in each of the extracts.

1   The letter he composed immediately, but the phone call he put off until later.
    – What is the basic subject–verb–object pattern in this sentence?
2   It was not that he was not keen on Pat, . . .
    – Did he like Pat at all?   YES/NO
3   While these fears should not be minimised, it should be observed that the lack of such comprehensive records in the past has never been any obstacle to the suppression of personal freedom.
    – Should one take any account of the 'fears'?   YES/NO
    – Have there previously been such comprehensive records?   YES/NO
    – Has there been suppression of people's freedom in the past?   YES/NO
4   It being not only possible but even quite simple to predict which youngsters are at greatest risk of growing up with sexist and racist attitudes to life, what action are we taking on the basis of this information?
    – Can we predict which youngsters will probably grow up with the attitudes described?   YES/NO
    – What is the 'information'?
5   Mordaci walked across the compound with a satisfied smile. It may be that had he known that Tony had spoken to him simply because it was part of his duty to detain him for as long as he could – or had he even guessed that, somewhere beneath his feet as he stood talking, the sacred soil of Italy was being excavated at the rate of more than a square yard a day – it is possible that had he known all this, his smile might have been less complacent.
    – Did he know why Tony had really spoken to him?   YES/NO
    – Whose duty is 'his' – Mordaci's or Tony's?
    – What two things does 'this' in the last line refer to?
6   The study of factors relevant to the historical development of verbal communication makes it clear that it became the usual manner of communication for most human interactive activities mainly because such activities themselves changed in nature.
    – What is 'it' (second 'it' in line 2)?
    – Did people always communicate in words?   YES/NO
7   The twin revelations of Parkinson's Law of Delay with its insights into human motivation and motives, and the Peter Principle, which makes clear the dubious validity of perceived status and apparent achievement in business or professional life, have called into question the traditional respect accorded to, and expected by, the more visibly successful members of society.
    – What is the subject of the verb 'have called'?

8 The announcement of the withdrawal of the Prime Minister's decision to resign by the Chancellor of the Exchequer must have had an extremely damaging, and indeed possibly disastrous, effect on the morale of members of the party.
 – What is the subject of the sentence?
 – Who made the announcement?
 – What was the announcement about?

9 Such a reaction is, when all is said and done, comprehensible if not entirely defensible, especially at a time of much corporate hysteria about the need to embrace information technology, to take the chip on board or go under, without the laudable generalisations having yet been translated (except in a few worthy instances) into practicalities.
 – Do we know exactly what the 'reaction' was?   YES/NO
 – Do 'embrace information technology' and 'take the chip on board' have similar meanings, or different?

10 Nobody who has not been orbiting the earth in a redundant Russian space capsule for the past ten years can fail to know that high fibre diets are good for you.
 – Who *can* be expected to know that such diets are good for you?

11 The principle has often been quoted that 'Opinions are free but facts are sacred'. This presupposes that 'facts' can be related with complete objectivity. That this is not the case is perfectly obvious.
 – Rewrite the third sentence beginning: *It* . . .
 – What is 'this' (line 2)?
 – What is 'this' (line 3)?

12 The sight of the Earth from the Moon forces us to think of it as small and fragile: it makes less sensible the arbitrary division of its surface into portions that we must think of as sacred.
 – What is 'it' (line 1)?
 – What is 'it' (line 2)?
 – What is 'its' (line 2)?
 – What is 'less sensible'?

13 As readers of popular literature, our main requirement is that the author gets on with the story and doesn't allow anything to interfere with the narrative, and this she invariably does.
 – Who is 'she'?
 – Who 'does' what?
 – What does 'this' refer to?

14 It is no disgrace not to find your favourite painting there.
 – If the painting you like most is absent, is this very bad?   YES/NO

15 The fact that there are often more police where the rate of certain types of crime has actually fallen has little to do with their success in controlling or even eliminating them.
 – To whose success does 'their' refer?
 – What are 'them'?
 – Rewrite the phrase 'has little to do with', to include the words 'connection' and 'much'.

16 (Talking about overcrowding on the London Underground)
 'We'd probably all kill each other if we had room to move. Only if we had room to move, we wouldn't want to, would we? You can't say London Transport haven't got it all figured, can you?'
 – What wouldn't we want to do?
 – London Transport haven't managed things very well.   TRUE/FALSE

7.2 Practice exercise

Read the following text and answer the questions which follow.

Unemployment

I first became aware of the unemployment problem in 1928. At that time I had just come back from Burma, where unemployment was only a word, and I had gone to Burma when I was still a boy and the post-war boom
5 was not quite over. When I first saw unemployed men at close quarters, the thing that horrified and amazed me was to find that many of them were *ashamed* of being unemployed. I was very ignorant, but not so ignorant as to imagine that when the loss of foreign
10 markets pushes two million men out of work, those two million are any more to blame than the people who draw blanks in the Calcutta Sweep. But at that time nobody cared to admit that unemployment was inevitable, because this meant admitting that it would
15 probably continue. The middle classes were still talking about 'lazy idle loafers on the dole' and saying that 'these men could all find work if they wanted to', and naturally these opinions percolated to the working class themselves. I remember the shock of astonishment it
20 gave me, when I first mingled with tramps and beggars, to find that a fair proportion, perhaps a quarter, of these beings whom I had been taught to regard as cynical parasites, were decent young miners and cotton-workers gazing at their destiny with the same sort of
25 dumb amazement as an animal in a trap. They simply could not understand what was happening to them. They had been brought up to work, and behold! it seemed as if they were never going to have the chance of working again. In their circumstances it was inevitable,
30 at first, that they should be haunted by a feeling of personal degradation. That was the attitude towards unemployment in those days: it was a disaster which happened to *you* as an individual and for which *you* were to blame.

1 Why did the author know nothing about unemployment before 1928?
2 What does the author blame for the rise in unemployment?
3 Does he consider the unemployed in any way responsible for their situation?
4 Rewrite the sentence 'I remember the shock . . .' beginning 'A quarter of . . .'. Keep your sentence simple.
5 What is the unemployed's attitude to their situation and how has this attitude been formed?

7.3 Summary exercise

Which sentence from the text best summarises the main idea?
a) I first became aware of the unemployment problem in 1928 (line 1).
b) When I first saw unemployed men . . . (line 5)
c) In their circumstances it was inevitable . . . (line 29)

For discussion

How would your life style have to change if you lost your job or other means of support? Do you think it would affect your relationships?

7.4 Practice exercise

Read the following text and answer the questions which follow.

George Smiley

Two seemingly unconnected events heralded the summons of Mr George Smiley from his dubious retirement. The first had for its background Paris, and for a season the boiling month of August, when Parisians
5 by tradition abandon their city to the scalding sunshine and the bus-loads of packaged tourists.

On one of these August days – the fourth, and at twelve o'clock exactly, for a church clock was chiming and a factory bell had just preceded it – in a *quartier*
10 once celebrated for its large population of the poorer Russian *emigrés*, a stocky woman of about fifty, carrying a shopping bag, emerged from the darkness of an old warehouse and set off, full of her usual energy and purpose, along the pavement to the bus-stop.
15 The second of the two events that brought George Smiley from his retirement occurred a few weeks after the first, in early autumn of the same year: not in Paris at all, but in the once ancient, free, and Hanseatic city of

Hamburg, now almost pounded to death by the
20 thunder of its own prosperity; yet it remains true that nowhere does the summer fade more splendidly than along the gold and orange banks of the Alster, which nobody as yet has drained or filled with concrete. George Smiley, needless to say, had seen nothing of its
25 languorous autumn splendour. Smiley, on the day in question, was toiling obliviously, with whatever conviction he could muster, at his habitual desk in the London Library in St James's Square, with two spindly trees to look at through the sash-window of the
30 reading-room. (The only link to Hamburg he might have pleaded – if he had afterwards attempted the connection, which he did not – was in the Parnassian field of German baroque poetry, for at the time he was composing a monograph on the bard Opitz, and trying
35 loyally to distinguish true passion from the tiresome literary convention of the period.)

Paragraph 1: 1 What is Paris like in August?

Paragraph 2: 2 Who did what, when, where?!
Now re-write the sentence simply, beginning, 'A woman . . .'

Paragraph 3: 3 What does the writer say about i) Hamburg and ii) the Alster?
4 What was George Smiley doing on that day?

7.5 Summary exercise

What is the topic sentence?

Vocabulary

Topic vocabulary: jobs and work

Look quickly through the following vocabulary bank and identify any problems. Then look at the exercise below to see if your problems are solved!

to apply for; an applicant; an application qualifications working conditions job satisfaction the working week the staff the management the work force an employer; an employee to be unemployed; the unemployed to be on the dole to lose your job	to be made redundant; redundancy to be laid off; lay-offs to go or be on strike to be dismissed, fired or sacked to get the sack or be given the sack to resign or hand in your notice industrial relations productivity to work overtime to be overworked	negotiations; to negotiate training an apprenticeship (to do) shift work part-time or full-time flexible working hours job sharing to be self-employed, freelance income, salary, wages tips, commission, bonus perks or fringe benefits to be promoted; to get promotion

7.6 Exercise

Choose the correct answer to complete the following sentences. Sometimes more than one answer is possible. (Discuss the differences).

1 I couldn't live on my salary alone. I rely on .... from the sales I make.
    tips   **fringe benefits**   **commission**

2 He .... last week in protest at the way the management handled the takeover bid.
    resigned   **fired**   **sacked**

3 She earns £40,000 a year as a lawyer but also has investments, so her total .... exceeds £60,000 p.a.
    salary   **income**   **wages**

4 As a nurse or a pilot, you have to be prepared to work ....
    part-time   **freelance**   **shifts**

5 Most of the work force were .... last week as orders for cars fell to an all-time low.
    given the sack   **made redundant**   **laid off**

6 In order to satisfy increased demand, the staff ....
    overworked   **worked over**   **worked overtime**

7 Jack lost his job last month and is now ....
    on strike   **on the dole**   **unemployed**

8 I am an electrician and I am my own boss. I am ....
    an employee   **an employer**   **self-employed**

9 It must be very soul-destroying to work in a dead-end job where there is no chance of ....
    job satisfaction   **promotion**   **working conditions**

10 It is important that people should receive the right .... for the jobs of the future.
    training   **apprenticeship**   **practice**   **qualifications**

11 Trade union leaders and management are negotiating about the possibility of a 35-hour ....
    work week   **time at work**   **working week**

Current questions

1 Do we live to work or work to live?
2 How will our working lives change in the next twenty years?

Verb combinations: 'down'   *Theme: work*

7.7 Exercise

Work out from the context an approximate meaning for the underlined verb combinations.

1 At the end of a stressful week at work, Tom Eaton needed the weekend in order to <u>wind down</u>.
2 The company advertised for a new sales manager. My sister applied for the job but unfortunately she was <u>turned down</u>.
3 We shall have to <u>cut down</u> the number of staff we employ if we want to make a profit this year.
4 The lack of communication between the different members of the department really <u>got John down</u> – so much so that he had a nervous breakdown.
5 The rate of income tax <u>went down</u> last year.
6 The company promised to deliver the new chairs by the end of last week. However, they <u>let us down</u> and we're still waiting for delivery.
7 The trade union official tried hard to get a precise figure for the wage increase but it was impossible to <u>nail the management down</u>.
8 After three years travelling around the world as a sales representative for a pharmaceutical firm, Mary decided to <u>settle down</u> in London.

Check with your teacher, or an English–English dictionary, that you have 'guessed' correctly.

- to wind down ....
- to turn down ....
- to cut down ....
- to get s'one down ....
- to go down ....
- to let s'one down ....
- to nail s'one down ....
- to settle down ....

Now write sentences of your own using the eight phrases.

Note also: a letdown

End of vocabulary

CHAPTER 8
Sentences and paragraphs

What to look out for

1 Words and phrases which can help you to *understand* what the writer is 'doing':
   a) contrasting things or ideas with each other:
      however, although, even though, yet, nevertheless, even if, whereas, while, despite, but,
      at best . . . , rather than . . . , it's not so much . . . ,
      on the one hand . . . , alternatively, it's not only . . . , etc.
      (SEE WRITING: CHAPTERS 1, 4 AND 5)
   b) making comparisons:
      **similarly, like, in the same way as . . . , just as . . . ,
      the same is true . . . , the same can be said . . . ,** etc.
      (SEE WRITING: CHAPTER 3)
   c) giving examples, or adding further ideas, to illustrate or strengthen what he or she is saying:
      so, thus, therefore, what is more, moreover, furthermore, or, in particular, at least . . . , illustrated by . . . , etc.,
      and the use of colons [:] to introduce such ideas.
      (SEE WRITING: CHAPTERS 3, 7 AND 8)
2 Words and phrases which can cause you to *misunderstand* what the writer is 'doing':
   since, as, nor, little, few, not least, other than, as if, no small . . . , etc.

8.1 Awareness exercise

Complete the following sentences in any way which is logical and possible, paying special attention to the 'marker' words (see 1a, b, c above)
e.g. The shortness of many newspaper articles, and frequent sensationalisation of news, often leave readers incapable of distinguishing between the trivial and the important. They are therefore . . . *not easily able to judge the real significance of what they read.*

1 There are those who believe that the effects of global warming have been greatly exaggerated. However, . . .
2 The most important factor contributing towards potential future criminal behaviour in children was having a parent with a criminal record, even if . . .
3 Rather than believe unquestioningly what I had read in the newspaper about the dangers of this particular road, . . .
4 It's not so much what she says in public about the education system that concerns me, . . .
5 Just as many people who live in attractive parts of the country may resent the presence of large numbers of visitors and tourists, so . . .
6 Young people who achieve sudden fame and fortune, for example through success in the world of pop music, often have problems in coping with the trappings of success: the same may be true . . .

7   We peered through the fog, desperately trying to make out a familiar shape, disorientated, very close to panic, stumbling about like …

8   The extent to which smoking can cause heart disease and other health problems has now been conclusively proved – at least that's what …

9   There are various good historical reasons why only a minority of British people speak many – or indeed any – European languages, with any great degree of competence: …

10 Theatre audiences in the North of England go for the play, a London audience goes for the interval, according to playwright Alan Plater. What's more, …

8.2 Awareness exercise

Look at the following paragraph, and answer the question which follows.

Our first idea as writers of this book was simply to select or write the texts, compile the exercises and leave the rest to the teacher's discretion. But to give no guidance about the different ways in which the material might actually be used would be to leave both teacher and student in the bewildered position of a tourist in a foreign city to whom the tour guide says, 'I'm afraid I haven't got any maps, but I'm sure you'll be able to find your own way round'. So we decided it was only polite to write an accompanying volume not only suggesting answers to the questions, but also offering ideas for exploitation of the material.

The description of the tourist in the foreign city is an illustrative comparison. Say in what way the teacher or student would be like the tourist.

8.3 Awareness exercise

Say whether the summaries of the following sentences are True (T), False (F), or whether it is impossible to say (?).

1   Jacques Cousteau played no small part in the French Prime Minister's abrupt decision to change his policy.
    – Cousteau played an unimportant part in the decision.   T/F/?

2   Many taxi drivers in Tokyo appear to have little knowledge of the geography of their city.
    – Tokyo taxi-drivers don't know their city's geography well.   T/F/?

3   He was only one of the 156 people involved in the riot to be arrested.
    – 156 people were arrested.   T/F/?

4   There are few things I don't understand about this software system.
    – I understand it pretty well.   T/F/?

5   Since I came here specifically to clean up the town, five daylight robberies in three days probably means my days as sheriff are numbered.
    – There have been five daylight bank robberies during my time here.   T/F/?

6   Q: What shall I do with this poster?
    A: Why don't you put it up down in the library?
    – The library is upstairs.   T/F/?

7   The chef lost his job not least because of his unwillingness to respond constructively to the adverse comments of those for whom he cooked.
    – Customers' complaints were an important factor in his dismissal   T/F/?

8   He was nothing if not handsome.
    – He was ugly.   T/F/?

9   We have no products other than those you can see.
    – You can see all our products.   T/F/?

10 I am not a little concerned at our Marketing Manager's lack of understanding of the services he is supposed to be selling for us, notwithstanding his expertise in selling them.
    – The fact that he didn't understand doesn't seem to me to be very important, since he sells them well.   T/F/?

11 It was no small feat on her part to have got the job in the teeth of massive male prejudice against her.
   – She was always certain to get the job.   T/F/?

12 We have a little time left before we go.
   – We must leave immediately.   T/F/?

13 As he went into the room after me, he saw her after she had taken her gloves off.
   – I saw her with her gloves off.   T/F/?

14 I don't believe that, nor does my wife.
   – My wife believes it.   T/F/?

8.4 Practice exercise

The aim of this exercise is to give you practice in *predicting* – anticipating what is going to come next, so that even if the words, when they come, are difficult, you already have some idea of what the writer is going to say.

Cover the whole text with a sheet of paper, and then slowly move the paper down to uncover one line of text at a time! Where there is a gap ..... in the text, write something that could logically continue the sentence. Then uncover the next line of text, where you will see the original sentence: how different was what you wrote? Did it have a similar meaning, even if the words were different?

Speaking your *own* language well is one thing, (1) .... using a foreign language idiomatically and feeling at home with it is quite another. Even native speakers of English who are used to the art of public speaking for example, (2) .... too often make mistakes of grammar or pronunciation. Listeners to (and viewers of) the proceedings in the British Houses of Parliament will doubtless have noticed such (3) .... misdemeanours in abundance. This observation, of course, is cold comfort for students of EFL for whom the first experience of the language would have been a standard school text book with the emphasis decidedly on the written word. Such students are probably well-advised to 'have-a-go' at speaking without worrying (4) .... too much about the inevitable mistakes. After all, trying to work out beforehand the perfectly constructed sentence does not lead to (5) .... a good conversation. Even those advanced students who can understand and even recite some of the great works of English literature when faced with a London taxi driver (6) .... have tremendous difficulty knowing what to say. So what's the answer to the problem? Well, it could be better use of material taken from original sources to help students understand 'real' English. Newspaper articles, for example, though intended for native speakers, (7) .... , are a good source of authentic language, as are (8) .... recordings from radio and television programmes. Of course there can be problems with using such material but these are probably (9) .... outweighed by the advantages. The user is exposed to 'real-life' language and situations within a framework of control. As a result, even the least confident student can, in theory, (10) .... be better prepared for the shock of having to speak when launched into the real thing.

8.5 Summary exercise

Write a title for the above passage.

For discussion

Do you think you can learn a language properly without spending some time in a country where it is spoken?

Vocabulary

Idiom/metaphor: adjective & noun collocation (1)

8.6 Exercise   Choose the correct adjectives to complete the collocations.

1   It was a terrible car crash and he was lucky not to have been killed. He had a .... escape.
    close   narrow   near
2   The result of the election was known before the counting even started. It was a .... conclusion that Mrs Hatchett would win.
    known   predicted   foregone
3   They have a(n) .... arrangement to meet every Wednesday at 12.00.
    long-standing   eternal   never-ending
4   The mountaineers had not intended to spend the night on the mountain, but darkness fell quickly and they took a(n) .... risk rather than continue their descent.
    calculated   estimated   mathematical
5   She was so unused to expressing her opinions it was a(n) .... struggle to get her to join in the discussion.
    mounting   uphill   difficult
6   When he returned to his home country after living abroad for ten years, he thought everything would be the same. However, he had a .... awakening.
    sudden   quick   rude
7   That's Paula Jennings, the new .... spark in the accounts department. She'll be financial director before long, you mark my words.
    shining   light   bright
8   You must have a very .... imagination to be able to make up all those stories.
    fertile   vivid   bright   deep (*2 possible*)
9   If the decision is split, the Chairperson has the .... vote.
    casting   latest   last
10 I gather the .... rate for private lessons is about £15 per hour.
    paying   giving   going

Special vocabulary: British life and institutions

8.7 Exercise   Who are the people and what is the significance of the places mentioned in the questions below?

1   Why would you expect to find the PM at Number 10?
2   Why would a PC be walking out of Scotland Yard?
3   Why might your GP suggest you went to Harley Street?
4   What would an MP be doing at Westminster?
5   Why would the Rev. Green think it an honour to be invited to Lambeth Palace?
6   Why would HRH occupy the Royal Box at Covent Garden?
7   Why would Alexandra Figgins, QC, be appearing at the Old Bailey?
8   Which House would the Chancellor announce his budget in?
9   Why might it be a surprise to see the MD on the shop-floor?
10 What would you be doing with a bookmaker at Ascot?

End of vocabulary

CHAPTER 9
Reading between the lines I

What to look out for

1 Exaggeration: the writer achieves a powerful or humorous effect by expressing something in language too extreme for it to be literally true.
2 Understatement: the writer conveys his or her meaning more strongly by expressing it in *less* strong words.
3 Irony: the actual words express the opposite of what the writer is really saying.
4 Ambiguity: words which have two possible meanings.

9.1 Awareness exercise

In these sentences, the writer is using one of the techniques in 1–3 above. In each case, identify the method used, and rewrite the meaning in a more literal way.

e.g.   a)   This is possibly the worst film that has ever been inflicted on the cinema-going public since the medium was invented.
Technique: exaggeration
Real meaning: it's an extremely bad film (but not that bad!)

b)   He was rather less than overjoyed at the prospect of spending two years studying rainfall patterns in the Gobi Desert.
Technique: understatement
Real meaning: he was extremely unhappy at the prospect...

c)   I am always impressed at the self-confidence with which male members of the government feel able to legislate on such matters as child birth.
Technique: irony
Real meaning: I find their self-confidence quite unjustifiable.

1   'Ah, another splendid British summer's day!' she exclaimed, drawing the curtains to reveal the rain lashing against the window pane.
2   'I can't go out in that!' he cried. 'I'd probably drown within a couple of yards of the front door.'
3   'I shouldn't go out just yet,' she warned. 'You might get just a trifle damp.'
4   A typical American shopping mall covers an area roughly the size of Liechtenstein, and has nearly as many stores.
5   If war *is* declared, it will be quite natural for the event to be signalled by special services of prayer and thanksgiving throughout the country.
6   Taking children to a modern art gallery requires nerves of steel.
7   Of course I should have protested at his behaviour, particularly when he lit a cigarette in the shadow of the *No Smoking* sign. But my station was approaching, and anyway, there are hazards involved in remonstrating with young men in large boots on late trains from London.
8   One of our political Masters recently uttered a profound truth. 'The year 2000,' he observed, 'is drawing closer every day'.
9   It is such a joy to discover, after you have spent many hours in many shops choosing a dress for a special occasion, that the one finally chosen for its interesting individuality is precisely the same as the one your neighbour will be wearing to the same event.

10   I had some slight doubts as to whether the new 'Eco-car' would sell very well –
I felt that the simultaneous operation of the sails, pedals and solar panels
would probably be a little too complicated for most normal people to manage.

9.2 Awareness exercise

English is a language in which it is comparatively easy to write sentences which
have two possible meanings. This is sometimes done deliberately (as in sentence 1
below), but more often unintentionally, sometimes with amusing or embarrassing
results.

Identify the two possible meanings of the following sentences; is there one word or
phrase which is the source of the ambiguity? Could you rewrite the sentence to
remove the double meaning, or alternatively say the sentence aloud in such a way
as to make the meaning clear?

e.g. 1 Nobody loves me because I'm tall.
  (i) nobody loves me: the reason for this is that I am tall.
  (ii) people may love me, but the reason for their loving me is not the fact
      that I am tall.
  key word: *because*
  The addition of a comma after 'me' would make meaning (i) unambiguous.

e.g. 2 The last thing we want is for them to die.
  (i) we want them to die, but we want this to happen after various other
      things.
  (ii) we certainly do not want them to die.
  key word: *last*
  Underlining or otherwise emphasising the word *last* would identify it as
  part of an idiomatic phrase with the meaning 'this is absolutely what we do
  not want.'

1   All of Europe was taken with this camera. (*advertisement*)
2   I didn't stop it because I didn't like it.
3   That's quite good for a foreigner.
4   He had pretty brown legs.
5   That's all I need!
6   I'm all right, really.
7   She had odd evenings off.
8   I do think an awful lot of you.
9   I had to survive, avoid that gruesome death by shooting.
10   They are bringing in a special anti-terrorist unit to guard skiers from nations
     allied against Moldania.
11   Perhaps he had drunk too much on the boat to boost his confidence, and was
     feeling ill.
12   Since I moved into my apartment, five people have stayed here; I didn't like
     one of them.
13   I know somebody called John.
14   **A:** I'm certain to spend at least five years in this dreadful place, even without
         loss of remission.
     B: That's a long sentence!
15   There are times when the area of moorland to the west of the hotel is closed
     off to the public and reserved for hunting and shooting guests.
16   She left her husband crying.

9.3 Practice exercise

Read the following, which is based on a TV comedy series about an imaginary politician called Jim Hacker. In his diary, Jim Hacker writes about the anxieties of waiting for a possible promotion. Annie is his wife. Answer the questions which follow.

Waiting for the phone to ring

I've been sitting by the telephone ever since breakfast. No potential Cabinet Minister ever moves more than twenty feet from the telephone in the twenty-four hours following the appointment of a new Prime
5 Minister. If you haven't heard within twenty-four hours, you're not going to be in the Cabinet.

Annie kept me supplied with constant cups of coffee all morning, and when I returned to the armchair next to the phone after lunch she asked me to help do the
10 Brussels sprouts for dinner if I didn't have anything else to do. I explained to her that I couldn't because I was waiting for the call.

'Who from?' Sometimes Annie really is a bit dense.

The phone rang. I grabbed it. It was Frank Weisel, my
15 special political adviser, saying that he was on his way over. I told Annie, who wasn't too pleased.

'Why doesn't he just move in?' she asked bitterly.

It's awfully difficult for Annie, I know. Being an MP's wife is a pretty thankless task. But now that I may be a
20 Minister, she'll at last reap the rewards!

Suddenly Annie screamed. 'Are you a bit tense?' I asked. She screamed again, and threw herself onto the floor. I thought of calling an ambulance, but was worried about the adverse publicity affecting my career at this
25 crucial juncture – NEW MINISTER'S WIFE TAKEN AWAY IN STRAIT-JACKET.

'Are you a bit tense?' I asked again. Carefully.

'No', she shouted – 'No, no, no, I'm not tense. I'm just a politician's wife. I'm not allowed to have feelings. I'm
30 just a happy carefree politician's wife.'

So I asked her why she was lying face downwards on the floor. 'I'm looking for a cigarette. I can't find any.'

'Try the cigarette box,' I advised, trying to keep calm. 'It's empty.'

35 'Take a valium.'

'I can't find the valium, that's why I'm looking for a cigarette. Jim, pop out and get me some.'

I explained to Annie that I simply didn't dare leave the phone. Annie betrayed her usual total lack of
40 understanding. 'Look, if the PM wants you to be in the bloody Cabinet, the PM will phone back if you're out. Or you can phone back.'

Annie will never understand the finer points of politics.

1 Which character, the Minister or Annie, uses
  a) exaggeration and understatement?
  b) irony (and its more insulting form, sarcasm)?
2 From the text, find
  a) an example of exaggeration
  b) an example of understatement
  c) an example of irony and/or sarcasm
  Explain why you have chosen these examples.
3 What picture have you built up of the Minister and Annie? For example,
  a) who likes politics?
  b) who doesn't want to play political 'games'?
  c) who is a realist?
  d) who doesn't enjoy their role?
  e) who understands the finer points of politics?

For discussion

What qualities does a politician need to have? Can you imagine yourself as the partner of a successful politician?

Vocabulary

Topic vocabulary: politics

Together with a partner, go through the following vocabulary bank, helping each other where possible with any problems.

democracy; democratic	an MP	a politician; politics;
the monarchy	backbench (*adj*)	political
a republic	the cabinet	a constituency
a one-party system or	a minister; a ministry	to vote; a voter
state	a civil servant	to call an election
the government;	a party	the electorate; to elect
to govern	right or left-wing	a referendum
the opposition		
a coalition		a policy
a coup	a (small, big,	a Bill, an Act
to overthrow	overwhelming)	to budget; a budget
parliament	majority	to lobby

9.4 Exercise

What can these people do? Use the following to help you talk about their roles.

1 A democratic leader: rule / govern / lead / consult / represent
2 A dictator: impose / dictate
3 A minister: discuss / form policies / head a ministry / budget
4 An MP: discuss / represent constituents / make laws
5 A voter: vote / elect / lobby / protest / demonstrate
6 A member of the opposition: vote against / bring down / discredit
7 The leader of a rebel group: stage a coup / overthrow
8 A civil servant: research / provide statistics / carry out government policy

Current questions

1 Politics is the servant of big business.
2 How much power has the individual?
3 Is democracy really possible?

Verb combinations: 'up' (1)   *Theme: politics*

9.5 Exercise

Work out, if necessary with the aid of a dictionary, the meaning of the underlined verb combinations. In some cases, you will find there is more than one meaning for the same combination; choose the one that fits the context of the sentences.

1   The meeting <u>broke up</u> in confusion when the military police arrived.
2   During the Cold War, it was normal for each super-power to <u>back up</u> its own allies with military and economic aid.
3   The defence budget has been spent on <u>building up</u> the supply of nuclear weapons.
4   During the pay talks, the question of a shorter working week <u>came up</u>: however, it was decided not to discuss the issue at that meeting.
5   The number of unemployed <u>went up</u> by 100,000 last month.
6   It was decided to <u>set up</u> a committee to discuss the problems of the homeless.
7   In 1605 Guy Fawkes tried to <u>blow up</u> the Houses of Parliament. Fortunately, or some might say unfortunately, he didn't succeed.
8   She was <u>brought up</u> by strict parents, studied chemistry at Oxford and <u>ended up</u> as Prime Minister.

- to break up ....
- to back up ....
- to build up ....
- to come up/to crop up (usually unexpected) ....
- to go up ....
- to set up ....
- to blow up ....
- to bring up ....
- to end up ....

Now write sentences of your own using the nine expressions.

Note also: a break-up; a build-up.

End of vocabulary

CHAPTER 10
Reading between the lines 2

What to look out for

1 Unusual punctuation: capital letters, sometimes used to indicate irony; 'quotation marks', to show something that should not be taken at face value; <u>underlining</u>, or *italics*, to emphasise a word or phrase; dots at the end of a sentence to show that the rest is left to the reader's imagination . . .

2 Humorous or powerful effects produced by sudden contrasts of style – for example, a change from abstract to concrete vocabulary, or from formal to colloquial language, or other unexpected combinations of words in the same sentence.

3 Connotations: reference to things, people, places, TV programmes etc. which are assumed to be known by the reader.

4 Satire: the aim may be to make the reader laugh at something the writer considers to be foolish or wrong; in addition to the techniques already described, the writer may do this by writing something that is clearly absurd or impossible.

10.1 Awareness exercise

In the following sentences, look for examples of the techniques described above, and answer the questions which follow.

1 When the Chancellor resigned, the pundits gathered, and mused, and offered up their conjectures and reflections, and it was called Political Speculation. When women gather to do the same, it is called gossip.
 – A 'pundit' is a great expert in a particular subject. Do you think the writer is using the word ironically here?   YES/NO
 – Is 'Political Speculation' in capital letters because the writer thinks it is important and serious, or because she wants us to laugh at those who do think it is?

2 Even in these supposedly enlightened days, most women who appear in TV commercials still wear one of four things – an evening-dress, an apron, a bikini, or a smile.
 – Why is the word 'smile' surprising?

3 The names of several of this company's best selling products imply appropriate foreign 'origins' as part of their brand imagery.
 – Does the writer believe the origins are foreign?   YES/NO

4 We succumb to the 'glamour' of mink, sable, fox, beaver, or lynx, parading our inhumanity while we develop 'humane traps' that cause 'less suffering' (and less damage to the fur).
 – Does the writer think that wearing furs is glamorous?   YES/NO
 – Does he believe that humane traps cause less suffering?   YES/NO
 – Does he think that our real aim in developing humane traps is to cause less suffering?   YES/NO

5 Soon on TV the politicians will be muscling in on Coronation Street and Eastenders, elbowing Michael Fish aside to stick Mori polls over his clouds.
 – From the word 'muscle', deduce the meaning of 'to muscle in on'.
 – What do you think 'Eastenders' and 'Coronation Street' are?

– What do you think Michael Fish's job is?

– What kind of poll do you think a 'Mori' one is?

6 Finally, let me be the first to say that Mrs Thatcher's outstanding contribution to the politics of our time is not in question. It has been remarkable. The issue now, however, is how to boot the old cow out as quickly as possible.

– Rewrite the last sentence in a style consistent with the first two.

7 I suppose what we're enduring at the moment is what they call A Momentous Week in Politics, and I wish I was somewhere peaceful, like the Gulf. Channels 1, 2, 3 and 4 plus every FM, MW, LW and SW station from here to Samarkand appear to be packed solid with politicians and their interviewers locked in the kind of intimate embrace you want to empty a bucket over in case the children see.

– Does the writer see it as a momentous week?   YES/NO

– Why is 'the Gulf' ironic here?

– Find two examples of exaggeration for effect (see Chapter 9)

– What word could you insert after 'embrace'?

– Explain the reference to the bucket.

8 Alcohol abuse – the West's socially acceptable agent of suicide and murder – has reached epidemic proportions in some countries.

– Why is the phrase 'socially acceptable' so powerful?

9 Jon had no trouble spotting Michael in the crowd at the terminal. He was wearing Levis, a clean white T-shirt, and a black and silver satin baseball jacket. And roller skates.

– Why does 'And roller skates', have a new paragraph to itself, and what is the effect of this?

10.2 Practice exercise   Read the text and answer the questions which follow.

A hot summer

I haven't dared mention the good weather for fear that it would immediately start to rain. But now that we're going on holiday it doesn't matter. It will rain anyway. Yet this summer has been a reminder of what life might
5 be like, a challenge to which the British public has risen magnificently.

The off-licence has run out of Perrier. Most of our local swimming pools are closed for repair. Entrepreneurial types, unaided by government grants,
10 are flogging buckets of water to old ladies at two quid a go. I actually know some people who *planned*, weeks ago, a party in their garden and were able to do so.

It has all reminded me of the Baron de Montesquieu (1689–1755). You too, I expect. Never mind that there
15 are worms in the tap water, and that the falling water table will crack the house foundations by September. Let's live for today and buy some luminous leisurewear at the new surf shop which has just opened on the High Road (where that over-priced antique business used to
20 be).

It is all a question of taste, of course. Friends who faithfully repair to Scotland every summer to escape the torrid heat of London have not enjoyed the real thing one whit: tropical heat, humid to boot (and sock),
25 mitigated only by evening breezes and the occasional short, sharp storm.

Myself, I love it, even when drenched in sweat and clothes with the tactile consistency of candy-floss. Heat that envelops you is one of life's luxuries, at least it is if
30 you are a Northern European. Kalahari bushmen probably feel the same way about a south-westerly depression. It has nothing to do with boring chores like suntans. It is the pleasure of heat, the kind that bounces off airport tarmac.

35 There are lots of us heat-freaks about too. We unburden ourselves with Latin candour while standing in line for a rumoured consignment of (Perrier-owned) Buxton spring water. Yes, I know you are going to say: 'What about the Greenhouse effect?' And: 'You'll be
40 sorry when it's like this in December.' But what we're talking about here is weather, not climate. One degree centigrade on the climatic global average constitutes a disaster in the making, not to mention falling house prices on flood-prone Canvey Island. One degree on
45 the weather won't make a blind bit of difference to swimming-pool sales or fleecing the tourists with over-priced ice-cream.

Put it another way, Edinburgh has the same annual

average temperature as Boston, around 48F. But the
50 Athens of the North ranges from averages of 38 to 58F
which makes you feel cold just to think about it, whereas
the Dublin of the West has a livelier spread, from 27 to
70F. Besides, my tenuous grasp of the Greenhouse
theory says that a warmer Britain will be a wetter one,
55 not Benidorm-on-Trent.

Back in mundane reality the changes are more
modest, but tangible. The British have broken out into
shorts, an art form which I had assumed we had lost
with the Empire. But they are no longer khaki and
60 baggy, they are lurid American Bermudas or fluorescent
bikers' lurex.

Then there's dining al fresco. Have you noticed how
those pathetic apologies for outdoor pub and restaurant
tables have flourished as confidence has grown in the
65 first British summer since 1976? For years now we've

come home from abroad resolving to be braver about
pavement life, only to retreat at about 7.30 p.m. as
petrol fumes engulf the table and the wind starts
whistling up the trouser-leg. This year the tables have
70 expanded over the pavement until our High Road –
next to the surf shop – looks like an Anglo-Saxon
Naples. Not up as late as Neapolitans, but 11 p.m. is
progress.

Which brings us to Montesquieu who pronounced
75 that 'liberty has its roots in the soil' and that temperate
islands (Britain) or mountains (Switzerland) were more
likely to sustain industry, moderation and healthy
individualism than sunny plains awash with lurex shorts.
Seems a bit hard on Aristotle but you know what he
80 means. A few summers like this and we'd all be behaving
like Italians. Myself, I could handle that better than
becoming a Norwegian.

1 Which word best describes the style of this text?
   a) humorous
   b) formal
   c) literary
   Find examples from the text to support your opinion.
2 Find two places in the text where the writer talks to you, the reader, directly.
   What effect does this have?
3 The words below all have 'connotations' for a native English reader. Say what,
   who, or where they refer to (you can try to deduce the answers even if you have
   not seen the words before).
   e.g. candy-floss (line 28) = something which is sticky and unpleasant to touch.
        (candy-floss is in fact a pink, sickly confection made of whipped sugar, and
        is eaten on a stick!)
   a) Perrier (line 7)
   b) the off-licence (line 7)
   c) Baron de Montesquieu (lines 13 and 74)
   d) the Kalahari (line 30)
   e) a south-westerly depression (lines 31–32)
   f) the Greenhouse effect (lines 39 and 53)
   g) Canvey Island (line 44)
   h) the Athens of the North, and the Dublin of the West (lines 50 and 52)
   i) Benidorm-on-Trent (line 55)
   j) the Empire (line 59)
   k) Aristotle (line 79)
   l) Norwegian (line 82)
4 Why is the word *planned* (line 11) written in italics, and what does 'able to do
   so' in the same line refer to?
5 Find examples in the text where the writer shows contrast of style; look in
   paragraph 2, paragraph 6, paragraph 10.
6 What do you infer about the British way of life in a 'normal' summer?

7   What techniques does the writer use to achieve his effect?
     a)   exaggeration
     b)   understatement
     c)   irony
     Find examples to support your opinion.

10.3 Summary exercise

Which would be the best alternative title for this article?
a)   The hotter the better
b)   How the greenhouse effect is affecting Britain
c)   Britain goes Mediterranean
d)   The problems of a British summer

Vocabulary

Topic vocabulary: weather

Look through the following and ask for explanations of any words you are not sure how to use appropriately.

wet	**hot**	**sunny**
a shower	to be boiling	sunlight
a downpour	to be stifling, oppressive,	shade
to drizzle	airless	shadow
to pour down	a drought	glare
dew	a heatwave	dazzling
to hail; hailstones	to be muggy, humid	
to be soaked to the skin;		**wind**
to be drenched; to be	**cold**	a hurricane
wet through	frost; frosty	a storm
	freezing	a gale
dull	ice; icy	(a biting, strong) wind
to be cloudy or overcast	chilly	a breeze
mist; misty	raw	to howl
fog; foggy	wintry	to blow
haze; hazy	bitterly cold	to whistle

10.4 Exercise

You are working on a film and have to describe the weather scene for the following clips – use your vivid imagination!

1   Two cowboys are riding across the desert.
2   It is a dark night in the middle of nowhere where strange things have been happening.
3   The railway station, and a parting between two lovers.
4   It's autumn sunrise, and young Anne Chambers has got up early to pick mushrooms from the fields.
5   Guests in the Largo Hotel on the coast are stranded because of a hurricane which has hit the area.
6   The mountain village has been in the grip of winter for 2 weeks, and the temperature has not risen above −10 C.
7   A palm-tree-lined beach on a South Pacific island is the idyllic setting for this musical number.

Currrent questions

1 How much does climate affect national character?
2 When scientists have learned how to control the weather, we shall all be much happier.

Special vocabulary: slang and colloquial English

The following exercise (like the text, 'A hot summer') shows current informal, spoken expressions. If you've got an up-to-date English–English dictionary, you will probably find them. This is the kind of language that changes with fashion.

10.5 Exercise

Look at the underlined expressions in the following sentences and, together with a partner, work out what they mean.

1 That jacket looks really expensive. It must have <u>cost a bomb</u>!
2 I <u>was ripped off</u> by that taxi-driver. I paid £20 for the journey from the station to the city centre.
3 What are you getting so <u>uptight</u> about? You're only being asked to make a short speech.
4 The trouble with you, Shirley, is that you're completely selfish. You <u>don't give a damn about</u> anyone but yourself.
5 I don't know whether I can be bothered to prepare a picnic. It's <u>a lot of hassle</u>, and then it'll probably rain. Let's just eat at home, it's simpler.
6 A: Can you imagine the confusion if our secretary mixed up the room reservations of the Wine Club and the Temperance Society?
   B: <u>The mind boggles</u>!
7 Don't <u>hassle</u> me – I'm doing it as quickly as I can.
8 Talk about luck! That goal by Gary Gascony was a complete <u>fluke</u>. The ball just happened to hit his leg at the right angle.
9 A: I've never tried raw fish before.
   B: Well, now's your chance. Go on, <u>give it a whirl</u>.
10 Have you managed to <u>suss out</u> what happened between Kim and Alan? They haven't said a word to each other for days.

Now take it in turns to set up situations where you and your partner can use these expressions.
e.g. You say: *Did you know Tony had passed his exam? Nobody expected him to, did they?*
Your partner says: *No, it was a bit of a fluke, I think.*

End of vocabulary

Writing

True ease in writing comes from art, not chance, As those move easiest who have learnt to dance.

Alexander Pope

INTRODUCTION

Writing compositions is a very examination-oriented activity. There are very few occasions in real life when you need to write a story describing a frightening experience, or record a discussion on the rights and wrongs of capital punishment. However, writing can be a very satisfying and creative experience.

What makes a good piece of writing?
– the content (ideas/thoughts – what you have to say).
– the language with which you express those ideas.
– the organisation of your ideas into a logical and convincing pattern.

Writing demands *accuracy*. Thoughts and ideas have to be expressed clearly and unambiguously so that anyone reading the work can understand what the writer wants to say.

The chapters in the writing section work on the different sentence structures used in writing, ranging from concession clauses to rephrasing, and in this way they provide the bricks to build the composition.

To help you with ideas and organisation, each of the chapters in the writing section provides systematic practice in tackling the different kinds of composition.

In each chapter, there is a model composition which is the focus for both the structural and composition work.

CHAPTER 1   Narrative

Text work

Before you read the model composition, can you predict ten verbs and their contexts concerned with either *actions* or *dealing with people* which you think might be in the story below? e.g. *chat to the relatives* or *rushed to her side*

Imagine you are a nurse in a busy hospital. Write a descriptive account of a working day.

As I made my way from the nurses' home over to St Luke's, I kept thinking and worrying about little Mark. However much we are taught not to get too emotionally involved, it is still difficult for me. As soon as I had reported for duty, I went along to check on him and was relieved to find his condition had improved.

For the next three hours my work consisted of giving out medicine, checking on the patients, accompanying the doctor on his rounds and carrying out his orders. This morning it was Dr Stephens who came to the ward and, much as I admire his skill as a doctor, I don't feel he is very good with children. He walked around without a smile on his face and I could see some of the younger ones looking frightened. By the time he had finished, I knew I was going to have to go around after him and reassure some of the kids. Not for the first time, I felt angry at the way this particular doctor seemed unaware of the effect he had on the patients.

It was only after I had calmed them down that I was able to sit down for the first time that morning for a quick cup of coffee with my colleagues. For about five minutes we managed to talk to each other about things other than work, but then the topic of conversation came back to the ward.

The rest of the morning passed without my really noticing. We were busy as usual but, for once, everything seemed to be going smoothly. I had lunch in the staff canteen with Sue, a friend working on the intensive care ward, and we swapped stories about our patients. We always find it hard not to talk shop, despite our good intentions.

On my way back to the ward, I bumped into Mark's parents who had just been to see him. They were really pleased with his progress and were actually smiling. One of the intensely satisfying parts of my job is seeing the relief and joy on relatives' faces when a child recovers.

For the remaining three hours I was rushed off my feet. There seemed to be a never–ending list of jobs to do – fetching, carrying, talking, comforting, filling in forms, helping children. Throughout all this activity I kept an eye on Mark. Walking past his bed, I suddenly noticed that his breathing was a bit irregular. I called the Sister and she immediately got Mark connected to a machine; before long his breathing had stabilised.

When I left the ward that afternoon, half of me wanted to stay and look after Mark and the other half of me wanted to go home and forget about everything. I know I'll never really be able to cope with seeing little ones suffer, no matter how many times it happens. For me this is the most difficult aspect of the job I love.

Language work

The underlined phrases in the model composition are examples of how you can move a narrative on, in a variety of ways, from one action to another. By using these phrases (particularly at the beginning of paragraphs) you can show clear thought and organisation in your writing.

Linkers and movers

1.1 Exercise

Look at the underlined phrases in the text and, together with a partner, agree:

1 Which phrase seems to be the most dramatic?
2 Three phrases which introduce the past perfect and past simple. Can you say why these two tenses are used?
3 Which three phrases contain movement and therefore act as linkers between one action and another?
4 Which four phrases describe the passing of time?

1.2 Exercise

In note form, write down how you spent yesterday. Make sure your ideas are in the correct time order (it doesn't matter if your day was not exciting!)

e.g. 1 *got up at 7.30 a.m.*

2 *went downstairs*

Using the linking phrases from the text, either tell your partner about your day or write up these points more fully.

e.g. *I got up at 7.30 a.m. and made my way slowly downstairs.*

For more practice, try the same exercise thinking about a day in the life of
– a prisoner
– an unemployed person
– a famous political person in your country

Contrast and concession

I admire his skill as a doctor.
I don't feel he's very good with children.

These two ideas taken from the model composition can be described as being in contrast, i.e. one is surprising or unexpected in view of the other. Look at the way the two contrasting ideas are joined into one sentence in the composition.

Find three other ways of joining contrasting or unexpected information in the composition (in paragraphs 1, 4 and 7).

1.3 Exercise

Below are ways of joining contrasting information together. Complete the sentences.

1 However much I like my job, …
2 However ill children are, …
3 Whatever happens next, …
4 He seems to bring out the best in people, whoever …
5 Wherever he goes, …
6 No matter how often it happens, …
7 Although he liked his job, …

8   She worked overtime, even though …
9   We find it hard not to talk about our work, despite …
10   In spite of having a sore throat, …
11   The parents looked cheerful in spite of the fact that …
12   Much as I admire his skill, …
13   Skilful though/as he is, …
14   For all his skill, …

1.4 Exercise

1   *It doesn't matter how confident you feel, it's always a good idea to check through your work.*
    Express this idea using
    a)   however
    b)   no matter

2   *It was a difficult job. I liked it.*
    Join these two contrasting sentences using
    a)   although
    b)   even though
    c)   in spite of
    d)   despite
    e)   difficult + though/as
    f)   for all
    g)   much as

3   Finish the following sentences using as many of the structures in Exercise 1.3 as you can.
    He always arrives on time …
    She agreed to marry him …

Composition work

Hints

1   Set the scene (who, what, where, when, why, how)
2   Plan how you're going to end – don't just drift on!
3   Think carefully about the first and last sentences (they create and leave a big impression).
4   Move the narrative on by using a variety of tenses, structures, vocabulary.
5   Use direct speech occasionally to add variety.

Getting ideas for compositions

Example 1: Think of who, what, where, when, why, how.
            for a story entitled: *The Fire.*

Who?   who saw it happen/who was involved, etc.
What?   what materials were involved/what was the end result
Where?   in the middle of town/factory/nuclear power station/house
When?   when was it spotted/when did it start and finish
Why?   cigarette/electrical fault/deliberately
How?   slowly/quickly

Let your imagination run free – don't try to think of the whole story until one of your answers sparks something off (it doesn't matter how silly your ideas are!)

Example 2: Write a short story which ends as follows: *'He woke up to find a grand piano on the lawn in front of his house.'*

Who?	famous pianist/gangster/my brother/road-sweeper
What?	a real piano/a toy/valuable/broken
Where?	Chicago/your town/Vienna/Buckingham Palace
When?	childhood/the future/Christmas/18th century
Why?	reward/punishment/purchase/surprise
How?	by helicopter/pushed/self-propelled

Now do the same with some of the following titles.
- *A journey that went wrong*
- *A day in the life of a prisoner/a farmer/a gambler*
- *Your visit to an international sporting event*
- *The smuggler*

Organisation of compositions

If you are telling a story, your composition has a natural, in-built organisation – you follow the sequence of events. It is, however, worth thinking about the first and last sentences in the composition. Write first and last sentences (where appropriate) for the above titles.

Composition titles

Choose one of the titles from **Composition work** above, or one of the following titles, and write a full composition of about 300–350 words.

- *Write a story, beginning: 'Nothing will ever be the same again.'*
- *Tell the story of the night the lights went out.*

Vocabulary

Topic vocabulary: health

As a group with your teacher, look through the following vocabulary bank and put any 'new' words or phrases into a sentence.

to examine s'one	to be mild	an overdose
to have a check-up	to be infectious	a virus
to treat s'one for; treatment	to be contagious	an injection
to operate on s'one	to be terminal	a vaccination
to have an operation	to be incurable	a prescription; to prescribe
to diet; a diet	to be chronic	tension
to diagnose; a diagnosis	to be acute	stress
to suffer from side effects	to be fatal	an allergy; to be allergic to
to be in good shape	surgery; a surgery	preventive medicine
to unwind	symptoms	alternative medicine
to be or feel run down	dosage; to dose	conventional medicine
to cure; a cure for	germs	

1.5 Exercise   Using some of the vocabulary from the above list, talk about the causes, symptoms and treatment of the following: heart disease, malaria, influenza, appendicitis.

1.6 Exercise   Fill in the gaps in the following text with words taken from the vocabulary bank.

Feeling unwell, I went to the doctor. Her .... hours were between 8.00 and 11.00 in the morning. She asked me what my .... were and I explained about my recurring sore throat. She .... me and .... a mild infection which could be .... by antibiotics. Unfortunately I am .... antibiotics – they work well on the problem but I .... from terrible .... as well.

In the end she gave me a .... for some pills and told me to come back in a week for a .... She also advised me not to let myself get ....

Current questions

1   Is the western approach to medicine the best one?
2   We are a world of pill-takers. Why?

Verb combinations: 'up'(2)   *Theme: health and medicine*

1.7 Exercise   Match the verb combinations on the left to their definitions on the right.

- to hold up =   to stop
- to take up =   to invent
- to own up =   to delay
- to make up =   to search for s'thg in a book
- to pick up =   to learn
- to look s'thg up =   to confess
- to give up =   to develop/stimulate s'thg
- to work up =   to begin a new hobby

Now put the correct forms of the phrases into the following sentences.

1   When she was working as a volunteer helper in St Ned's Hospital, Jenny .... a bit of medical knowledge which was very useful later in her life.
2   If you're not feeling well, it is possible to think about your symptoms and then .... in a medical encyclopaedia. However, be careful as it is very easy to imagine that you're suffering from everything in the book!
3   Sitting in an office all day made me feel very lethargic, so I .... jogging as a way of getting some exercise.
4   Swimming is supposed to be very good for you but I find it .... my appetite. I always need a big meal afterwards!
5   Some doctors have .... prescribing drugs for their patients. Instead they have recommended alternative treatments, like acupuncture.
6   One of the junior doctors .... to giving Mrs Smith the wrong dosage of penicillin. As a result of his mistake, she suffered very bad side-effects.
7   The opening of the new psychiatric ward has been .... due to staff shortages.
8   In the old days, quack doctors travelling around the United States used to prepare their own medicines and then .... fantastic stories about how wonderful they were.

Give yourself a task: next time you are doing some writing in English, make a determined effort to use at least three verb combinations instead of single words e.g. **pick up** instead of **learn**

End of vocabulary

CHAPTER 2   Descriptive

Text work

You are going to read a composition entitled 'The family next door' (Mr and Mrs Taylor and their three children). Before reading, look at the following phrases taken from the text and, in a group, build up your story incorporating these words. They are not necessarily in the right order!

– might have been a soldier
– on the surface
– littered with
– look good in a sack
– a relatively short time
– well-ordered life
– despite their differing ages

Now see if any of your ideas are similar to those in the model composition.

The Family Next Door

The Taylors have lived next door for a relatively short time. They moved in on the hottest day of last year when the neighbours were all sunbathing or working in their gardens, and so the entire street felt they knew every detail of their life before they had been there a day! However, things <u>are not always as they seem</u>.

Mr and Mrs Taylor are in their thirties with three children aged ten, eight and five. John Taylor is a tall man who <u>looks as if</u> he might have been a soldier at some time. He stands very straight and walks with a determined step. <u>In fact</u>, we discovered later that he is an actor in second-rate war films, who prides himself on his bearing. His wife, Caroline, is slim and always elegant, even when she goes to the local supermarket, which really annoys everyone else in the street as we tend to go shopping in our oldest, shabbiest clothes. Caroline would look good in a sack.

In view of this <u>apparently</u> well-ordered life, it comes as a shock to find that they <u>actually</u> live in chaos. Their house is littered with papers, books, toys and coffee cups, but the entire family <u>appears to be</u> oblivious to the mess. Caroline and John <u>seem</u> very relaxed with the children, who thrive on their easy-going upbringing, and the atmosphere in the house is always warm and welcoming. Some people in the street judge the Taylors solely by what they see in their home and fail to appreciate the genuine friendliness and generosity that exists.

The children have been brought up to like each other – and they do most of the time. It is not unusual to see the three of them playing happily together for hours, despite their differing ages. However, they are not always angels – the middle one can be very stubborn and this can lead to friction in the group.

<u>On the surface</u>, then, everything is wonderful about the Taylors next door. But occasionally there is a look on John's face that makes us wonder if everything is <u>as rosy as it appears</u>.

Language work

Appearance/impression + reality

The underlined phrases in the composition highlight this area of written language.

2.1 Exercise Complete each of the following sentences. While doing this, think of a real person in your life (e.g. a teacher, friend or colleague) to make the examples more genuine, or look at the photos.

Appearance/impression
1 He/She looks (or seems) as if ......
2 He/She appears (or seems) to be ......
3 He/She seems (or appears) ......
4 He/She often stands by the window, apparently ......
5 To all appearances, he/she is ......
6 She gives the impression of ....
7 He gives people the feeling that ....
8 He very often strikes people as ....

Contrast with reality
9 On the surface, he/she ...... , but ....
10 At first sight he/she ...... , but when you get to know him/her, ...
11 In theory his/her life ...... , but in practice ....
12 He/She isn't as ...... as ....
13 He/She looks ...... , but actually ......
14 He/She seems ...... , but in fact ......

2.2 Exercise

For further practice, use the different structures above to write about:

a) a character in a book or film

b) yourself, or others, just before a nerve-racking event (e.g. an examination, a visit to the dentist)

c) a place you know which is not immediately attractive to someone seeing it for the first time.

Composition work

> **Hints**
>
> 1 A descriptive composition should include most, if not all, of the following:
> – people (physical description and characteristics)
> – place
> – scene/activity
> – atmosphere
> – impression
> – the effect on your senses
> 2 This is the place where you can really show off your rich descriptive vocabulary!
> Think of synonyms
> – instead of *nice*, how about *wonderful*?
> – instead of *walk*, how about *stroll*?
> – instead of *quietly*, how about *silently*?
> 3 Vary the use of words: change adjectives into nouns, nouns into verbs, etc.
> e.g. *I was shocked to see . . .*
> or *The shock of seeing her made me . . .*

Look at point 1 in the Hints Box.

Write, in note form, what you want to include in those categories for the following compositions.

- *Describe the scene in a busy airport departure lounge.*
- *Describe someone who has had a big influence on you.*
- *Describe the place (village, town, city) where you grew up.*

Composition titles

Choose one of the titles from **Composition work** above, or one of the following titles, and write a full composition of about 300–350 words.

- *Write a descriptive account of the scene after an earthquake.*
- *Describe the most beautiful sight you have ever seen.*
- *Describe yourself in thirty years' time.*
- *Describe the scene from the window of the room where you have been confined for a long period of time.*

Vocabulary

Topic vocabulary: people

2.3 Exercise

Below are some 'positive' (+) and some 'negative' (−) adjectives which can be used when describing people. Together with a partner, read through the 'positive' words and find a matching 'negative' attribute: e.g. *generous – mean*

+	−
cautious	vague
decisive	cool, reserved
easy-going	lazy
energetic	dull, boring
entertaining	tactless
even-tempered	shy
flexible	reckless, impetuous
generous	narrow-minded
open-minded	moody, touchy
sociable	mean, selfish
tactful	stubborn, obstinate
warm	uptight

2.4 Exercise

The following poem paints a slightly unconventional picture of which attributes may be desirable, and which may not be.

If I had my life to live over

I'd dare to make more mistakes next time. I'd relax.
I would limber up. I would be sillier than I have
been this trip. I would take fewer things seriously.
I would take more chances. I would take more
trips. I would climb more mountains and swim
more rivers. I would eat more ice cream and less
beans. I would perhaps have more actual
troubles, but I'd have fewer imaginary ones.

You see, I'm one of those people who live
sensibly and sanely hour after hour, day after day.
Oh, I've had my moments and if I had it to do
over again, I'd have more of them. In fact, I'd try
to have nothing else. Just moments, one after
another, instead of living so many years ahead of
each day. I've been one of those persons who
never goes anywhere without a thermometer, a
hot water bottle, a raincoat, and a parachute.
If I had to do it again, I would travel lighter
than I have.

If I had my life to live over, I would start barefoot
earlier in the spring and stay that way later in
the fall. I would go to more dances. I would ride
more merry-go-rounds. I would pick more daisies.

(Nadine Stair, 85 years old, Louisville, Kentucky)

Nadine Stair thinks she would have different values if she had the opportunity to re-live her life. Look at the following adjectives, and decide whether she would see them as 'positive' or 'negative' (you may find some interesting contrasts with Exercise 2.3).

reckless	prudent	sensible
responsible	adult	open-minded
cautious	adventurous	serious
daring	silly	

2.5 Exercise

Social attributes: how well do you present yourself to other people? What do you think are your social strengths and weaknesses, and do other people see them in the same way? (Unfortunately for international communication, what is considered a 'strength' in one culture may be seen as just the opposite in another, and it may be useful to discuss this if you find examples when doing the exercise.)

Look at the following lists and write down those strengths and weaknesses that you consider apply to you. Then work in pairs and write down those you think apply to your partner. After, compare your perceptions of yourself and each other!

Strengths

witty	enthusiastic
able to hold people's attention	humorous
able to maintain eye contact	patient
knowledgeable	confident
able to stand my ground	articulate
sympathetic	perceptive
quick-witted	sincere
able to raise my voice if necessary	able to show empathy
calm	lively
friendly	sensitive
cheerful	approachable
able to establish a good rapport	good at reassuring people

Weaknesses

unable to think logically	not good at 'selling myself'
dour	hesitant
unable to hold eye contact	long-winded
tactless	easily pressurised
judgemental	opinionated
easily embarrassed	sarcastic
unable to raise my voice	pompous
unable to disagree or argue	hostile
unsympathetic	impatient

Current questions

1 Is it possible that birth signs can determine a person's character, i.e. are there common characteristics among all Scorpios, or, in the Chinese system, all people born in the year of the Rat?
2 Is assertiveness a good thing?
3 Can one be too nice?

Verb combinations: 'on'(1)   *Theme: family life*

2.6 Exercise   Match the definitions to the verb combinations.

- to look down on =
- to get on (with) =
- to carry / go on =
- to count / rely / depend on =
- to look on s'one/s'thg =
- to pass on =
- to splash out on =
- to take on =

to accept / agree to s'thg
to consider s'one / s'thg to be
to regard s'one / s'thg as inferior
to spend money extravagantly
to have a friendly relationship (with)
to continue
to give / tell s'one s'thg
to put your trust in s'one / s'thg

Now put the correct verb combination into each of the following sentences.

1   It is rare for all members of a family to .... equally well together.
2   'Mixed marriages', whether of class, culture or language, can be difficult enough at the best of times; they're even more so if one of the families .... the other because it considers it to be inferior.
3   Nowadays it is normal for women to .... working after they have had children.
4   In large families, older children have to .... the responsibility of looking after the younger ones.
5   How often is it possible to .... your father or mother as a friend?
6   In many traditional societies, the older generation .... the stories of the tribe to their children.
7   In Britain, even though many families are not well-off, they usually .... toys for the kids at Christmas.
8   It's important for children to know they can .... the love and support of their parents.

To help remember these phrases, choose one of the combinations and make (mime) a gesture that you can associate with it. The rest of your group will try to guess your choice.

End of vocabulary

CHAPTER 3
Fantasy / hypothetical

Text work

Before you read the text entitled '*Describe your ideal house*', think of your own ideas on the subject under the following headings:
– *position*
– *style*
– *high/low priorities*
– *special features*

Now see if you have anything in common with the writer of this composition.

Describe your ideal house

The first priority is its position. It must be overlooking the sea. Without this, the house, however perfect, could not be ideal.

The house itself would be modern and spacious. The principal room would have a high ceiling and it would be painted in pale colours to give the effect of space. One side of the room would be made of glass so that I could look at the sea, and outside there would be a terrace where we could eat on summer evenings. In addition, the room would have a polished wooden floor with exquisite Persian rugs scattered around. The dominant features in the room would be an open fire for cooler evenings and a large table where I could seat at least eight people for dinner. Apart from that, the only other essentials in the room are plants – lots of large, healthy green plants. Besides being a room where I could entertain, it would also be the room where I would relax and contemplate the magnificent scenery.

I'd like the kitchen to have a tiled floor and, needless to say, there would be plenty of space. I'm not that particular about having all the latest electrical gadgets – I would get far greater pleasure from having traditional cooking utensils around than from switching on the latest wondertoy.

The other room downstairs would be a work room. Here I could set up my pottery with a wheel, kiln and space for all the equipment. Just as my living room would have a large window overlooking the sea, so my workroom would have a similar view which would inspire me.

From the living room a spiral staircase would lead up to the first floor. Here you would find the bedrooms and bathrooms. The floor would be carpeted throughout. The main bedroom would be slightly bigger than the others and would have its own bathroom. I know carpet is not half as convenient as tiles in a bathroom but still I would prefer something soft underfoot. In common with the rest of the house, the first floor rooms would be painted in pale colours.

Last but not least, music. I'd like there to be a music system which could be heard in every room in the house if and when required. These are some of the features of my ideal house.

Language work

Expressing similarities and adding points

The underlined phrases in the model composition express the above two areas of language.

3.1 Exercise

Practise the following structures by completing the sentences in any way that makes sense.

Similarities
1 Both the elderly and the very young ...
2 The new tax is similar to the old one in that ...
3 The USA and Britain have one important thing in common: ...
4 In common with many other traditional industries, coal-mining ...
5 Neither France nor Germany ...
6 Just as the horse was once used for everyday transport, so today the ...
7 Dogs, like cats, ...

Adding points
8   In addition to being quick, the plane ...
9   Apart from having a house in Monte Carlo, she ...
10 Besides being a constantly available source of power, solar energy ...
11 Besides your brother, who ...?
12 It's much safer for a child to play in his or her own back garden. Moreover, ...

3.2 Exercise

Use the 'Similarities' phrases to talk about features, rooms, decoration in your house or flat.

e.g. Both the kitchen and the bathroom have tiled floors.

3.3 Exercise

Use the 'Adding points' phrases to express the following information differently:

– The three-bedroomed house is very modern. It is situated near the town centre.
– The house has a garden and a patio for relaxing on or eating outside.
– The kitchen is large and is well-equipped.

3.4 Exercise

1 Write a paragraph describing your ideal bathroom. Use language from the 'Adding points' section.
2 Compare your paragraph with a neighbour's and find any similarities. Write these down using language from the 'Similarities' section.

e.g. My bathroom is similar to Maria's in that it has a sunken bath.

Composition work

Hints

1 The composition is fantasy, so **would** and **could** are natural choices for the main verb tense.
2 Make it personal – include expressions of personal likes, preferences, dislikes.
3 Back up your ideas with reasons and/or explanations.

Think of your ideas for the following two titles.
- *Imagine you could have three wishes. What would they be and why?*
- *Describe your ideal job.*

Remember the points from the Hints Box. Now tell your neighbour about your three wishes and your ideal job.

Composition titles

Choose one of the titles from **Composition work** above, or one of the following titles, and write a full composition of about 300–350 words.

- *If you woke up and found you could make yourself invisible at will, how would you spend your first day?*
- *Do you think your life would be different if you were of the opposite sex?*
- *How would you survive if you were stranded on a desert island?*
- *What would be your policy priorities if you were made Prime Minister?*

Vocabulary

Topic vocabulary: homes and homeless

Identify the new vocabulary and check it out.

a detached, semi-detached or terraced house	a slum	a landlord, a landlady
a bungalow	a shanty town	a tenant
a cottage	cardboard city; to live on the streets	————
a mansion	to be evicted	a mortgage
a stately home	to be homeless	rented accommodation
a flat; a block of flats	a down-and-out	subsidised housing
a high-rise building	————————	redevelopment
a bedsit	an estate agency	in the suburbs
a hostel	an estate agent	on the outskirts
a squat; to squat	a home-owner	a commuter town

3.5 Exercise

Correct the underlined phrases in the following sentences.
1. Living in a <u>semi-detached</u> house, I can easily hear both sets of neighbours through the walls.
2. Because he had no job and therefore no money, he broke into an empty property and <u>rented</u>.
3. A <u>landlord</u> has to pay rent to a <u>tenant</u>.
4. In Britain, people on low incomes live in <u>their own houses</u>.
5. The tenant was <u>welcomed</u> by the landlord for not paying her rent.
6. They lived in a <u>high-rise building</u> in the sleepy village of Wilton.
7. Around Rio de Janeiro, thousands of poor people live in makeshift accommodation in <u>leafy suburbs</u>.
8. In London everybody lives in <u>the centre of the city</u>.
9. At the beginning of this century, redevelopment of the <u>luxury houses</u>, that is those properties without water or electricity, took place.

10   He became a home-owner when he could no longer pay the fees to the bank.
11   She couldn't climb stairs so she bought a three-storey house.
12   Students can usually only afford to live in detached houses, where the bedroom and sitting room are one.

Current questions

1   Should the state be obliged to provide cheap housing for those who need it?
2   What are the causes of the rise of homelessness?

Verb combinations: 'in/into'   *Theme: homes*

3.6 Exercise

Work out the meanings of the underlined verb combinations in the story.

Steve and Rebecca were not well-off but they managed to save enough money to get a mortgage on a house which needed a lot doing to it. After moving into their new house, they had central heating put in and felt very cosy for the first time. Unfortunately, one problem remained – some of their old furniture was too big to fit into the small rooms. Steve was very reluctant to get rid of it but finally he gave in. One day, Steve bumped into an old friend, Jane, who was into antiques, and he asked her to come and have a look at their stuff.

Jane couldn't believe her eyes when she saw their wardrobe – it was a sixteenth century antique worth thousands of pounds. At first they couldn't take in what she was saying but then they realised that, if they sold it, they could at last afford to renovate the house exactly as they wanted to. Jane talked them into letting her sell it for them and they began to plan their dream house.

Jane spent the next week looking into the history of the wardrobe and then took it to an auction in London. There it sold to an American collector for £50,000. Ironically, Rebecca and Steve realised that they could now afford to move into a larger house where they would need larger furniture!

Check with your teacher, or an English–English dictionary, that you have 'guessed' correctly.
1   to put in ....
2   to fit into ....
3   to give in ....
4   to bump into ....
5   to be into ....
6   to take in ....
7   to talk s'one into ....
8   to look into ....
9   to move into ....

Now write sentences of your own for practice.

End of vocabulary

CHAPTER 4   Personal

Text work

Read the title and the first paragraph of the following model composition. Then cover up the rest of the text except for the first line of the second paragraph. Together with a partner, see if you can predict what is going to come on the next line. Continue in the same way, line by line, for paragraphs 2, 3 and 4. You will have to look at the first line of each paragraph in turn.

How does the weather affect your mood?

In England, where the weather seems to change every minute, you might imagine that people's moods would reflect these changes. But the English are regarded as an undemonstrative and rather placid race.

For myself, I know I am affected by the weather. There is a big difference in my energy levels during the different seasons. In winter I have nothing like as much enthusiasm for doing things as I have in the summer. Even on sunny days I find it difficult to make myself do anything more than I have to. While not getting particularly depressed during winter, I do feel rather like a hibernating animal. The one exception to this is when I go to the mountains – in spite of the freezing temperatures, I feel exhilarated by the fresh, clear air and once more ready for anything.

Unlike most people, I love the wind. I have never experienced a tornado or a real hurricane, just a strong gale, and I find it thrilling. The wind gives me both physical and mental energy. It sweeps away all my stale thoughts and gives me the feeling of being able to start again. It makes me feel much more creative, but at the same time slightly mad.

In contrast to this happy feeling produced by the wind, my lowest time is on days of grey skies and constant rain. Then, it doesn't take much to make me short-tempered with people; also, the ability to make sensible decisions seems to go out of the window at this time.

My wet weather mood contrasts greatly with my sunny day behaviour. I notice two changes in me – one which is more dramatic than the other. If we have a period of dull weather followed by a bright sunny day, it is almost as if I have won £1m – I feel cheerful, happy and full of joy, as if a burden has been lifted from me. If this one sunny day is followed by more and more sunny days, my mood settles down into one of contentment, openness and a feeling of physical well-being. My face relaxes, as does my body, and I feel able to cope with everybody and everything.

There is no doubt that the weather plays an important part in my behaviour. Sometimes, however, it is difficult to distinguish between a weather-related mood and just a bad temper. It's very easy to blame the weather!

Language work

Expressing differences and contrasts

The underlined phrases in the composition highlight this area of written language.

4.1 Exercise

Think about contrasting aspects of your own country and then use the following incomplete sentences to write about some of these contrasts in as interesting and as full a way as possible.

e.g. There is a (slight, big, enormous, marked, etc.) difference in people's ways of thinking. In the north, they are much more open-minded.

1   There are big differences ....
2   ...... is different from ....
3   ...... differ from ...... in that ....
4   .... distinguish .... from ....
5   .... distinguish between .... and ....
6   It is nothing like as .... as ....
7   Unlike ....
8   Instead of .... in the ...., there is/are .... in the ....
9   It is .... rather than ....
10 In contrast to ......, ...
11 Contrary to popular belief, ...
12 ...... contrasts greatly with ....
13 The (west) is .... as opposed to the (east), which is ....
14 The (north) is ......, whereas (*or* while) the .... is ....

4.2 Exercise

Fill in the blanks in the following text, using structures from the previous exercise and from the model composition 'How does the weather affect your mood?' In some cases there is more than one possible correct answer.

When you travel around Britain, you'll see big (1) .... the landscape: for example, it is easy to (2) .... the west coast (3) .... the south coast. The west has rocky cliffs (4) .... the south, which is flatter and more gentle. The west coast gets the full force of the Atlantic Ocean (5) .... the southern coast has only the Channel to contend with. (6) .... expectations, however, the Channel between England and France can sometimes be very rough and one of the worst gales this century occurred in the normally calm southern counties.

The hills in southern Britain are rounded, (7) .... the ones in northern Britain, which are more like wild mountains. Scotland, of course, is (8) .... populated as England so there is much more natural countryside to be seen.

(9) .... the rather gentle, almost domesticated landscape of England, you will find yourself in magnificent, dramatic scenery. (10) ...., the cities of Edinburgh and Glasgow are important cultural centres.

Composition work

> **Hints**
>
> 1 Remember that this is an examination exercise: nobody is judging you, or your opinions – just your English. It is not necessary to tell the truth!
> 2 Since you're writing directly from experience, ideas and general organisation should not be a problem; however, it is important to have very clear first and last paragraphs.
> 3 Everything you write obviously relates to you, personally, but try to limit the number of sentences beginning with '*I*'.

For the three titles below, write a first sentence which does NOT contain the words *I, myself* or *me*. (If you have difficulty, look at the first paragraph of the model composition.)

- *How do you feel about the way your country is governed?*
- *Earth, air, fire, water: which of the four elements do you find strikes the most personal note in your life?*
- *What do you do to get yourself out of a bad mood?*

Composition titles

Choose one of the titles from **Composition work** above, or one of the following titles, and write a full composition of about 300–350 words (except for the last one below).

- *What do you hate most?*
- *How much does someone's appearance influence you?*
- *You are applying for a new job, and are asked to summarise your strengths and weaknesses on the application form. Do this in two separate paragraphs, each of 150–180 words.*

Vocabulary

Idiom/metaphor: nature and weather

4.3 Exercise

Look at the following conversation, paying particular attention to the underlined idioms. As you are reading, try to work out what the expressions mean.

A: You seem to be <u>making very heavy weather of</u> this exercise. It's not at all complicated.

B: It's OK for you to talk. You're a genius at maths, you get through these exercises like <u>greased lightning</u>.

A: The secret is, don't listen to what the professor says – that's <u>a lot of hot air</u>. Just think logically for yourself.

B: To tell the truth, I'm <u>a bit under the weather</u> today, so my brain is less active than usual.

A: I'll help you. Look, all you do is multiply by 2.3 and then divide by 3.5 . . .

B: Oh I see. That's the first time I've understood what to do. Gosh, you're like <u>a breath of fresh air</u>. Thanks a lot. I owe you a favour.

A: <u>Save it for a rainy day</u>.

Below are the definitions of the underlined idioms (not in the right order!). How close were your definitions?

1   to feel unwell
2   refreshing
3   a lot of words but with not much substance
4   extremely quickly
5   to make something more difficult than it really is
6   to keep it for another time when it might be needed

Descriptive verbs: liquids

4.4 Exercise   With the help of a partner and a dictionary, put the verbs in their correct forms into the sentences.

gush   lap   drip   seep   soak   pour   drift   spill   trickle   drench   spray

1   I didn't sleep a wink because the tap was .... all night long.
2   She was trying to .... the wine into the glass but unfortunately .... some on the tablecloth.
3   The tanker was holed below the water-line and oil .... into the sea at an alarming rate.
4   It was a perfect day. The water gently .... against the sides of the boat as we .... downstream.
5   His head hit the pavement with a crash and blood began to .... slowly from a wound on his forehead.
6   The poisons and pesticides used on plants slowly .... into the soil and eventually get into the streams and rivers.
7   In order to remove that stain, you should .... the shirt in cold water.
8   I forgot my umbrella this morning so I was completely .... by the time I reached the office.
9   She .... herself from head to foot with perfume.

As a group, discuss the characteristics of these words and the kind of situations when you can use them, e.g. blood can *gush* from a wound.

End of vocabulary

CHAPTER 5   Discussion

Text work

'Discuss the role of sport in the modern world'. Before reading the model composition, talk about this subject with your neighbour – why do we do sport nowadays, is it the same as it always has been, etc.?

Now read the composition and see if any of your points are included.

5.1 Exercise

After reading, look at the structure of the composition and say what the main point/ theme is in each paragraph.

Introduction . . . .
Paragraph 1 . . . .
Paragraph 2 . . . .
Paragraph 3 . . . .
Paragraph 4 . . . .
Conclusion . . . .

Discuss the role of sport in the modern world

Sport has played an important part in our lives for many centuries. For some it seems as necessary and natural an activity as eating and sleeping, for others it is just entertainment on television.

Today it is easy to forget that sport is supposed to be for enjoyment, for the good feeling that is produced when the body has done some physical work. Many people nowadays work in offices where they have to sit at desks for six or eight hours a day. For this reason, we feel the need for exercise at the end of the day and turn to sport. How better to get rid of tension or let off steam than to hit a ball hard or go running?

Sport, then, should provide an opportunity for people to express themselves in a way that is not always possible in work life. It can provide a challenge and can break down economic and social barriers. Thus a participant can become good at something purely through his or her ability.

However, these ideals do not always stand up when we look at professional sport. In this situation, sport seems less to do with enjoyment and more to do with making money. Top sports people appear to view their sport as a way of making as much money as possible in as short a time as possible. As a result of this desire, some particpants are prepared to take drugs to help their performances – and therefore help their bank balances. On the other hand, without these potential record-breaking performances, sport would not be as attractive to watch on TV. There is no doubt that televised sport is great entertainment.

But sport has become too connected to big business. Sponsorship, advertising and appearance money for top sports people have all led to a situation where it sometimes seems that the athlete comes second to the accountant.

To sum up, sport at an amateur level should be for enjoyment and fitness, and should provide an outlet for surplus energy. At the same time we have to say that professional sport seems to have lost these aims and is now being used by some purely as a way of making money.

Language work

The underlined phrases in the composition express two areas of written language, developing a balanced argument and expressing cause and effect.

Developing a balanced argument

5.2 Exercise

Read the following mixed comments on the participation of children in top-class international sports, like tennis, gymnastics, swimming. Add some of your own if possible.

It's unnatural for young people to earn so much money.
It's natural to exploit their talents.
They wouldn't do it if they didn't want to.
Their parents are pushing them.
They miss out on all the other enjoyments of youth.
They have fun and see the world.
They learn to be independent very early.
They don't have many friends of their own age.

Use these ideas to practise the 'balance' phrases below.

1   ....., but on the other hand .....
2   On the one hand ....., while on the other hand .....
3   .....; however, ...
4   ....., but .....
5   .....; at the same time, ...
6   For some ....., whereas for others .....

Expressing cause and effect

5.3 Exercise

Read the following about the athlete, Ben Johnson.

Traces of a steroid drug were discovered in Ben Johnson, the 100m record-breaking athlete, after the 1988 Olympics in Seoul. He was stripped of his medals and banned from the sport for three years. He changed almost overnight from being a national hero to being a national embarrassment.

Use the information to practise the 'cause and effect' phrases below.

1	....., and for this reason	5	.... because of ......
2	As a result of	6	...... owing to ......
3	......; consequently, ...	7	.... due to ......
4	.... and therefore (or thus)	8	.... led to ......

Composition work

Hints

1 Be clear in your mind what words in the title are the important discussable ones.
2 There are always two sides to a discussion. It is not necessary to find both sides of every point you make, but evidence of some balance should be visible.
3 Avoid making your points too personal – keep it objective (except perhaps in the conclusion). Use variations on 'Some people think that ...' or 'It is felt that ...' etc.
4 Think of your points (approx. 4) before you begin. When writing, make sure you know which are your main points, and which are expansions or illustrations of them.
5 Getting started is hard: one way is to use some kind of general 'historical' statement in the introduction:
   e.g. 'Killing is never justified. Discuss.'
   Since the beginning of time, man has killed in order to survive.
6 Make the conclusion by summarising in one or two sentences your main arguments. Add a personal opinion if you wish, or perhaps a hypothetical question.

Getting ideas for compositions

1 Look at point 1 in the Hints Box.
   Find the 'extreme' words in the title, which may make it easy for you to express counter arguments or compromises.

   Example 1: 'Killing animals is wrong.'
   Wrong? Always? In some circumstances? Which animals?
   Example 2: 'The Individual has no power to control his/her life any more.'
   No power? How much? In what circumstances? How much should (s)he have?

What is discussable in the following?
- *Old people are no longer valued members of society.*
- *We would all be a lot happier if aeroplanes had never been invented.*
- *Discuss the role of prisons in society.*
- *The smoking of pipes, cigars and cigarettes should be banned.*

2   Think of the subject at different times: Past Present Future
    Example: 'Large scale unemployment is now a permanent feature of our society. Discuss.'

    Past: *Industrial Revolution/mass employment/cheap labour, coal etc.*

    Present: *time of change/foreign competition/whole areas with little work*

    Future: *different patterns of employment/leisure*

    Now do the same with *Old people are no longer valued members of society.*
    Past: . . .
    Present: . . .
    Future: . . .

3   Think of opposites and unlikely interpretations of the title to stimulate ideas.
    Example: 'We would all be a lot happier if aeroplanes had never been invented.'

    Happier/unhappier: *think who would miss aeroplanes most*
    Had never been invented: *what if they had always been part of life and somebody had invented an alternative, such as the horse?!*

    Now try the same idea with: *Describe the lifestyle of those who work while others sleep.*

Organisation of compositions

1   List approximately four ideas to include in each of the above compositions.
    Example: (for the model composition)
    – amateur versus professional sport
    – sport for enjoyment, but also for health (too little physical activity today)
    – way of expressing your real self
    – professional sport equals money (drugs, sponsorship, etc.)

2   When you have made some notes on the points you want to include, decide which is your main point (consider writing this first after the introduction, or possibly last for maximum effect).

3   Support your point through illustration or example, i.e. go from abstract to concrete.

4   A new paragraph indicates some kind of change – an introduction of a new point, or a contrast to a point made previously. Wherever possible, make some kind of link with the previous paragraph – often the last sentence. Look at the model composition and identify the links at the beginning of paragraphs 2–5. Do the links emphasise similarities, differences, contrasts or the general theme; do any of them connect to the last sentences of the previous paragraphs?

5   Look at point 5 in the Hints Box. Write short introductory paragraphs for some of the above compositions (look back to the model composition for an example).

Composition titles

Choose one of the titles in **Composition work** above, or one of the following titles, and write a full composition of about 300–350 words.

● *'Life is getting better all the time.' Discuss.*
● *Discuss the role of drugs, both legal and illegal, in our daily life.*

Vocabulary

Topic vocabulary: sport

Look through the following vocabulary bank and give a context for each one.

to take or do exercise	to be disqualified	a drug test
to be healthy, fit	to sponsor; sponsorship	a fitness fanatic
to run the risk of injury		a referee
to be injured; an injury	**Places**	an umpire
to set or break a record	a football pitch	amateur; an amateur
to win; a winner; winning	a golf course	professional; a
to draw	a boxing ring	professional
to beat, to defeat, to be	a sports centre	officials
unbeaten	an athletics track	players
to lose	an ice rink	a trainer
to train	a swimming pool	a coach
to coach	a tennis court	an opponent; the
to support; support		opposition
to compete; competitive	strength	an athlete
to score	endurance	supporters or fans

5.4 Exercise

Complete the following text about a football player. Use some of the above words, changing the form where necessary.

John Charlesman is a member of Charlford United football club. Every day the lads (1) .... together in order to improve their game. John is being (2) .... by an ex-international at the moment. They are working specially on his ball-passing skills. Charlford United are a very (3) .... team, they do not like losing. At home matches, they receive good (4) .... from their (5) .... and usually manage to (6) .... the opposition, or at least (7) .... with them. Last Saturday, John (8) .... the (9) .... goal in a thrilling victory for Charlford United. John earns his living from football. He is a (10) .... player and the team is (11) .... by a large computer firm. Without this (12) ...., the club would not be able to keep going. At 21 John feels (13) .... and healthy. He earns a lot of money but he needs to make as much as possible now in case an (14) .... forces him to stop playing.

5.5 Exercise

Complete the following sentences, using the vocabulary above.

1 The football match had to be cancelled because the .... was water-logged after the heavy rain.
2 The champion .... his .... by three sets to one, and was once again through to the final.
3 Some sports, like weight-lifting, are a test of .... whereas others, like marathon running, need ....

4   At the Seoul Olympics Ben Johnson .... a new world record for the 100m, but later he was ...... because of a positive ....

5   Most professional sports people now receive .... from commercial concerns.

6   To make the top in any sport you have to have a .... instinct.

7   When a football player's playing career is over, he often turns to .... younger players.

8   Why is it that football .... are so much more violent than those who watch baseball?

9   If you push yourself beyond your limit, you .... serious injury.

10   Golf is a popular way for older people to ....

11   She goes jogging every day, does weight training twice a week and cycles to work. She's a real ....

12   The sports facilities in our town are very poor – we have no athletics ...., only two tennis ...., and an indoor sports .... which is too small.

Current questions

1   How much should professional sports people be paid?
2   Is it possible to have international amateur sport?
3   Can sport ever be drug-free?
4   How important is sponsorship in sport?

Verb combinations: 'off' (1)   *Theme: sport*

5.6 Exercise

Below are ten infinitives. Can you put them (in the correct form) into the ten sentences?

to display one's talents in a too-obvious way
to become worse
to isolate
to get rid of (unwanted feelings, etc.)
to become less intense
to cancel
to have a short sleep
to distract/disturb
to leave (a means of transport)
to begin (a journey)

1   So much snow fell over the weekend that the skiing village of Greenforth was ......

2   His opponent was so slow that Boris Ivanov, chess champion of the world, was seen to .... between moves.

3   Sport is the best way of .... surplus energy.

4   The standard of play has .... in recent years and the team is no longer attractive to watch.

5   Snooker is a game which requires great concentration. It's very easy to be .... by someone in the audience coughing.

6   His enthusiasm for aerobics will soon .... He never manages to keep up an interest for very long.

7   The match was .... owing to fog in the second half.

8   The challenger was late for the fight because he travelled to the stadium by bus and, unfortunately, ... at the wrong stop.

9   They .... from base camp at dawn and hoped to reach the summit by lunchtime.

10   He is very skilful with the ball so why does he have to ......? Maybe it's to impress his fans.

Now see if you can match the following verb combinations to the definitions above. Work with a partner, or an English–English dictionary.

- to set off ....
- to cut off ....
- to work off ....
- to show off ....
- to go off ....
- to nod/doze/drop off ....
- to call off ....
- to put s'one off ....
- to wear off ....
- to get off ....

Finally, put the verb combinations into the original ten sentences, and then write examples of your own.

Note also: a show-off (a person); off-putting (adjective)

End of vocabulary

CHAPTER 6
Discuss + opinion

Text work

Look at the title of the model composition and say what you think before reading the text. How are we exploiting the earth and are there any signs that we are learning to be more careful? What is your general feeling – are you optimistic or pessimistic for the earth's future?

Now read the text and see if the writer agrees with you.

If we continue to exploit the earth in the way we have been doing, the planet will soon be destroyed. Do you agree?

Man has always regarded himself as the most important species on earth and has used whatever the planet can provide for his own good. It is only recently that we have begun to question this behaviour and to realise that it cannot continue.

The second half of the twentieth century has seen many dramatic changes in the way we live, particularly in industrialised countries, and our environment is now paying the price for this. Scientists tell us that there are holes in the ozone layer caused by excessive production of CO_2, and this is likely to lead to a warming of the earth's climate. It is quite conceivable that the polar ice caps will begin to melt and this might well result in large areas of land being flooded. Many people will, consequently, lose their homes and their livelihoods.

The dangers of the warming-up of the earth, or the greenhouse effect as it is called, is something which it is becoming 'fashionable' to discuss and worry about. However, there are other less fashionable aspects of the problem which, unless controlled, will lead to dramatic changes in the life of our planet. The destruction of large areas of forests is not only reducing the oxygen supply but destroying the natural habitat of thousands of different plants, animals, birds and insects.

Apart from these examples, the animal world has suffered greatly from man's greed. Our attitude seems to be: if we can use an animal either to make money from or to use for our own benefit, then we have the right to do so regardless of whether this causes the species to become extinct.

In my view, we will have to reassess our way of living and question whether continued growth at the expense of other creatures and of the planet itself is acceptable. Personally, I believe that the worsening situation will in all probablility force us to change our behaviour both at an individual and a national level. The developed world, which is responsible for the majority of the environmental problems we are now facing, also has a responsibility to help the underdeveloped countries not make the same mistakes.

It is my opinion that our exploitation of the earth has already put its survival at risk; but I think there is a chance that, if we all work together, we will be able to save our planet from destruction.

Language work

Speculating and expressing personal opinions

The underlined phrases in the composition highlight these two areas of written language.

6.1 Exercise

Complete the sentences using the topic of possible future developments in medical knowledge (e.g. cures for all kinds of cancer? laser surgery? transplant surgery? choosing the sex, character etc. of your baby?)

e.g. *It is quite conceivable that we will be able to choose the sex of our babies.*

Speculating
1   ...... is likely to ......
2   It is likely that ...... will ......
3   There is every/little likelihood that ...... will ......
4   There is every/little likelihood of ......
5   It is conceivable that ......
6   It is inconceivable that ......
7   In all probability ......
8   ...... may/might well ......
9   There is a chance that ......

Expressing personal opinion
10   As I see it, ...
11   In my opinion/view, ...
12   Personally, I ......
13   To me, ...
14   It is my opinion that ......

Composition work

> **Hints**
>
> 1   This is similar to the other discursive composition (see Chapter 5), but this time your personal opinion is being asked for.
> 2   Try to back up your points with concrete examples/illustrations.
> 3   The best place to express your personal opinion is towards the end of the composition, probably in the conclusion.

For the following titles, write
a)   the introductory paragraph
b)   your points for the discussion and
c)   your opinion

● *Too much emphasis today is put on physical appearance. Do you agree?*
● *Life one hundred years ago was much more stressful than it is today. How true do you think this is?*
● *Upbringing is more important than parentage in shaping a child. Do you agree?*

Composition titles

Choose one of the titles from **Composition work** above, or one of the following titles, and write a full composition of about 300–350 words.

- *'People who break the law forfeit their right to be treated in a civilised way by society.' Do you agree?*
- *Rail before road? Assess the relative merits of these two methods of transport in the life of your country.*
- *The world is one community, and the primary responsibility of national governments is a global one. How true do you think this is?*

Vocabulary

Descriptive verbs: light and fire

6.2 Exercise

Working with a partner, and a dictionary when necessary, match the following verbs with the situations below.

e.g. strong sun on a fair skin *burn*

glow smoulder blaze dazzle burn flash sparkle shine flicker scald sweat

1   a blue light on top of a police car
2   a big, beautiful diamond
3   full-beam headlights of a car coming towards you at night
4   a light or flame showing an unsteadiness
5   a pair of shoes that have been well-polished
6   a fire that has been put out but may burn again
7   the steam from a kettle if it makes contact with flesh
8   a person who is very hot, maybe from running
9   a big, welcoming fire on a cold winter's day
10   your face when you come inside after a walk in the frosty air

Check with your teacher that you have identified the verbs correctly.
Now write illustrative sentences for the above, using the relevant verbs.

e.g. I looked through my driving mirror and was alarmed to see a police car behind me with its light...

Topic vocabulary: animal world and natural world

6.3 Exercise

Talk for one minute abut some of these aspects of the natural world using the words given. You can change the form of the words if you wish.

elephant	to poach
	ivory
	a threatened species
tiger	to hunt
	fur
	an endangered species
	to wipe out
trees	the rain forests
	to cut down
	the natural habitat
	to destroy; destruction
desert	(a) drought
	(a) crop failuure
	(a) famine
	a natural disaster
whales	whaling
	to become extinct
	to ban
seals	to slaughter; the slaughter
	skins
	to club
wildlife reserves/zoos	conservation
	to breed
	survival
	to do research into
	to die out

Current questions

1   Why should humans have the right to use or kill animals?
2   How can people be educated to take care of the world better?
3   Does it matter if some species become extinct?

HOW dINoSauRS beCAMe eXTiNcT

End of vocabulary

CHAPTER 7   Speeches

Hints

1   State your reason for making the speech, or its purpose.
2   Address the audience (*'you'*, *'ladies and gentlemen'*).
3   Vary the style of your language depending on your listeners – is it a formal speech, should it be relaxed and humorous, do you want to exaggerate in order to be more forceful, etc.?

Composition work

Think of a) first and last sentences and b) the style you would use for the following speeches.

- *You have been asked, as student representative, to make a speech welcoming a group of foreign students to your college. The group are part of an exchange system between their college and yours.*
- *You are leaving your company after working there for ten years. A colleague has just presented you with a gift from all your co-workers. Make the speech in response.*
- *You are standing for election in your local council. At a public meeting, attended by both supporters and the opposition, outline your reasons for wanting to represent the people, and some of your proposals.*

Now read the model composition.

There is a public enquiry for a new sports complex which is being planned in your town. Write two speeches, one as a representative of the local residents, who are against the proposal, and the second as a representative of the local council, which favours the scheme.

First speech

Good evening, ladies and gentlemen. I represent a group of local residents and we would like to express our opposition to the proposed building of a sports complex in Burbury Road.

To begin with, we feel Burbury Road is the wrong place. This is a residential area and we do not feel it is appropriate for a large, commercial building to be put up in our midst. Why can't it be built in a more suitable place, near the city centre, for instance?

In the second place, we know that there will be an increase in the amount of noise and traffic in the area and we are not prepared to tolerate a disruption to our peaceful existence. Besides, where are all these cars going to park?

Above all, we believe that the centre will be a waste of money here. Most teenagers, surely the most important potential customers, will not be able to use the place because they haven't got cars and there is no bus service in this area.

In short, the proposal should be abandoned.

▶

Second speech

I would like, as a representative of the local council, to answer some of Mr Pratt's questions and to reassure you all about this proposed development. First of all, the architects have designed a building which will blend in well with the neighbourhood and, furthermore, the council has undertaken to landscape the car park with trees and shrubs. As a result, the residents will hardly know that the centre is there.

Secondly, as everyone knows, there is no land available for development in the city centre so we are forced to look elsewhere. With regard to transport, the council will be running a regular bus service from the city centre throughout the day and evening to cater for all those without cars, so everyone – young and old – will be able to use the facilities.

In conclusion, the council is confident that the centre will be a financial success and will fill a need in the community.

Language work

Sequencing points and giving examples

The underlined phrases in the speeches highlight these two areas of language.

7.1 Exercise

Think of four reasons, and one supporting example, *either* for *or* against the following:
– *compulsory military service for men and women*
– *living in the country of your birth*
– *making school optional*

Now tell your neighbour these points, or write them down, using the following language. Keep the most important point until the end (no. 4) and then write a short conclusion (no. 5).

1 To start/begin with ... First of all, ... First(ly), ...	3 Besides, ... Furthermore, ... In addition, ... Moreover, ...	5 In short/brief, ... In conclusion, ... To sum up, ...
2 In the second place, ... Secondly, ... Then, ...	4 Above all, ... Finally, ...	

Composition titles

Choose one of the titles from **Composition work** on page 83, or one of the following titles, and write a speech of about 250–300 words.

● *As the boss of a small company, you have to announce some bad news to your colleagues/employees (e.g. poor financial results, redundancies, economies). Write the speech you would make to them.*
● *You are taking part in a debating competition and have been asked to speak in favour of smoking. Write the speech you would make.*

Vocabulary

Idiom/metaphor: games and sports

7.2 Exercise   Fit the following into the sentences below, making any changes that are necessary.

to take unnecessary risks
to start with
to deal with
to be up-to-date with
to start prematurely
to tell a secret
to be in the same difficult situation
to start again from the beginning
to be extremely unlikely
to accept (something) without considering it to be a problem
to be legal
to perform well

1 I'm sorry you were disappointed with his performance. Normally, he's much better than that. He wasn't really .... tonight.
2 It is necessary to .... the problem of inflation before we can bring down interest rates.
3 The fact that we have no more orders for our product affects us all, both management and workers. For once, we are all ....
4 Oh bother! You've interrupted me in the middle of counting the number of words in my essay. Now I'll have to ....
5 We were going to give Dad his breakfast in bed on Sunday as a big surprise, but Tom ....
6 Right, now we have got a very full agenda for this meeting so let's .... the first item, which is executive expenses.
7 Going to the dentist is something that most people ...., but I get incredibly nervous beforehand.
8 If we want to be the market leaders, we have got to .... the latest developments in our field.
9 The transfer of the company assets to a tax haven in the Bahamas was in no way suspicious. It is all completely ....
10 To go sailing in the oceans of the world without wearing a life jacket is ....
11 Nobody thought she had a chance; her success was ....
12 I don't think the others are ready yet; be careful not to ....

Now match these expressions to the sentences.
● to dice with death
● to start from scratch
● to be against all (the) odds
● to tackle
● to kick off with
● to be in the same boat
● to give the game away
● to keep pace with
● to take s'thg in your stride
● to jump the gun
● to be above board
● to be on form

Verb combinations: 'with'   *Theme: social problems*

7.3 Exercise

Look at the following infinitives and then put them (in the correct form) into the sentences below.

to escape punishment for
to stay at the same level as
to need
to receive and to process
to support/approve of s'one
to continue doing s'thg regardless of distractions
to tolerate/bear
to be separated from s'thg/s'one

1 At one stage, the Citizens Advice Bureau .... a hundred complaints a day about the old Community Charge.
2 London .... more hostels where homeless young people could sleep.
3 It's time pensions were increased to .... the rise in the cost of living.
4 Despite having to live on the streets, the young girl would not .... her dearest friend – her dog.
5 People who are unemployed find it hard to .... their low standard of living when all around them advertisements are encouraging people to spend, spend, spend.
6 Most people who throw litter on the streets seem to .... it. I don't know anyone who has been prosecuted.
7 When it comes to controlling football hooligans, I .... the police. I think they have a really difficult job and deserve our support.
8 In the Eighties there was an increasing tendency for people just to .... their own lives, and ignore the problems of those less fortunate.

With the help of your teacher (or an English–English dictionary) match the infinitives to the following verb combinations.
* to part with s'thg ....
* to deal with s'thg ....
* could do with ....
* to put up with ....
* to get on with ....
* to get away with s'thg ....
* to keep up with s'thg/s'one ....
* to be with s'one ....

Now write sentences of your own using the eight verb combinations.

End of vocabulary

CHAPTER 8   Letters

Hints

1   The first paragraph should set the scene, and give the reason for the letter.
2   The last paragraph should state the action needed or reiterate the purpose of the letter.
3   Keep control of the paragraphs in between – try to be clear about the 'function' of each paragraph.
4   Correct display of addresses is not always necessary in an exam, but correct forms of salutation (*Dear Sir*, etc.) and signature (*Yours faithfully*, etc.) are.
5   Think about who you are writing to and how this should affect the 'tone' of your letter.

Composition work

1   Write one or two sentences to express each of the following as you would in a letter – but first think who you are writing to. Some of the situations are obviously more 'businesslike' and require a degree of formality, others may be interpreted as either formal or informal situations. Where this is the case, discuss with your neighbour the differences in the way you would express yourself.
  – ask for information about accommodation
  – express a complaint about your car
  – give a reason for writing
  – ask s'one to send you details
  – enclose something with your letter
  – make an arrangement/appointment
  – thank s'one for their help
  – change/put off an arrangement
  – apologise for making a mistake
  – express your anxiety about your elderly next-door neighbour
  – ask for an early reply to your letter

2   Write the first and last paragraphs for the following letters (think about what 'action' is required).

  ● *You saw an advertisement in the newspaper for a tour guide for groups of holidaymakers visiting your capital city. Write a letter applying for the job.*

  ● *You are thinking of setting up a small business in London. Write a letter to an estate agency stating your requirements and inquiring about property for rent.*

  ● *You stayed in a first-class hotel in New York recently and were very disappointed with several aspects of the service. Write a letter to the manager to inform him of your feelings.*

  ● *Use the situation above (the hotel in New York) and write a letter to a friend to describe your experiences at that hotel.*

Now read the model composition.

You live two doors away from a cinema and you wish to complain about the behaviour of some of the patrons. Write a letter to the manager.

Dear Sir

　　I live at No 24 Cabbage Street, two doors away from your cinema, and I would like to draw your attention to the behaviour of some of your patrons, <u>especially</u> on Saturday nights.

　　It is pointless for me and my husband to go to bed before 1.00 a.m. as we know we will not be able to get a wink of sleep, owing to the noise in the street. On more than one occasion I have been obliged to ask people to make less noise, but my requests have been ignored – your customers seem incapable of talking quietly, <u>let alone</u> closing car doors without slamming them.

　　<u>As well as</u> noise, we have to put up with <u>litter – litter</u> that is thrown into our front garden as if it were a convenient dustbin. We get crisp packets, chewing gum, hamburgers, chips, used tickets, <u>not to mention</u> large quantites of Coca Cola cans, and this is <u>not just once</u>, <u>but every</u> Saturday night.

　　<u>Needless to say</u>, I do not wish to stop people enjoying themselves at the cinema but I would like <u>you, as the manager,</u> to ask your patrons to consider the neighbours when they leave.

Yours faithfully

Language work

Intensifying and emphasising

The underlined phrases in the letter highlight the above area of written language. This is particularly useful when trying to make a point forcefully e.g. in 'strong' letters, speeches or discussion.

8.1 Exercise

Complete the following sentences using the topic of food.

1　I really like Italian food, especially ....
　　　　　　　　　　　　　particularly ....
　　　　　　　　　　　　　in particular ....

2　If you suffer from high blood pressure, then obviously/clearly you ....

3　She's keen on fruit, not just ...., but also ....

4　He's quite useless in the kitchen. He can't even butter a piece of toast, let alone .... (*used after a negative, and the second point must be more 'extreme' or 'difficult' than the first*)

5　For their golden wedding celebration they had a five course dinner, not to mention .... (*used after a positive, when you want to add extra information which emphasises even more strongly the point you are making*)

6　The first western-style restaurant to open in the USSR was, needless to say, ...

Composition titles

Write one of the letters from the **Composition work** on page 87, or one of the following letters. Use between 200–250 words.

- *Write a letter to your local newspaper describing how somebody helped you recently when you had an accident, but went away without giving their name; express your gratitude.*
- *A local café of which you are very fond is threatened with closure by property developers. Write a letter to your local council saying why you feel they should oppose this in the interests of the local community.*

Vocabulary

Topic vocabulary: life in the 90's

What is life in the latter part of the 20th century like? What are people's priorities in the northern and southern hemispheres? Discuss your ideas before looking through the following.

communism, socialism, capitalism	to be uncaring	to be environmentally friendly
consumerism	the rat race	
to look after number one	a/the welfare state	the standard of living
to opt out of	an image	the quality of life
the haves and the have-nots	a status symbol	the way of life
to be materialistic	a lifestyle	the cost of living
	to 'go green'	

8.2 Exercise

'It's alright officer, I'm not an anarchist, I'm a property developer'.

Choose a word or phrase from the above vocabulary bank, changing the form where necessary, to complete the following text.

How will life in the 90's be different from life in the 80's? Certainly in Europe, life has changed a great deal in recent years. We have seen the end of the communist states, but this does not automatically mean that (1) .... has triumphed. Most of the Eastern European countries are trying to hold on to their (2) .... principles and still believe in the (3) ...., where government supports the old, sick and unemployed.

In Western Europe, the USA and Japan, the 80's were dominated by money and the rise of the individual. Those of us with money have become even more greedy and (4) .... But at the same time we have seen a growing division between the (5) .... and (6) .... The attitude towards those people who cannot take part in the consumer boom is very often an (7) .... one. The philosophy of the 80's seems to have been rather self-centred, a case of (8) .... There are some who have reacted against this kind of society and have decided to (9) .... They have decided that their (10) .... of (11) .... is more important than their (12) .... of (13) ..... . They have chosen to live more simply and not to worry about their (14) ....., nor about acquiring the latest (15) .... Maybe this kind of (16) .... will become more common in the 90's.

One change which has been noticeable in our (17) .... of (18) .... is our awareness of environmental problems and how these affect our daily lives. Many consumers are (19) '....... ....' and only buying (20) .... products. Is this reflecting real concern or is it just another fashion? The 90's will tell us.

Current questions

1 We are not an uncaring society – just look at the amount of money people give to charities.
2 Do you think the 90's will see a rejection of materialism in the developed world?
3 'Enough is enough' – how much *is* enough?

Special vocabulary: collectives

The following collectives (**a** . . . **of** . . .) are used figuratively – one, '*a wink of sleep*' was used in the letter of complaint.

a mine of information
a clash of cultures
a flash of inspiration
a battle of wits
a wink of sleep (not get)
a piece of cake (it's a . . . [*colloquial*])

a load of rubbish
a breath of fresh air
a flood of tears
a round of applause
a sea of faces
a bag of nerves

8.3 Exercise

Put each of the above collectives in its correct sentence.

1 You can ask Tim anything, he seems to have a tremendous amount of knowledge. He is . . . .
2 Most of what you watch on TV these days is . . . . . . I don't know why we bother to pay the licence fee any more.
3 On hearing that she had been rejected by the drama school, she spent the evening in . . . .
4 Seeing a Macdonalds in the middle of Beijing seemed to me to be . . . .
5 After boring old Mr Atkins, the new head teacher is . . . .
6 When he stood on the platform in order to give his first-ever public speech, he almost fainted when he saw . . . . . . looking expectantly at him.
7 Someone next door was playing heavy metal music all night long. I didn't get . . . .
8 While I was sitting in the bath last night, the solution to our problem came to me in . . . .
9 'Cambridge Proficiency? No problem, it's . . . . . . ,' he boasted.
10 Some of the discussion programmes on TV are quite entertaining, especially when you get good speakers who have opposing views. It very often turns into . . . .
11 'Could we have . . . . . . for our most marvellous speaker? She really did keep us absorbed for the whole evening.'
12 He chain smokes, never sits still and is always giving little coughs. He really is . . . .

End of vocabulary

CHAPTER 9
Instructions and explanations

Hints

1 Be clear, logical and sequential whenever possible.
2 Don't attempt to answer this kind of question in an exam if you're not able to get your thoughts clear.
3 Imperative forms (without *you*) should generally be used.
4 Make rough notes before you start so you don't forget part of the procedure.
5 If you feel you don't know the correct vocabulary for an object or action, don't panic. You can usually get your meaning across by using phrases like **'it's a kind of . . .'**, **'it's a bit like . . .'** etc.

Read the model composition.

Describe the process involved in making something.

How to make a pot on a wheel.

First of all, you have to prepare the clay. To do this you have to knead it to remove all the air, in other words, press and pull the clay many times rather like preparing bread, until you are sure that all the air bubbles have gone. If you don't do this, there is a danger, when the pot is in the kiln, that the former might explode!

Take a piece of prepared clay of the required size and throw it firmly onto the moving wheel head. Then, making sure your hands are wet, place them around the clay to begin the centring process. It is impossible to produce a good pot unless the clay is properly centred, and many people find this the hardest thing to do. According to experts, it can take up to ten years to learn how to do this well! The process consists of a series of movements which alternately squeeze in and press down the clay.

When you are satisfied that the clay is centred (and as I said before, this is a crucial part of the process), make a hole in the centre with the index finger of your right hand – if you're right handed – and at the same time keep your left hand against the side of the clay. With your index finger, enlarge the hole by pulling the clay out towards your left hand. You have now got the beginning of the base of the pot.

To build up the sides, place one hand inside the pot and the other outside. Then, working from the base, pull up the excess clay between your hands in order to form the 'wall'. It is at this point that the pot begins to take shape.

And that's all there is to it! When you're satisfied with your efforts, remove the pot from the wheel by passing a wire under the pot while the wheel is still turning. Leave the pot to dry and then decorate it and cover it with a glaze, that is the mixture which gives the pot its shine when it is finished. Finally, put it in a kiln and 'fire', or 'cook', it at a high temperature. With a bit of luck, you will see a wonderful pot when you open the kiln some hours later.

Composition work

Make notes, in point form, for two of the following.

- *Tell someone how to get on a bicycle and start riding.*
- *Give someone an explanation of how to play a card game or board game.*
- *Tell someone how to open a bottle of wine with your corkscrew.*
- *Tell someone how to plait long hair.*
- *Explain how you make a really good cup of coffee.*

Language work

Giving instructions, rephrasing, referring

The underlined phrases in the composition highlight the above areas of written language.

9.1 Exercise

Look at the notes you made for one of the topics in **Composition work** above. Tell your neighbour how to do one of these things, using some of the phrases below.

First of all, …   Don't forget to …
Then, …   When you've …
To do this, … until …   At this point …
If you don't do this, …   At the same time, …
Make sure … .   Finally, …

Rephrasing: you might need to explain something in another way; if so, use one of the following.

…, in other words …
…, that is …
…, or …

Referring: (use this when giving written instructions/explanations)

According to …, (people, articles, sources of information etc.)
Referring to what …
As mentioned before, … / As I said before …
the former …, the latter …

9.2 Exercise

Draw a simple shape, picture or diagram like the one here.
Without being too mathematical about size, length, etc. give your neighbour instructions as to how to draw the same. Use the phrases for instructions and explanations and be prepared to rephrase if you can see your neighbour having difficulty in understanding what you want!

Composition titles

Choose one of the titles from the **Composition work** above, or one of the following titles, and write a full composition of about 300–350 words.

- *Explain how you teach someone either to swim or to knit.*
- *Write a set of instructions to give to your neighbour, who has promised to look after your rather highly-strung cat while you are away for a week.*

Vocabulary

Idiom/metaphor: bodies (foot and hand)

9.3 Exercise

Hands (and feet) are useful for other things, not just making pots! Match the expressions on the left to their definitions on the right.

- to put your foot in it =
- to pull s'one's leg =
- to have/get cold feet about s'thg =
- to put your feet up =
- to twist s'one round your little finger =
- to keep your fingers crossed =
- to come in handy =
- to be a dab hand at =
- to be a handful =
- to live from hand to mouth =

to have doubts about a decision you've made
to be difficult to control
to be useful
to be very good/skilful at
to hope things will turn out right
to have hardly enough to live on
to tease someone
to relax
to cause embarrassment by saying s'thg inappropriate
to be able to persuade s'one to do anything you want them to

Now look at the following situations and use your imagination in order to extend each one to include one of the above idioms.

1 Life for the peasants was hard. Harvests often failed and profits were non-existent.
2 If you're going climbing, take some extra rope with you.
3 You can tell Mark anything and he'll believe you.
4 Why on earth did you start talking to Jean about Tom?
5 **A:** You look exhausted.
 B: Yes, I've been Christmas shopping for six hours!
6 **A:** Do you think Charlie's father will give him the car for the weekend?
 B: . . .

7   **A:** I've got my driving test on Saturday.
    B: ...
8   I'll put the shelf up for you, if you like.
9   Why did I say 'yes' to that new job? It'll mean a lot more responsibility.
10   Good heavens! I didn't realise you had six children!

Verb combinations: 'for'   *Theme: the arts*

9.4 Exercise

Below are ten infinitives. Put them (in the correct form) into the sentences.

to participate in
to fall in love with
to mean
to come to s'one's house (and collect them)
to go in the direction of (literally)
to go in the direction of (metaphorically)
to take into account
to like
to accept (reluctantly)
to want very much

1   'When you come on, ... the door at the back of the stage, avoiding the body on the floor,' the director said.
2   BBC .... British Broadcasting Corporation.
3   The exhibition was a financial disaster because the organisers had not .... the cost of advertising and catalogue production.
4   When he saw the life-size sculpture, he .... it immediately and bought it.
5   The performance lasted four hours and at the end I .... a drink.
6   I don't really .... classical music; jazz appeals to me much more.
7   My son is keen on photography and is .... a Young Photographers Competition.
8   He wasn't given the starring role; he had to .... a less important part.
9   After three consecutive productions which played to half-empty houses, the opera company was .... financial disaster.
10   The film starts at 7.30, so I'll .... at 7.00.

Now match the following verb combinations to the definitions above and then fit them into the correct sentences. Work with a partner or an English–English dictionary.

●   to allow/bargain for ....
●   to be dying for (*informal*) ....
●   to make for ....
●   to call for ....
●   to settle for ....
●   to go for ....
●   to head for ....
●   to stand for ....
●   to fall for ....
●   to go in for ....

End of vocabulary

CHAPTER 10
Extracting and re-presenting

Extracting information – summarising

> **Hints**
>
> 1 Read the text through at least once.
> 2 Look at the summary task – what information do you have to summarise, and how long should the summary be?
> 3 Return to the text and underline the relevant points.
> 4 Write down the points in note form, rephrasing where possible. Make sure your points relate to the task.
> 5 Write up the points into a paragraph.

10.1 Exercise

1) Read the following text by Robyn Davidson about training camels.

Camel training

During this time, I also had to begin training Zeleika for riding and carrying pack. This was not easy – I had no money to buy equipment, no saddle to put on her back so that I wouldn't fall off every time she bucked, and I
5 had lost most of my nerve at Sallay's. So I rode her bareback, quietly, up and down the soft sand of the creek, not asking her to do too much – just trying to win her confidence and keep her quiet and protect my own skin. She was in such poor condition that I constantly had
10 to balance the need for training against not allowing her to worry herself back into a skeleton. Camels always lose weight during training. Instead of eating, they spend all day thinking about what you are going to do to them. Zeleika also had a lovely gentle nature which I did not
15 want to spoil. I could walk up to her anywhere in the wild, whether she was hobbled or not, and catch her, even though I could feel her muscles tighten into hard lumps with tension and fear. Her only dangerous fault was her willingness to kick. Now, a camel can kick you in
20 any direction, within a radius of six feet. They can strike

with their front legs, and kick forward, sideways or backwards with the back. One of those kicks could snap you in half like a dry twig. Teaching her to accept hobbles and side-lines was not an easy business. In fact, it
25 was ulcer-inducing if not death-producing and required infinite patience and bravery, neither of which I was particularly blessed with, but I had no choice. To quieten her I had to tie her to a tree on the halter and encourage her to eat rich and expensive hand-feed,
30 while I groomed her all over, picked up her legs, played loud music on a tape recorder and got her used to having things around her feet and on her back, all the time talking talking talking. When she did let fly with one of those terrible legs, it was out with the whip. She soon
35 learnt that this kicking got her nowhere and that it was easier to be nice, even if that niceness didn't come from the heart.

2) Collect points under these two headings.
– What problems did she have training Zeleika?
– What methods did she use to train Zeleika?

3) Look at the suggested points for the first heading, and the way these points have been written up into a paragraph of approximately 85 words.

What problems did she have training Zeleika?

– no money to buy equipment so had to ride bareback
– camel was in bad condition and she didn't want to make it worse
– had to be, for her, unnaturally patient and brave
– had to avoid being kicked

> Robyn Davidson had no money to buy equipment so she had to ride Zeleika bareback, which was difficult. Unfortunately, this particular camel was very thin and, in order not to make her condition worse, the author had to be very careful not to let the camel get too worried. Perhaps the biggest problem she had was to avoid being kicked – something that Zeleika was good at. She had to find a lot of patience and courage in herself, neither of which came naturally to her, in order to train the camel.

4) Now write up your points under the second heading into a paragraph of approximately 90 words.

Re-presenting information

In this example we are dealing with interpreting statistics from graphs, charts etc. and re-presenting the information in written form. The language used to write about these areas is very specific. Look at the following.

Nouns (& associated verbs)	Adjectives (& associated adverbs)
an increase in the number of (people)	dramatic
an increase in the amount of (money)	sharp/rapid
a growth in	marked
a rise in	steady
a decrease in	gradual
a fall in	slight
a drop in	
a reduction in	
a decline in (standards/popularity)	

how much / how many	Adjectives & associated adverbs
the majority / the minority	overwhelming
one in ten (or one out of ten)	considerable
a third of . . . / half of . . .	significant
twice / three times as many / much (as)	small / tiny
twenty per cent	
threefold	
double the number	**Time periods**
x has doubled	over the last five years
by far the most	since 1979
as many as / as much as	in the next ten years
among the highest	
a proportion of	**Reference**
an average of	According to . . . (the survey)
on average	The survey found
fewer than	The statistics show/reflect . . .

10.2 Exercise

Read the following short extracts, underlining the language used to express the trends and statistics. Then complete the task after each one, using another way of expressing the same information. The first one has been done as an example.

> Most British teenagers spend up to three hours a night watching TV but <u>fewer than one in ten</u> spend more time than that doing homework. <u>As</u> <u>many as</u> one in five 11-year-old boys and one in ten girls of the same age claimed to spend more than five hours watching TV.

e.g. Who watches most TV, 11-year-old boys or girls?

Twice as many 11-year-old boys as girls watch more than five hours' TV a night.

> Public concern on environmental issues has increased almost fourfold, according to opinion surveys for the Department of the Environment.

1 Re-express this using the words 'dramatic rise'.

> Young love is getting younger, with a third of 11-year-olds claiming to have a steady boyfriend or girlfriend, according to the latest survey. It found that 32.6 per cent of 11-year-old boys and 31.2 per cent of 11-year-old girls had 'a regular boyfriend or girlfriend'.

2 Re-express the percentage figures in the last sentence.

> Men will be retiring relatively earlier than women by the end of the decade, as more women go to work. The labour force is expected to grow by one million in the next ten years, with women accounting for 90 per cent of the growth.

3 What can be said about women and work in the future?

> British men worked 43.5 hours a week in 1987 on average, more than in any other European Community country. The EC average was 40.7 hours. British women worked an average of 29.8 hours (EC average was 33.4 hours).

4 Express the comparisons, without using percentages.

> Almost three-quarters of all cash withdrawals from banks in 1988 were from cash card machines. Only 27 per cent of withdrawals were by cheque, compared to 97 per cent in 1976.

5 What can be said about the use of cheques and cash cards?

> The number of homeless families in temporary accommodation rose 45 per cent between the end of 1986 and the end of 1988.

6 What adjective could describe the rise?

10.3 Exercise

Look at the table which shows the percentage of children who consider themselves to be smokers in Britain. Fill in the gaps in the text below.

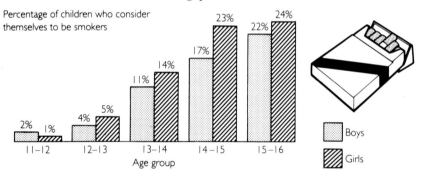

Percentage of children who consider themselves to be smokers

Overall, a higher (1) .... of young girls (2) .... boys consider themselves to be smokers. It is only in the age range 11–12 that (3) .... boys (4) .... girls smoke. At that time (5) .... as many boys smoke (6) .... girls, but this is only a tiny percentage. The survey (7) .... that the (8) .... rise (9) .... numbers of smokers occurs between the ages of 13 and 15 for both boys and girls. By the time girls reach the age of 15, approximately one (10) .... of them smoke.

Now write a similar paragraph about children and alcohol.

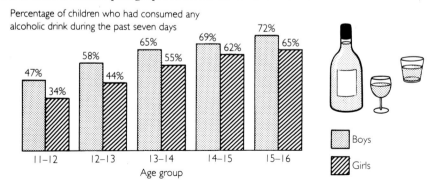

Percentage of children who had consumed any alcoholic drink during the past seven days

10.4 Exercise

Using some of the language from above, make statements about life in your community. You obviously do not have statistics available, but you can say something general about trends.

e.g. In Oxford, there has been a steady increase in the amount of traffic in the city centre over the last five years.

Use the following topics to help:
– the cost of living
– the number of people out of work
– the change in the pattern of crimes committed
– elderly people
– the video-watching and/or cinema-going habits among young people
– the growing/declining popularity of some sports

10.5 Exercise

Prepare a rough graph or table (it doesn't have to be beautiful!) of one of the following:
– temperature variations in your country (in different seasons and/or regions)
– percentage of your income spent on food, transport, accommodation, entertainment over the last five years
– percentage of your time spent on sleep over the years as a child/teenager/adult
Present your information to a classmate or the group.

Vocabulary

Idiom/metaphor: number

Here are some more statistics – this time metaphorical ones!

$1/2$ to go halves

1 (go) back to square one

2 to be in two minds; to have second thoughts about; to put two and two together

4 on all fours

9 nine times out of ten

10 ten to one

19 nineteen to the dozen

10.6 Exercise

Match the above to the underlined phrases in the following sentences.

1 In order to pass the window without being seen, he had to go <u>on his hands and knees</u>.
2 If a man and a woman with the same qualifications and experience go for the same job, <u>it is usual that</u> the man gets it.
3 I <u>can't decide</u> whether to do another degree or travel for a couple of years.
4 If we plan a picnic for the weekend, <u>I bet</u> it'll rain.

5 Unfortunately, their design for a wingless plane didn't work so they had to start again from the beginning.
6 Normally the Prime Minister was very clear about what she wanted for the nation, so it was surprising to read that she was thinking again about her proposed tax policy.
7 You can't afford to take me out for dinner so why don't we each pay for ourselves.
8 Despite the fact that they couldn't speak each other's language, the two five-year-olds were soon chatting without stopping.
9 It didn't take a genius to work out what had happened. Her tears said everything.

Special vocabulary: paired words (mixed)

The 'camel lady' referred to walking her camel 'up and down'. Here are some more pairs of words joined by and.

10.7 Exercise

Substitute the correct paired phrase for the underlined definition in the sentences below.

e.g. He's the kind of person who will change his mind a dozen times before making a decision.

    Answer: chop and change

trial and error	short and sweet	by and large
sick and tired of	chop and change	hard and fast
touch and go	few and far between	hit and miss
safe and sound	black and blue	

1 I'm fed up with your noise!
2 Sunny days are rare in January.
3 If you want your letter to be published in the newspaper, keep it concise.
4 The only way to learn something is by experimenting.
5 There are very few strict rules about English grammar.
6 I slipped on the ice yesterday and now my bottom is badly bruised.
7 It's doubtful whether Simon will pass his final exam next week.
8 His performance as an actor is very unpredictable – sometimes he's brilliant, other times he's awful.
9 On the whole, it has been a successful conference.
10 While their mothers were telephoning each other frantically at four in the morning, the two girls were alive and unharmed at the house of a friend.

To help remember these phrases, choose one of them and make (mime) a gesture that you can associate with it. The rest of your group will try to guess your choice.

End of vocabulary

Listening

It takes two to speak the truth – one to speak and another to hear.

H D Thoreau

INTRODUCTION

Why is listening a problem?

Listening in a classroom to a cassette requires different skills from listening in real life.

In real life, listening takes place when you want to find out some information, for example from a lecture, a radio news broadcast, at a station or airport, or when you are in conversation with somebody. It very rarely takes place as an isolated skill – most of the time, there is an interaction between the speaker and the listener and much of the time there is face to face communication.

Listening in the classroom, especially connected to listening comprehension exercises, can be unrealistic and causes different problems:

– there is no possibility of interrupting the flow
– there are no gestures, facial expressions etc. to help with comprehension, especially of mood
– the listener has no prior knowledge of the topic (and may not even be interested in it)
– the 'speech' may be long and cause problems of concentration
– words may cause problems (new ones, cultural reference, slang, collocation)
– there may be unfamiliar accents
– it is impossible to say, as you would in real life, *'Hang on a minute, I don't understand. Could you explain what you mean?'*
– the tasks that follow listening texts may have less to do with listening comprehension than with reading skills
– 'listening skills' which are natural in your own language, e.g. predicting, may have to be re-learnt

CHAPTER I
Sounds of English

1.1 Exercise

R1

Can you underline the word that is being said in the following pairs of sentences? The differences are sometimes minimal, but important.

1 She'll be leaving / living here in six weeks' time.
2 Ask for the bell / bill, please.
3 It's perfectly possible to write with a pin / pen.
4 We passed the man / men on the way to town.
5 He spent many hours wondering / wandering about the city.
6 There's a puddle / paddle in the boat.
7 Some ports / parts are more interesting when visited for a second time.
8 I've worn / won this medal and now I'm going to retire.
9 He was old and had naughty / knotty fingers.
10 Did you know she was training to be a belly / ballet dancer?

11 The collar / colour is wrong, I'm afraid.
12 We need to test / taste the product before we sell it.
13 You'll have to work / walk faster if you want to finish.
14 Water was escaping from the leak / lake.
15 Three cheers / chairs please for the Kennedys.
16 The mice ran through the hall / hole and escaped into a cupboard.
17 We found / phoned John last night after supper.
18 He patted / batted the ball across the net.
19 We need new drains / trains. The system cannot cope.
20 My ankle / uncle is much better, thank you.
21 If you touch me, I'll sing / sink.
22 This plant stinks / stings when you get near it
23 The ban / bang surprised everyone.
24 Could you collect / correct the homework for me?
25 The farmer had to rescue the ram / lamb from the river.

26 First of all, you must eat / heat the chocolate.
27 Don't go too close to the hedge / edge.
28 The children laughed at the thin / tin man.
29 The mountain pass / path was used by the refugees.
30 The cause / course of the war can only be clearly seen in retrospect.
31 The prize / price was better than expected.
32 Can I take this sheet / seat, or is someone using it?
33 Our cat is almost a person / Persian.
34 I'm interested in real life / live documentaries on TV.
35 Please take a photograph of / off the pile of things on my desk.
36 Gosh you are lucky! It's a vast / fast car.
37 The van / ban started first thing this morning.
38 Genghis Khan's last fort / thought was dedicated to his wife.
39 Her shin / chin hit the table as she fell from the ladder.

40 I washed / watched him in the bath.
41 He was choking / joking because he had just eaten some sheep's eyes.
42 The fans jeered / cheered their team at the end of the game.
43 The wine / vine is a very fine one and should be kept.
44 Oh dear! We can't use that yolk / joke, it's a bad one.
45 He breathed / breezed in.
46 It seems worse / worth doing it slowly.

Now, with a partner, take it in turns to say one of the sentences. Write down the word you think your partner says, and then check it.

Vocabulary

Idiom/metaphor: preposition collocation (1)

e.g. Sentence 30 in Exercise 1.1: *The cause of the war can only be clearly seen in retrospect.*

1.2 Exercise

Which one goes in which sentence?

1 He is .... burst into tears if you mention that name.
2 He passed the test .... some last minute revision.
3 He was given a loan .... the normal conditions of repayment.
   subject to   liable to   thanks to

4 When we arrived, the party was ....

5 Having been in the same job for twenty years, she felt ....

6 It's much easier to understand, ..., why it happened.

in a rut   in retrospect   in full swing

7 I'm exhausted. I've been .... since 4 o'clock this morning.

8 I know we haven't booked but let's try .... They might have some tickets left.

9 He spent ten years working on his theory and was .... of a breakthrough when he died.

on the offchance   on the go   on the verge

Together with your neighbour, work out synonyms/explanations for the expressions. Check them with your teacher, or a dictionary.

Descriptive verbs: communicating

1.3 Exercise

R2

Listen to ten utterances and decide which communicating verb is appropriate.

tease   blurt out   mutter   stammer   whisper   chat
hesitate   yell   mumble   croak

Put the verbs, in the correct form, into the sentences.

1 The old man walked out of the shop .... to himself about the price of bread.

2 A: What were you talking about on the phone?
   B: Oh, nothing special. We were just .... about this and that.

3 Try to speak a little more clearly. You'll never learn to be an actor if you .... like that.

4 When he was taken to the police station for questioning, he .... the name of his accomplice.

5 'Would you two in the back row stop .... together. If you've got anything interesting to say, say it so we can all hear.'

6 'But ... but ... how did you find out?' the girl ....

7 His favourite pastime when drunk seemed to be sitting by the roadside and .... at all the cars as they passed.

8 It was a difficult question and she .... before answering.

9 At the end of a long and tiring campaign with many speeches, the Presidential candidate was only able to .... his thanks to his supporters.

10 'You didn't really buy me a toothbrush for my birthday, did you? Come on, stop .... me, tell me what you really bought.'

Put the above verbs with their definitions.

● to speak almost without any voice, due to pain, emotion or dryness
● to speak quietly, often to yourself and often complaining
● to say something suddenly
● to pause for thought
● to speak loudly, to shout
● to talk informally about not very serious things
● to speak quietly to someone so no-one else can overhear you
● to try playfully to make someone believe something that's not true
● to speak with hesitation and repetition due to nerves or speech defects
● to speak indistinctly so as a result others can't hear or understand

End of vocabulary

CHAPTER 2
Contractions / weak forms

2.1 Exercise

R3

Say the following sentences.

Joe and Paul went to town.
Joseph and Paula went to town.
Jonathan and Christopher went to town.
Antonia and Emmanuel went to town.

In English, the stressed syllables in a sentence are important – they carry the main message. Two things happen to the remaining syllables:
1   they must be 'squashed' together, since their job is mainly to connect together the important sounds
2   they must not be pronounced too strongly.

In the above sentences, it takes roughly the same time to say sentence 4, with its increased number of syllables, as it does to say sentence 1. Because of this need to 'squash' the unimportant parts in order to keep the stressed parts clear, contraction and weak pronunciation take place.
Now listen to the above four sentences and repeat each one, concentrating on keeping the same rhythm, stress and timing.

2.2 Exercise

R4

Listen to the next set of sentences and repeat after each one, concentrating on keeping the stressed syllables clear and the weak syllables squashed!
Discuss with your teacher the differences between the pronunciation of the full and weak forms.

2.3 Exercise

R5

For this exercise, when you have repeated what you hear on the cassette, write the sentence in order to check that you have heard correctly!

Vocabulary

Idiom/metaphor: water

Remember what you were doing with contractions and weak forms. Make sure you pay similar attention to these phrases when saying them aloud.

2.4 Exercise

Replace the underlined phrases with one of the idioms below, making any changes that are necessary.

1   Nobody's talking to anyone. We need a game to get the party going.
2   We decided to do something a bit risky and start our own business.
3   The children needed to use up some energy after having sat quietly for three hours.
   to take the plunge   to let off steam   to break the ice

4   My contribution is only small but every little bit helps.
5   The problem she mentioned was only the most obvious one; there were many other reasons too.
6   She felt awkward being the only woman in the parliament.
   the tip of the iceberg   like a fish out of water   a drop in the ocean

7 Two years ago he walked out leaving her <u>helpless</u>.
8 The Minister was really <u>given a difficult task</u> having to negotiate with the unions on her first day in the job.
9 I feel completely <u>lost</u> when people start talking about quantum physics.

to leave s'one   to be thrown in at   to be out of
high and dry   the deep end   one's depth

For discussion

When do you feel
– like a fish out of water?
– out of your depth?
– like taking the plunge?
What do you do
– to break the ice?
– to let off steam?
– when you are thrown in at the deep end?

Special vocabulary: containers

2.5 Exercise

What other things can you put in the following containers?

e.g. a bottle   wine, …
Answer: *gin, milk, perfume*

For practice, make sure you don't pronounce the 'of' too strongly – it should have a very weak pronunciation.

1	a jar	jam, …, …	7	a pot	paint, …, …
2	a box	chocolates, …, …	8	a tin	soup, …, …
3	a packet	cigarettes, …, …	9	a barrel	beer, …, …
4	a sack	potatoes, …, …	10	a crate	oranges, …, …
5	a sachet	shampoo, …, …	11	a carton	cream, …, …
6	a tube	toothpaste, …, …	12	a bag	sweets, …, …

2.6 Exercise

Use these words to ask for the following items when you go shopping.

book   loaf   ball   pad   pair   bar   pack   bunch

1 a ……. of soap, chocolate
2 a ……. of flowers, bananas
3 a ……. of string, wool
4 a ……. of cards

5 a ……. of gloves, scissors
6 a ……. of bread
7 a ……. of stamps
8 a ……. of paper

End of vocabulary

CHAPTER 3
Stress = meaning

When listening to extended passages, do not try to understand every word – not only is it unnecessary, it is impossible: some words are new, some are indistinct and, above all, speech goes too fast for this kind of comprehension (you probably don't actually *hear* every individual word clearly when listening to a passage in your own language). Instead, concentrate on listening for the *stressed* words – these are the ones that carry the important parts of the message. You may notice that the voice often 'moves' down or occasionally up in its intonation on the stressed words.

3.1 Exercise

 R6

Look at the following stressed words that have been extracted from a news item. Can you work out what the piece of news is?

Stressed words: liner QE2 / way / Norwegian fiords / called in yesterday / rescue / 49 oil workers / trapped / oil platform / North Sea. Platform / damaged / gale-force winds / danger / breaking up. None / men / injured.

Now listen to the extract to confirm what you thought.

3.2 Exercise

R7

Listen to the following four news items and identify the stressed words. In the first extract, the stressed words have been missed out of the transcript, so you have to fill them in.

1   Richard Bleasdale has been .... for .... in .... on .... of .... to .... He was said to have .... the .... of .... to .... in .... It is .... known .... the .... were smuggled out of the .... and .... of .... are .... being .... by the ....

Practise reading the item aloud, making the stressed words really clear.

The second item is written out in full. As you listen, mark the stressed words.

2   Details of an accident in 1968 at the Hellabeach nuclear power station were disclosed yesterday. The accident, which was not made public at the time, was caused when a pipe burst under pressure and radio-active steam escaped into the plant. The quick action of the station supervisor prevented what could have been a major disaster. Questions about current safety standards at Hellabeach are to be raised in Parliament today.

Again, try reading the item aloud. Now try reading it at the same time as the voice on the cassette!

3   For the remaining two items (the first is about education standards and the second about flooding), just write down the stressed words. From these words you should be able to build up a picture of the complete item.

3.3 Exercise

R8

Listen to the following short extract, 'A Letter Home from Vietnam'. Write down the stressed words and build up the story from them.
Pre-listening vocabulary: 'a purple heart' is a medal given to members of the US Armed Forces who have been wounded during battle.

Vocabulary

Topic vocabulary: media

The press
a journalist, an editor, a critic, a reporter, a reviewer
an article, a leader, a review, a column, an editorial, a feature
the tabloids, the gutter press, quality papers, the heavies
a headline, to print, to publish, the circulation, the readership
a periodical, a magazine, a comic

TV/radio
to broadcast, transmit, put on
channels – independent, commercial, state-owned, satellite
a broadcaster, a newsreader, a script writer, a chat-show host,
a presenter
a serial, a soap, an episode, a series
peak-viewing

General
sensationalism, cheque-book journalism, invasion of privacy
to be biased, neutral, objective
to form an opinion, to have an influence on
censorship, freedom of the press

3.4 Exercise   Fill in the gaps with one or more of the choices given.

1   The Daily Mirror has a .... of 3 million.
     coverage   readership   publication   circulation
2   The person who goes out to find the news stories, to interview people and dig
     up the stories behind the stories, is ....
     an editor   a reviewer   a reporter   a critic
3   On the front page of yesterday's *Guardian* there were only three ....
     printed across all eight ....
     articles   editorials   leaders   columns
4   Here's a good .... of Alan Parker's new film by my favourite critic.
     feature   article   review   letter
5   In Britain there are eleven national daily papers, six of which are printed on
     small-size sheets and are called the ....
     quality papers   heavies   tabloids
6   Newspapers or magazines which contain stories about people's private lives
     and scandals are often criticised and referred to as ....
     the Press   sensational   comics   the gutter press
7   The broadcasting organisations were attacked by the government for being
     .... against them.
     biased   neutral   objective
8   The story of an oil-rich family from Texas became the most popular .... on
     TV in the 80's.
     serial   series   soap   episode
9   At the moment in the UK there are two .... TV channels (ITV and Channel 4,
     whose revenue comes from advertising) and two .... ones (BBC1 and
     BBC2, whose income derives from a licence fee); there are no .... channels.
     independent   commercial   state-owned
10   The nation's favourite chat-show was .... at peak-viewing time.
     broadcast   put on   transmitted

Current questions

1 The role of cheque-book journalism.
2 Invasion of privacy by the media. (see cartoon below)
3 Freedom vs. censorship.
4 How responsible are the media for forming our opinions?
5 How much does TV affect our daily lives?

☺ We bring you — live, from the scene of the tragedy..... ☹

Verb combinations: 'on'(2)   *Theme: media*

3.5 Exercise   Match the verb combinations on the left to their definitions on the right.

- to turn on s'one =   to employ
- to sleep on s'thg =   to encourage s'one to do s'thg daring
- to egg s'one on =   to mention briefly
- to fall back on =   to be shown/broadcast
- to dawn on s'one =   to become clear suddenly
- to take on =   to use (knowing it's 'safe')
- to touch on s'thg =   to attack unexpectedly
- to be on =   to consider overnight before making a
                                 decision

Put the verb combinations in their correct form into the sentences below.

1   The news .... at 9.00 p.m.
2   The editor was given a copy of a secret document which gave details of the
    government's plan to cut the education budget. He didn't know whether to
    print it or not, so decided to .... and give his decision the following day.
3   It was even said that some journalists in the crowd had .... young men to
    throw stones during the demonstration.
4   When there is nothing happening in the news, journalists tend to .... stories
    about the Royal Family.
5   Last week I was stopped in the street by a woman from an opinion research
    agency. She was in the middle of explaining the survey to me when it suddenly
    .... that I was being filmed.
6   The circulation of the new Sunday paper grew steadily and the management
    were able to .... ten new staff.
7   The TV interview with the Prime Minister started well, but when the interviewer
    .... the question of privatisation, the Prime Minister suddenly .... her and
    demanded an end to the interview.

End of vocabulary

CHAPTER 4
Unusual stress

4.1 Exercise

R9

Listen to this sentence said in four different ways.

Kate bought a black skirt.
1 (*not Carol*)
2 (*she didn't make it*)
3 (*not blue*)
4 (*not a shirt*)

By changing the stress position in the sentence, the speaker can communicate a different message.

4.2 Exercise

R10

Now listen to the following sentences. Identify which word is being stressed and discuss the significance of this – what has been said before to produce this, and/or what is being implied, and/or what might come next?

1 I'd no idea she was such an impatient person.
2 No, it's double 39602.
3 I painted the walls white.
4 The Industrial Revolution started in the 19th century.
5 He's a very kind person.
6 We were supposed to be going to the cinema.
7 I'm not flying to Edinburgh.
8 They might have called.
9 They might have called.
10 I thought it was going to rain.
11 I thought it was going to rain.
12 I hoped you would understand.
13 I hoped you would understand.
14 **John**: We were both on time, surely!
    Mary: You were.
15 **Dick**: But you promised me some!
    Anna: That's true.
16 **Fred**: Did you find your gloves?
    Joan: My umbrella.

4.3 Exercise

R11

Listen to ten different remarks or situations on the tape. After each one, say the sentence given below, paying particular attention to the stress pattern.

1 Excuse me, I ordered a rare steak.
2 I've had one.
3 John borrowed it.
4 I knew you'd buy the red one.
5 9.30.
6 California.
7 I was going away.
8 I bought her the flowers and him the chocolates.
9 Carol bought a black skirt and I bought a black shirt.
10 He might have helped.

Vocabulary

Idiom/metaphor: adjective & noun collocations (2)

When you say these phrases, make sure you put equal stress on the adjective–noun combination.

4.4 Exercise

Choose the correct adjectives to complete the collocations.

1 After working for the company for twenty years, she received a .... handshake. As a result, she was able to buy a house in the south of France.
   gold   golden   silver   diamond

2 He's the .... image of his father. Even their gestures are similar.
   exact   spitting   reflecting   same

3 Health inspectors are allowed to visit any hotel or restaurant without advance warning to do a(n) .... check.
   spot   dot   immediate   spark

4 There are, at a(n) .... guess, about two hundred different kinds of bird in Britain.
   approximate   gross   rough   about

5 It's no good going on about what you'd say if you ever met him. You know it's only .... thinking.
   wanting   wishful   hopeful   optimistic

6 .... journalism (that is, buying human-interest stories) is what many newspapers seem to be interested in these days.
   speculative   financial   credit-card   cheque-book

7 Working as a police secretary, she was able to pass on .... information about future drugs raids.
   inside   internal   inner   interior

8 The debate about public spending developed into a .... argument.
   hot   boiling   heated   warm

9 It's very important to read the .... print before you sign a contract.
   minute   little   tiny   small

10 I know she doesn't work very hard, but I've got a .... spot for her.
   kind   soft   nice   gentle

With a partner, make up a short (2–4 line) dialogue which illustrates (but doesn't use) one of these collocations. Your classmates must guess which one you are talking about. (The example below introduces a new collocation.)
e.g. I'm afraid this is only a .... visit; I have to leave by 5 o'clock.
   running   flying   fast   speeding

   A: My girlfriend's coming down next week.
   B: Is she staying long?
   A: No, she has to go back to Yorkshire the same day.
      (Guess: *It's a flying visit.*)

Verb combinations: 'about'   *Theme: feelings*

4.5 Exercise   Together with a partner, match the underlined verb combinations with the definitions below.

1   Oh, do stop <u>messing about</u> with your food. Just eat it!
2   Having mastered Russian by the age of 50, he then <u>set about</u> learning Chinese.
3   When she starts discussing quantum theories, I haven't a clue what she's <u>on about</u>.
4   The continued criticism of his work <u>brought about</u> his resignation.
5   Since her stroke, she has found it difficult to <u>get about</u> without a stick.
6   There's no point making yourself ill by overworking. You should <u>see about</u> getting an assistant.
7   What's she doing, <u>nosing about</u> in the staff room? I'm sure she's spying on us.
8   Did you realise that John has been <u>hanging about</u> on the corner for the last two hours? Don't you think you should go and talk to him?

- to cause ....
- to begin to do s'thg ....
- to wait aimlessly ....
- to say ....
- to move/walk/travel ....
- to play/not be serious ....
- to take an interest in s'thg that is not your business ....
- to arrange for s'thg to be done ....

Can you relate these feelings to the above sentences?
depression, suspicion, irritation, boredom, frustration, enthusiasm, bewilderment, stress.

End of vocabulary

CHAPTER 5
Prediction

There are many clues which can help you to understand what you are listening to by enabling you to predict what you are likely to hear next. It is important to recognise these clues when they occur – they may be in the form of individual words, topics, conjunctions such as but, phrases such as on the other hand, and so on – all of these help your mind to anticipate what is to come. In your own language, this ability to predict using clues from what you hear is a natural process; in a foreign language, the ability has to be cultivated.

5.1 Exercise

R12

Listen to the following sentences and try to predict a possible ending. The first one is shown as an example.

1   She came to see me because . . . *she was worried.*

For further practice, make some similar examples and try speaking them to your neighbour, who will (with a bit of luck!) finish your sentence.

5.2 Exercise

R13

You are going to hear an interview with Richard, an actor who is suffering from AIDS. Before listening to the tape, consider as a group what you already know about AIDS and then try to predict in very general terms some of the things you may possibly hear Richard saying.

The tape will be stopped every now and again during the conversation for you to predict the sort of thing that Richard is going to say next. You do not have to be word-for-word accurate in your prediction – that would be almost impossible in some places. Say either *the words* you think Richard is going to use or *the idea* that is going to be expressed. The tape will be stopped 8 times.

Vocabulary

Topic vocabulary: prejudice

Look through the following and identify the phrases that you are not sure about. Consult the group, your teacher or a dictionary for explanations.

equal rights; equal opportunities	to be prejudiced or biased against	to feel superior or inferior to
to treat s'one as an equal	to have preconceived ideas about	to patronise
equality		to suppress
discrimination (against)	to be narrow-minded	to be considered on merit
to discriminate between or against	to have a closed mind	
	to open your mind to	to be supportive
to be sexist, racist, ageist	to be open-minded	to jump to conclusions
apartheid	to categorise s'one as	to twist
to be intolerant	to pigeonhole s'one	to be dogmatic
race or gender issues	to look down on s'one	to be one-sided

5.3 Exercise
Read the following text, paying particular attention to the underlined words and phrases which are selected from the vocabulary bank.

The Thoughts of Lizzy

Ronnie Carter never <u>treated her as an equal</u> or even a real person, just as a useful object. She knew if he had a male secretary, he would not be able to behave like that. She knew she was good at her job and she hated being <u>patronised</u>. In some way he seemed to think he <u>was</u> naturally <u>superior to</u> her and she wondered, not for the first time, what sort of relationship he had with his wife.

The company prided itself on offering <u>equal opportunities</u> to men and women, but only at management level, she thought sadly. There was definitely <u>discrimination</u> as far as promotion was concerned. No secretary had ever been promoted to executive level. Only last month, Charles Taylor's secretary had been turned down because the Board had been too <u>narrow-minded</u> even to consider that a secretary could make a good executive.

It was difficult for her to <u>suppress</u> her natural inclination to say what she thought but, along with her colleagues who were very <u>supportive</u>, she had decided to try and <u>open Ronnie's mind to</u> the fact that women were people and should not be automatically <u>categorised</u> as a sub-species. Everyone should be <u>considered on their merits</u>, not on their sex. <u>Having preconceived ideas about</u> anyone was just not acceptable in the 1990's. In the meantime, however, a girl couldn't help imagining a bit of revenge!

Look at the underlined words in *The Thoughts of Lizzy* and use them, together with any others from the list on page 115, to talk about other forms of prejudice e.g. racial prejudice or 'ageism'.

Current questions

1 There is no person alive who has no prejudice.
2 What prejudice have you encountered in your life so far?
3 Prejudices are very convenient.

Descriptive verbs: walking

e.g. 'I've got a series of walls that I'm able to sit on to have a rest before I slowly trudge home.' (Richard, the AIDS victim)

5.4 Exercise

Look at the underlined verbs and, together with your neighbour and a dictionary when necessary, agree on a definition of the word. Check your definitions with the teacher, or an English–English dictionary.

1 His injured foot made him limp badly.
2 Be careful or you'll slip on this icy pavement.
3 She wasn't looking where she was going and tripped over the dog.
4 The exhausted men had to trudge for five miles through the snow.
5 The boxer staggered to his feet just before the count of ten.
6 In order not to wake his sleeping parents, he crept upstairs to bed.
7 We strolled arm in arm along the promenade watching the people on the beach.
8 My bus leaves in five minutes so I'll have to dash.
9 Normally a baby will crawl around the floor before it learns to stand up and walk.
10 The old woman was found wandering through the streets, not really conscious of where she was or what she was doing.

Discuss how these verbs can be used and the different situations you can use them in.

e.g. *creep* can be used to describe someone trying to move quietly and slowly without being noticed, although its literal use is normally for the movement of insects; *crawl* is used literally in the example, but is often used metaphorically to describe the slow movement of traffic.

Take it in turns to move around the room in the manner of one of the above verbs. The other members of your group will identify your action and speculate on why you might be walking in this way!

End of vocabulary

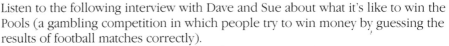

CHAPTER 6
Listening for 'gist'

An important skill to acquire in listening is the ability to listen to an entire piece and, at the end, have some general idea what it was about and what the general tone was. This listening for gist should precede anything else you might be asked to do in listening comprehension exercises.

6.1 Exercise

 R14

Listen to the following interview with Dave and Sue about what it's like to win the Pools (a gambling competition in which people try to win money by guessing the results of football matches correctly).

Remember you are listening for a general impression, so don't stop the tape during the first listening.

Now answer these two questions.
1   How do Sue and Dave feel about the money?
2   How has it changed their lives?

6.2 Exercise

 R14

You are now going to be asked to listen in more detail.
Play the tape again and, during the second listening, answer the following TRUE / FALSE questions.
Look at the questions before you listen.

1   Dave would like to have won £1m.   T/F
2   Dave was a builder.   T/F
3   They lost their real friends.   T/F
4   Dave won the money.   T/F
5   Sue feels a bit guilty about winning money.   T/F
6   Sue doesn't talk about things she's bought anymore.   T/F
7   Dave feels he will win again.   T/F
8   They were not short of money before their win.   T/F

Together with a partner, or in a small group, take it in turns to explain why you made the choice by referring to what you heard on the tape.
e.g. 'I thought the first statement was … because on the tape it said that …….'

Vocabulary

Topic vocabulary: personal money

Look through the following vocabulary bank, identify any phrases you cannot explain and check them with your partner, your teacher or a dictionary.

to economise	a mortgage	to put a deposit on
to make ends meet	pocket money	credit cards or plastic
to go on a spending	fees	money
spree	an overdraft; to be	the hole in the wall or a
to come into money	overdrawn	cash point
a loan	to pay by instalments	to get into debt

6.3 Exercise

Say why the underlined words are wrong and then choose the correct ones from the list above.

1. We'll have to get <u>a mortgage</u> to buy the new car.
2. <u>Cheques</u> are an example of the 'live now pay later' philosophy.
3. With an income of £300 per week and a minimum expenditure of £290, it is very difficult to <u>get into debt</u>.
4. She unexpectedly came into some money and decided to <u>economise</u>. She bought presents for everyone in the family and several for herself!
5. When I was a child, my parents used to give me 50p a week <u>fees</u>.
6. The shop promised to reserve the freezer for her if she put <u>an instalment</u> on it.
7. 'We regret to inform you that your account is showing a deficit of £200. We wish to remind you that you do not have any agreement for <u>a loan</u> with us.'
8. With the incredible rise in the popularity of cash cards and credit cards, most people now get their money from <u>the cashiers</u> at the bank.

Current questions

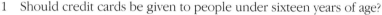

1. Should credit cards be given to people under sixteen years of age?
2. 'Money makes the world go round'.

Special vocabulary: newspaper headlines (e.g. 'Local Couple Win Pools Jackpot')

1. The simple present usually refers to a recently completed past action:
   e.g. *Peace talks fail   Union sacks boss*
2. The infinitive expresses the future:
   e.g. *Film star to wed   PM to resign*
3. The past participle expresses the passive:
   e.g. *Hostage released   Suspicious package blown up*
4. Articles, personal pronouns and the verb 'to be' are generally omitted:
   e.g. *Japanese angry over trade deal   Minister resigns after son's conviction*
5. Words take on unusual functions, and strange combinations appear:
   e.g. *Women man winning yacht   Egg talks – Ministers to meet*
        General flies back to front
6. Certain prepositions recur:
   e.g. *in* = involved in   *for* = in favour of   *over* = about, concerning, because of
        Ford management for pay settlement
        BBC in row over interview
7. Certain punctuation adds to the meaning:
   e.g. *Ministers in bomb plot?* (it is not sure if they are or not)
        'Ministers' in bomb plot (they are not real ministers)
        'Ministers in bomb plot' (this is a quote from someone)

6.4 Exercise Make headlines for the following articles.

1
A gale which blew across Southern England last night destroyed thousands of trees.

2
The President of Santa Montego has announced that he will visit Argentina next month.

3
Neighbours are anxiously searching for a four-year-old boy who has disappeared from his home in Oxford.

4
The ceasefire between rival militia groups broke down last night and fighting is now described as 'fierce'.

5
The police think that the escaped prisoner, Danny Nab, might have flown to Brazil.

6
The Finance Minister has been sacked because of his refusal to lower interest rates.

7
One hundred people are believed to have died when an explosion occurred in the Kintalk mine, South Africa, on Monday.

End of vocabulary

CHAPTER 7
Listening for information 1

7.1 Exercise: first listening

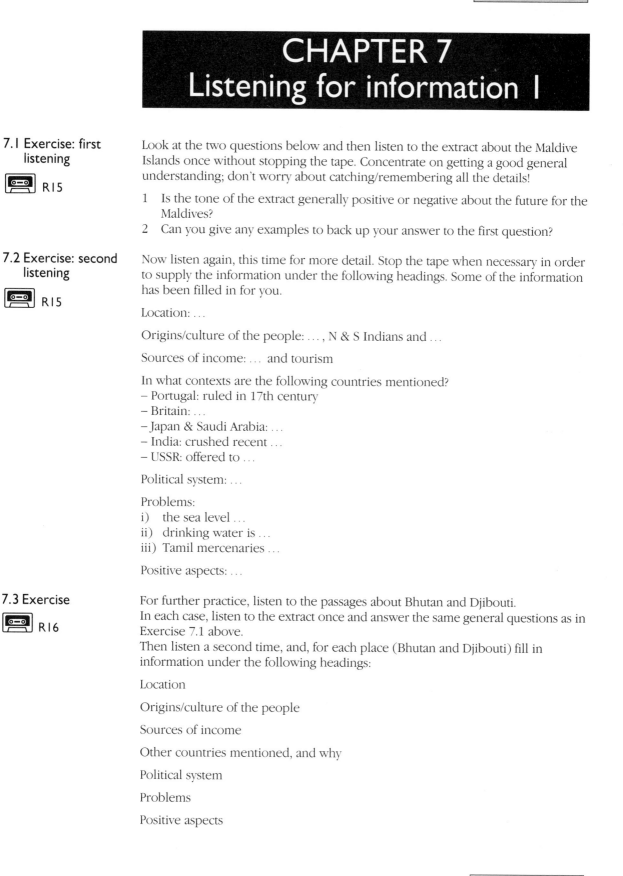 R15

Look at the two questions below and then listen to the extract about the Maldive Islands once without stopping the tape. Concentrate on getting a good general understanding; don't worry about catching/remembering all the details!

1 Is the tone of the extract generally positive or negative about the future for the Maldives?
2 Can you give any examples to back up your answer to the first question?

7.2 Exercise: second listening

R15

Now listen again, this time for more detail. Stop the tape when necessary in order to supply the information under the following headings. Some of the information has been filled in for you.

Location: ...

Origins/culture of the people: ..., N & S Indians and ...

Sources of income: ... and tourism

In what contexts are the following countries mentioned?
– Portugal: ruled in 17th century
– Britain: ...
– Japan & Saudi Arabia: ...
– India: crushed recent ...
– USSR: offered to ...

Political system: ...

Problems:
i)   the sea level ...
ii) drinking water is ...
iii) Tamil mercenaries ...

Positive aspects: ...

7.3 Exercise

R16

For further practice, listen to the passages about Bhutan and Djibouti.
In each case, listen to the extract once and answer the same general questions as in Exercise 7.1 above.
Then listen a second time, and, for each place (Bhutan and Djibouti) fill in information under the following headings:

Location

Origins/culture of the people

Sources of income

Other countries mentioned, and why

Political system

Problems

Positive aspects

Topic vocabulary: environmental issues

7.4 Exercise   Read the following text, looking particularly at the underlined words.

How long can we continue polluting and destroying our planet before even those who benefit most from the ransacking of its resources realise that time is running out? The average global temperature is now almost one degree Fahrenheit higher than a century ago, and the number of natural disasters – floods, storms, drought, famine – has risen appreciably even in the last thirty years.

Global warming is largely the result of what is called 'the greenhouse effect'. This term describes the absorption of solar heat – which should naturally be re-radiated into space after striking the earth's surface – by various gases of which carbon dioxide (CO_2) is the commonest. Every litre of petrol used – whether lead-free or not – represents the emission of 2.5 kilos of CO_2 from your car exhaust. Burning fossil fuels – oil, coal, wood – to produce energy in power stations results in the release not only of CO_2 but also of sulphur dioxide, the principal cause of acid rain.

As far as the destruction of our immediate environment is concerned, the effects of 'progress without responsibility' are there for all to see: chemical fertilisers and pesticides pollute our rivers, untreated sewage and radioactive waste are discharged into the sea to contaminate beaches and disrupt marine food chains, acid rain from industrial activity kills forests and lakes, and in some parts of the world widespread burning of forests catastrophically depletes the oxygen supply and accelerates the release of CO_2 into the atmosphere.

But it is no use the rich nations of the world trying to moralise: they themselves are the countries that have produced the greenhouse effect. Our duty to the huge and expanding populations of the Third World is to pass on the bitter lessons we have learnt, to implement our own programmes of energy saving, and to help others develop the alternative low-energy technologies on which human survival will depend.

Check the meanings of the words and phrases with your dictionary, or your teacher.

1   Write sentences of your own incorporating what you consider to be the most useful words.

   e.g. During the petrol crisis in the early 1970's, the USA had to implement many energy saving policies in order to conserve fuel.

2   Discuss the following questions.
   – What can individuals do?
      suggestions: private car/public transport
                  recycle certain materials
                  buy 'green' products, etc. etc.
   – What can be done internationally?
      suggestions: monitor the changing situations
                  make agreements on certain issues (aerosols, nuclear waste, exploitation of Antarctica), etc. etc.
   – What can the rich nations of the world do?
      suggestions: write off third-world debts
                  limit activities of multi-national corporations
                  give development aid, etc. etc.

Current questions

1 Is the interest in the environment just another fashionable cause?
2 Everybody thinks we should do something, but nobody is prepared to change their way of life in order to do it.
3 Do people believe the scientists' warnings?

Verb combinations: 'back'   *Theme: business*

7.5 Exercise

In the following sentences, the underlined words *do not fit* into the sentences – in fact they are contrary to the meaning being conveyed. Give a better alternative.

1 His business suffered badly in the recession, but the following year he <u>failed to recover</u> with a new product which swept the market.
2 We've really been spending far too much every month. If we want to survive as a company, we're going to have to <u>spend more</u>.
3 I've taken £100 from the petty cash, but I promise I'll <u>take it out</u> within a week.
4 The loss of our design team has <u>given us a push forward</u>, but I am sure we'll recover in time for the next trading year.
5 'In business, as in life, there is no point <u>thinking of the future</u>. Tomorrow is what we must concentrate on,' said the sales manager.
6 If you want to rise to the top in this company, you'll have to learn not to <u>speak out</u>. We like people who are not afraid to say what they think.
7 I wish I could <u>express</u> all those things I said about the new finance director. I think she is going to be a great asset to the company, after all.
8 Shopkeepers are often reluctant to <u>sell</u> unsatisfactory goods if you haven't got the receipt to prove you bought them in their shop.
9 You can't just <u>be active</u> and wait for customers to appear, you've got to find them and then persuade them to buy from you.

The alternative phrases that you suggested for the above are the definitions of the following verb combinations; put them together.

* to cut back . . . .
* to take back s'thg (1) . . . .
* to take back s'thg (2) . . . .
* to look back . . . .
* to set s'one back . . . .
* to bounce back . . . .
* to sit back . . . .
* to pay s'thg back . . . .
* to hold back . . . .

Note: a setback, a cutback

End of vocabulary

CHAPTER 8
Listening for information 2

The aim of this exercise is to train your ear to listen for information. The following interviews are with women serving sentences in Holloway Prison, London, for smuggling drugs into Britain.

8.1 Exercise

  R17

First, read Estella's story and extract the information necessary to fill in the table opposite.

Estella

Estella, serving nine years, was in no doubt she was breaking the law. It took the thirty-nine year old Colombian two full days to swallow the 72 condoms containing four hundred grams of cocaine, which she was to carry inside her stomach on the flight from Bogota to Heathrow. She said she felt fine during the trip, as did her companion, who had 123 of the condoms inside him. The contents of their stomachs were worth £168,000. After her arrest, it took eight days in detention at Heathrow before all the condoms passed through her system.

She did not know she was pregnant at the time. But, as we spoke, the result of that pregnancy – a baby girl born on Christmas Day – was learning to crawl beside us in the mother-and-baby unit at Holloway. Estella will be able to care for the child until she is nine months old, when she will be taken from her and put into foster care for the rest of the mother's sentence.

Through a Spanish interpreter, she explained with matter-of-fact dignity how her situation came about. She said she had married at sixteen and lived with her husband for seventeen years until he died, leaving her to bring up two boys and a girl, now aged twenty, nineteen and eleven. The debts mounted and the cost of sending the older children to college was crippling. She started to live with the man who was to become the father of her new baby, but there was no prospect of solvency.

They were offered one thousand pounds each if they made the condom run to London, although no cash changed hands. The money was to be paid on their return. 'I had never taken drugs, never been in trouble with the law. I did this thing out of necessity, although it was never going to help that much. The sums of money were too small.'

Estella and her man were arrested at Heathrow. They have refused to name the people who would have made the serious money if they had escaped detection. 'They've said that if we do, they'll kill my children in Colombia. I believe them.'

'Now my children are on their own. The older boys are looking after my eleven-year-old daughter, but they have to work at nights, so she is left alone. I get a letter from the kids every four or five months. I wish I could serve my sentence in Colombia so I could be nearer them, but there is no chance . . . The sentence is so long. It is too big.'

Now do the same by *listening* to four other women describing their experiences. Listen to the interview for the first time without stopping the tape; you will be able to catch some of the information required. Then listen again, this time stopping the tape when necessary, in order to complete your own information table like the one shown opposite.

	Estella	Woman 1	Woman 2	Woman 3	Woman 4
Name					
Age					
Nationality					
Family/children					
Sentence					
Type of drug					
Weight/value of drug					
Supplier of drug					
Reasons for doing it					
How she carried the drug					
Her knowledge of her actions					
Her feelings now					
Any other information					

8.2 Exercise: discussion

Imagine you are all members of a prison board of governors. You are meeting to discuss possible changes in the sentences given to these women. Each of you must represent one of the women. In groups of five, be prepared to put the case of one woman for the others to listen to and discuss.

Vocabulary

Topic vocabulary: law and order

Look through the following vocabulary bank. When you come to something you don't know or are not sure about, ask. Another student may be able to give you a definition.

to be law-abiding to commit a crime or an 　offence to punish; punishment to accuse s'one of to be arrested for to be charged with to be tried for to go to court or appear 　in court to be put on trial to plead guilty to to be released on bail to be granted or refused 　bail	to be remanded in 　custody ——— to keep the peace to check to investigate to control ——— a suspect the accused a judge a jury a magistrate a defence or prosecuting 　lawyer	a case a verdict to be acquitted to be found guilty to be convicted of; a 　conviction to be sentenced to . . . 　for . . . to appeal against the 　sentence a suspended sentence to ban s'one from to fine s'one capital punishment; the 　death penalty

8.3 Exercise

Choose from the above vocabulary bank in order to complete the following, changing the form where necessary.

1 Jon Stringer appeared in .... yesterday, ... of shoplifting. He was found
   .... but, because this was the first .... he had committed, he was given a
   suspended ....

2   The .... of the so-called 'Gripper' ended sensationally yesterday when Judge Pickler .... Mark Pockton .... life imprisonment for the murder of his wife, Jane. The jury returned a unanimous .... of guilty and Judge Pickler had no hesitation in issuing the severest punishment. The .... lawyer, Tony Andrews, said they would appeal.

3   Pop star Lenny Neal has been .... bail following his arrest last week .... possession of heroin. He is due to appear in court next month.

4   Rachel Connors, ... with driving while over the legal limit, was .... £2,000 and .... from driving for two years.

5   A man with a string of previous .... appeared before local magistrates yesterday. He was .... custody until his trial next week.

6   Jim Wilson was .... by Oxford Crown Court yesterday. The prosecution had been unable to prove that there was a .... against him.

Current questions

1   Do the police have too much or too little power?
2   Is prison the best place for all criminals?
3   Is the law fair to all citizens?
4   Is capital punishment ever justified?

Verb combinations: 'off' (2)   Theme: *law and order*

8.4 Exercise

Look at the underlined verb combinations in the following sentences and work out their approximate meanings.

1   The drunk was abusive to the police so they put him in a cell overnight in order to <u>cool off</u>.
2   The judge was suddenly taken ill so the trial was <u>broken off</u> in the middle.
3   Mr Smith's car was completely <u>written off</u> in a head-on collision.
4   John ('The Grass') Biggs <u>tipped the police off</u> about the planned burglary and they were able to catch the thieves red-handed. (*informal*)
5   Despite being found guilty of drinking and driving, she <u>got off</u> with a fine.
6   The bomb planted in Chinchila Airport <u>went off</u> injuring thirty people.
7   I paid £20 for what I later discovered was a £5 ticket for the concert. I <u>was really ripped off</u> by the ticket agency. (*informal*)
8   'If he can't learn to keep his mouth shut,' said Al Dopino, 'we will have to arrange for him to <u>be bumped off</u>.' (*informal*)
9   The lawyer's plan to make the jury sympathise with his client didn't <u>come off</u>. They sentenced him to life imprisonment.

Check with your teacher, or an English–English dictionary, that you have 'guessed' correctly.

Now finish the following sentences in any way that shows you have understood how the verb combinations are used.

- The hijackers broke off ...
- One of the accused got off but the other ...
- I wrote it off when ...
- The plan never came off, despite ...

- He was bumped off by ...
- The police were tipped off about ...
- 'Cool off or ...'
- It was timed to go off ...
- I remember being ripped off ...

Note also: a tip-off; a rip-off; a write-off

End of vocabulary

CHAPTER 9
Note-taking/summarising

9.1 Exercise: superstitions

 R18

Do you have any superstitions in your country connected with what pregnant women eat, or with magpies (big black and white birds)?

In this radio programme on 'Superstitions', listen to two people describing strange events. After each, write in *one* sentence what superstition could develop from the story. The first extract is short and you will probably be able to remember the details in order to fulfil the task; the second extract, about magpies, is a bit longer, so you may find it helpful to write down any *key words* while you are listening.

1   The pregnant woman and the oranges
2   The magpies

9.2 Exercise: Frederick Forsyth

R19

Listen to Frederick Forsyth talking about his life as a best-selling writer and his feelings about the money he has earned. The books he mentions are *The Day of the Jackal*, *The Odessa File*, *The Dogs of War* and *The Devil's Alternative*.

As you are listening, take notes in order to be able to summarise in one paragraph: **'Frederick Forsyth – his career and his money'.**

First listening: write down key words. Second listening: add necessary details. Use these headings.

Career (facts & feelings) ....
Money (facts & feelings) ....

Compare the information that you have extracted with your neighbour to check that neither of you has missed any important points.

Before you write the notes into a summarising paragraph, consider the order of the points.

Suggestion: i)   factual details about him
              ii) information about his life before he was an author
              iii) information about his money and his attitudes to it

Vocabulary

Idiom/metaphor: animals (2)

Superstitions have grown up around magpies, but the characteristics of some animals have led to some interesting idioms.

to be peckish	to badger s'one
to duck	a stag night
the rat race	a hen party
to be pig-headed	a bookworm
the underdog	to hound

9.3 Exercise

Put the above idioms into the sentences in place of the underlined phrase.
1   I'm feeling <u>a bit hungry</u>. I fancy a sandwich or something.
2   Will you please stop <u>going on at</u> me? I've said I'll do it, and I will!

3 Paul was late for his wedding because his <u>men-only party</u> went on until the early hours.

4 She always seems to have her nose in a book. She's a <u>keen reader</u>.

5 Why is it that in any contest or competition we always seem to support <u>the person who has less chance of winning</u>?

6 While he was famous, journalists and photographers <u>followed</u> him constantly.

7 <u>Lower your head!</u> The ceiling is very low.

8 They decided to give up their high-powered jobs and live simply on the money they could make selling their own garden produce. They had had enough of <u>the pressures and competition of modern life</u>.

9 The men are having an all-men party so why don't we women have <u>a women-only party</u>?

10 You really are the most stupid, ignorant and <u>stubborn</u> person I've ever met!

Try your artistic talent. With a partner, take it in turns to draw one of the idioms. It doesn't matter if you can't draw well – in fact it makes it more fun trying to guess!

Verb combinations: 'By / at'   *Theme: the natural world*

9.4 Exercise   Put the following infinitives (in their correct form) into the sentences below.

to support and comfort	to acquire/obtain/get
to follow/trust	to reach
to manage to survive	to criticise continually
to accept an opportunity enthusiastically	

1 When I was in Kenya recently a friend offered to take me out into the countryside. Needless to say, I .... of seeing the animals in their natural habitat.

2 How did you .... that ivory carving? I thought there was a ban on the import of ivory goods.

3 When an elephant is dying, the other members of the group will .... him/her until the end.

4 'Red sky at night, shepherd's delight.
Red sky in the morning, shepherd's warning.'
Unfortunately, you can't always .... this old country saying about the weather.

5 Most of the conservation organisations are charities and receive no government help. Public donations are their main way of ....

6 By stretching its very long neck, a giraffe can .... the topmost leaves on a tree.

7 The only way to stop the killing of whales is to .... the countries who use whale products until they agree to give up.

Check with your teacher that you have made the right decisions.

Match the following verb combinations to the definitions. Then fit them into the sentences, making any necessary changes.
- to come by s'thg ....
- to jump at the chance of ....
- to stand by s'one ....
- to keep on at s'one ....
- to get by ....
- to get at s'thg ....
- to go by s'thg ....

Note also: a standby (also adj)

End of vocabulary

CHAPTER 10
Listening between the lines

Often listening involves not just understanding the words that are being used but also interpreting other things – the circumstances around the conversation, the mood of the speakers, the events leading up to and following the speech etc. The listener has to learn to pick up 'clues' to help understand what is, and isn't, being said.

10.1 Exercise

R20

Listen to the following monologue once, without stopping the cassette, and see if you can guess what is being talked about.

Look at the questions below before you play the tape again. Now listen, stopping at frequent intervals to write down any words or phrases that might help you: e.g. *plop*.
Are there any unusual stressed words which might tell you what is being implied? Write them down, too.

Now answer the following questions. (Afterwards, be ready to justify your answers – what words/feelings/intonations helped you to decide?)

1   What is it that they've been waiting for?
2   Who's talking, and to whom?
3   Where does the conversation take place?
4   Why are 'he and Michael' going to phone later this morning?
5   Describe the mood(s) of the speaker.
6   What two parts tell you something about the relationship between the speaker and Jim?
7   Do you think the news is good or bad, and why?

10.2 Exercise

R21

Now follow the same steps for the next monologue. Once you've guessed the situation, answer the questions.

1   What's 'down there' or 'up there'?
2   What was the weather like?
3   Why does the speaker say 'thanks'?
4   What did the listener say that prompted the speaker to say 'No, I can't do that – you're not . . . '?
5   Why does the speaker say 'Ahh, that's better'?
6   Who was keener to come today, the speaker or the listener?
7   Describe the mood(s) of the speaker.

Again, be prepared to justify your answers.

Vocabulary

Verb combinations: 'to'   *Theme: implied relationships*

When you were listening to the monologues, you had to work out what the relationship was between speaker and listener.

10.3 Exercise

Look at the following sentences, and, with a partner:
a) work out the approximate meanings of the underlined verb combinations
b) suggest what the relationship between the speaker and the listener might be (e.g. husband and wife). Explain why you think this.

1 'Don't you think it's time you <u>got down to</u> doing some revision?'
2 'You're awfully quiet in there. What <u>are you up to</u>?'
3 'I wonder why it took me so long to <u>get around to</u> asking you out?'
4 'Look! You <u>stick to</u> your half of the room and I'll <u>stick to</u> mine.'
5 'I don't really <u>feel up to</u> going back to work yet. Could you give me another note?'
6 'We'll just have to <u>face up to</u> the fact that it's not working.'
7 'Your predecessor set such incredibly high standards, I'm afraid you're going to find them hard to <u>live up to</u>.'
8 'See to that call would you, Miss Jones.'
9 'I didn't really <u>take to</u> you at first, but now . . . !'

Together with your teacher, or with the aid of an English–English dictionary, check your ideas.

Now write nine sentences of your own to show you can use the phrases.

Descriptive verbs: noises

10.4 Exercise

R22

Which of the following noises do you think might have been heard in the situation of the second monologue?
Listen to the noises on the cassette and see if you can identify the sound being made from the following list.

squeak snap pop creak tick whistle slam sizzle rumble rattle roar

Put the verbs, in their correct forms, into the following sentences.

1 Mind that stair! It .... if you tread on it.
2 It was silent apart from the clock .... in the background.
3 There's someone following me. I just heard a twig ....
4 She stormed out of the room, ... the door behind her.
5 The champagne corks .... and the steaks .... on the barbecue.
6 There's a terrible draught .... under the door.
7 The sky darkened and we could hear thunder .... in the distance.
8 The plane .... overhead and made all the windows in the house ....
9 You can always tell when John's coming. His bike is so old and rusty you can hear it ....

Now discuss what other things can make these noises.

End of vocabulary

Speaking

A child
should
always say
what's true,
And speak
when he is
spoken to.
R L Stevenson

INTRODUCTION

Speaking is an *active* skill. It doesn't really matter how much you know in your head, it's how you use it that is most important – it is the time when language comes alive.

To speak well you need to:
– be *accurate*.
– be able to choose the *appropriate* words for the situation.
– be *confident* and *reasonably fluent*.

One of the main aims of the speaking section is to extend the range of your spoken language so that you are no longer limited to expressing ideas or thoughts in the same way as you have always done.

Each chapter in this section includes:
– intensive work with the appropriate language (for awareness & accuracy).
– controlled & then freer practice (for building confidence & fluency).
– practice linked to the format of CPE Paper 5 (Interview).

The recorded conversations contain natural, spoken language. However, for the purposes of practising the target language, some natural features of conversation, e.g hesitation, unfinished thoughts, two people speaking at the same time, have been omitted.

CHAPTER 1 Socialising

1.1 Exercise: listening & responding

 R23

You are going to hear lots of different remarks made in normal social situations – greetings, compliments, exchanges of news, goodbyes, etc. They are all part of everyday communication (including a remark about the weather!) Respond to the stimulus in as natural a way as possible.

Were your ideas similar to the ones shown below? For further practice, look through the list, then listen to the cassette again and say the appropriate response (they are not in order).

I hope so too.

Fine thanks, and you?

Not so bad/could be worse.

Well, it's hard work but interesting.

Good to see you too.

Yes, very cold.

No, what's happened?

Still at the same place.

How do you do? (*more businesslike*)

Yes, it was very sad.

Yes, it's time I went too.

And you.

Yes, it must be two years.

You too.

Thanks, I feel good.

I will. 'Bye for now.

THE FAR SIDE By GARY LARSON

11-5 © Chronicle Features, 1983

"So then Sheila says to Betty that Arnold told her what Harry was up to, but Betty told me she already heard it from Blanche, don't you know . . ."

1.2 Exercise: intensive dialogue practice

 R24

You will be given some cut-up lines of a 'Hello and goodbye' dialogue. With your partner, organise them into a coherent conversation.
Listen to the recording to see if you're correct.
Take turns to speak the roles of A and B. Try not to read your part in a monotone – put some enthusiasm and interest into your voice: you really are pleased to see each other!

1.3 Exercise: initiating & responding

Do you remember what the stimulus was that prompted each response in Exercise 1.1?
Working in a pair, one of you should look at the responses above and the other say what the stimulus was. Then reverse roles.

1.4 Exercise: further practice

Get up and move around the class, greet another student, socialise for a moment or two and, when you hear the teacher's signal, say your goodbyes and move on to someone else. Give yourself practice as both an initiator and a responder in these practice situations.

Vocabulary

Topic vocabulary: reactions and feelings

There is a lot of rich idiomatic vocabulary in the following lists – choose to remember the items that appeal to you and you feel you can use.

happiness
to be overjoyed, delighted
to be over the moon
to be in a good mood

sadness
to feel like bursting into tears
to have a lump in your throat
to be moved by s'thg
to be dejected
to feel blue, down or low
to lose heart

doubt
to have qualms about
to have second thoughts about

to have mixed feelings about
to distrust

fear
to be petrified, terrified or scared stiff
to turn pale
to be as white as a sheet
to be frightened out of your wits
it makes your hair stand on end
to have goose pimples
it takes your breath away
it makes your flesh creep
to be haunted by
to be panic stricken
not to turn a hair

surprise
it came out of the blue
it took me by surprise

disbelief
words fail me
to be at a loss for words
I was taken aback by

nervousness
to be a nervous wreck
a nerve-racking experience
to shake in your shoes
to tremble like a leaf
to be tongue-tied
to dry up

1.5 Exercise Work with a partner and take it in turns to imagine yourself in the following situations: describe your feelings/reactions. Your partner's role is to sound suitably interested, sympathetic, etc. using language like *'You must have felt awful' 'Really?' 'Lucky you'*, etc.

1 Someone whom you haven't seen for years rings up with what sounds like an incredible business proposition.
2 You're walking home late at night along a deserted street and you suddenly become aware of footsteps behind you.
3 You have reluctantly agreed to speak to a local travel club about your experiences travelling up the Amazon. When you walk into the hall, you discover there are two hundred people eagerly awaiting you.
4 The manuscript of your first novel has just been rejected by the twentieth publisher.
5 The postman has just delivered a letter telling you that you have won a new car in a national lottery.
6 Your boss has just called you into her office and told you that, as from next month, your salary will rise by 25 per cent.

Current questions 1 Men have more difficulty in expressing and valuing their feelings than women do.
2 Can fear be unlearnt?

Descriptive verbs: body movements

A way of communicating without words!

1.6 Exercise Find out what the underlined verbs mean and show you understand by performing the actions!

1 She <u>nudged</u> her neighbour on the bus and said, 'Just look at that man!'
2 'Stop <u>fidgeting</u>. Can't you sit still for just a minute?'
3 'Do you know where he's gone?' I asked. Mary <u>shrugged</u> and turned away.
4 When asked whether he had passed his driving test, Tony sadly <u>shook</u> his head.
5 Just looking at snakes makes me <u>shiver</u>.
6 When she went in, he was <u>kneeling</u> on the floor trying to light the fire.
7 He got out of the bath and <u>rubbed</u> himself dry.
8 I felt myself <u>blushing</u> at what I saw on the screen. (Difficult to mime!)
9 Only by <u>leaping</u> out of the way did he avoid being run over by the Ferrari.
10 When he finished the four-hour exam, he sat for a few minutes <u>slumped</u> in his chair.

Give examples of other situations where you can use these verbs.
e.g. 'shiver' can be associated with fear, cold, or illness. If someone went swimming in the North Sea in the winter, they would shiver when they got out of the water.
Work in pairs to make an illustrative sentence for each of the ten verbs and then share them with your group.

End of vocabulary

CHAPTER 2   Afterthoughts and red herrings

Look through the following phrases.

Incidentally, . . .
By the way, . . .
Talking of . . .
Anyway, . . . (to change the topic, sometimes to divert attention)
That's made me think of . . . (you've got a story to tell about this subject too)
That reminds me, I . . . (the topic of conversation has made you remember s'thg)
Before I forget, . . .
Can we talk about . . . ? (often used when you're fed up with the existing topic)
Shall we leave that for now and move on to something else? (useful in a more 'structured' debate or discussion)
Well, as I was saying. . . .
Now, where was I? (a question to yourself to restart what you were saying after an interruption)

2.1 Exercise: listening/ discussing

Now listen to the conversation and tick any expressions that you hear from the above list.
Discuss with your teacher how these phrases are used and write the agreed definitions, similarly to the ones already done.

R25

2.2 Exercise: speaking

Using the phrases above, complete the following mini-dialogues.
Discuss with your neighbour which phrase is appropriate (sometimes more than one is possible). The punctuation will help you make your choice.

1   **A:** How are you *really* feeling now?
    B: Not so bad, I suppose. . . . . . ., what about you , that's much more interesting.
2   **A:** I had the best chips I've had in my life last night.
    B: . . . . . ., I must buy some potatoes on my way home tonight.
    A: Yes well, ..., they were absolutely superb – crisp, light and not at all oily.
3   **A:** Well, he finally left at 4.00 in the morning and we fell into bed completely exhausted.
    B: . . . . . ., there was a message for you to ring home.
4   **A:** I would like to bring up for discussion at this meeting the problem of dog mess in the streets.
    B: Yes, thank you Mr Medley, but . . . .
5   **A:** I really enjoyed seeing them again, didn't you?
    B: Yes I did. Oh . . . . . ., Sarah's news is a secret, she doesn't want anyone to know.
6   **A:** I just didn't recognise him. He'd had so much done to his face he wasn't the same person.
    B: . . . . plastic surgery, did you see that programme on TV about it last night?

2.3 Exercise: Just a Minute

One-minute talks
On separate pieces of paper, write down three different topics which you would like someone in the class to talk about e.g. your holiday photos, an accident, the current political situation in your country. On other pieces of paper, write down six

phrases from the list at the beginning of this unit. Put the two sets of papers in two piles in the centre of the room.

One student picks up a topic card and the other students pick up a 'diversion' card. Student A begins to talk on the topic and the others interrupt when appropriate, using the phrase on their card. When you have used your card you may pick up another. After one minute, student A stops talking and a new topic is chosen by another student.

2.4 Interview exercise

With a partner, look at the photographs and
1 describe/compare
   – the people
   – the settings
   – the relationships between the people
2 put yourself in their shoes: imagine the conversation that is taking place in each of the scenes. Where appropriate, use the language from this chapter and from Chapter 1, Socialising.

Vocabulary

Idiom/metaphor: colours

2.5 Exercise

Discuss the meaning of the following 'colour' idioms. Then put them into the sentences in place of the underlined phrases, making any necessary changes.

to catch s'one red-handed	to give s'one black looks
once in a blue moon	a red herring
(to be) off-colour	black market
out of the blue	in the red
red tape	

1 I hadn't heard from my ex-boyfriend for years and then one day, completely <u>unexpectedly</u>, a letter arrived from him.
2 Did you notice Jane <u>staring angrily at Ron</u>? I wouldn't like to be him when they get home!
3 The <u>illegal trade</u> in tickets for the Brazil–Italy football game was stopped by the police.
4 A man was <u>arrested while in the middle of</u> robbing the chief inspector's house.
5 One way to stop potential football hooligans from travelling to international matches would be to make all the <u>paperwork and bureaucracy</u> so difficult that people wouldn't bother.
6 Do you often go to discos? No, <u>very rarely</u>.
7 There's nothing particularly wrong with me, I've just been feeling <u>less than 100 per cent</u> for a couple of weeks.
8 Why is it normal for nations to be <u>in debt</u>, but for me it's a crisis?
9 Introducing the question of shorter working hours at this stage is just <u>an attempt to side-track the discussion</u>.

Can you see any logic in the choice of colour for the expressions? Select the idioms you like and try to use them at least twice in the next forty-eight hours!

Descriptive verbs: hand actions

2.6 Exercise

With a partner and a dictionary, put the verbs in their correct form into the following sentences. Then perform the actions with your neighbour (carefully!)

poke   tap   tickle   smack   pat   beat   scratch   punch   stroke   point

1 The nurse .... the child's forehead to comfort him.
2 My idea of hell is someone .... my feet with a feather.
3 Daley .... him hard on the nose.
4 The rash will disappear much faster if you don't .... it.
5 He .... gently on the table to attract the waiter's attention.
6 He was sent to prison for repeatedly .... his wife.
7 Apart from anything else, it's very dangerous to .... a child on the head.
8 If you .... a dog several times on its head, it'll know you are friendly.
9 Careful! You almost .... my eye out with your finger then.
10 It's your turn. The receptionist is .... at you.

Now write some example sentences of your own.

End of vocabulary

CHAPTER 3
Likes, dislikes and preferences

3.1 Exercise:
listening

R26

First listening. Look at the following questions and answer them after listening to a short conversation between two people discussing holidays.

1   Where would Speaker 1 choose for a holiday?
2   What 'activity' does Speaker 1 like on a holiday?
3   How does Speaker 2 differ in her desires for a holiday?

Second listening. Ask the teacher to stop the tape when you identify any phrases that are used to express the speakers' *likes, dislikes and preferences.*
These phrases, together with other ways of expressing likes, dislikes and preferences, are included in the following list.

3.2 Exercise:
speaking

What kinds of holiday do you prefer? Look at the photographs for some ideas and, together with a partner, finish each of the statements below. Look carefully to see what structure is needed.

I (quite, really, particularly) like/love/enjoy . . . +-ing
I'm (not particularly) keen on . . . +-ing (often negative)
I don't like/hate/can't stand . . . +-ing
I'm not mad about . . . +-ing (informal – usually in negative form)
There's nothing I enjoy more than . . . +-ing
You can't beat . . . +-ing (informal)
What I like most is . . .
(The above 3 phrases show the strength of your feeling)
. . . 's not my scene/cup of tea
I find . . . quite amazing/superb/revolting, etc.
. . . appeals to me/doesn't appeal to me
I'd much rather . . . + inf. (*Note: no 'to'*)
I prefer . . . + -ing
Given the choice, I'd . . .
If I could choose, I'd . . .
(in response to a question) **I'd prefer** . . . + inf

3.3 Exercise:
intensive
dialogue
practice

Student A look at page 241 and Student B look at page 242. You will find different blanked-out versions of the holiday dialogue. Complete the dialogue *orally – do not write anything!* If you get stuck, your partner will be able to help you. Do the same activity with another student and, when you feel confident, change roles. If possible, move around the class practising with different partners until the dialogue is flowing fluently and with good rhythm.

3.4 Exercise:
pairwork

Choose an occupation e.g. road sweeper.
Student A writes down 5–6 likes/dislikes/preferences that a person in this profession might have, then says them one at a time to Student B.

e.g. *This person would much rather work when it's not raining.*

This person can't stand litter.

Student B tries to guess the profession that is being described.
Then reverse the roles.

3.5 Exercise:
discussion

For freer practice, discuss as a group your ideas for a good meal, a good film, or a good evening out.

3.6 Interview
exercise

Look at these paintings and in pairs/groups:
1 describe/compare
    – what you can see
    – the effect it has on you
2 discuss
    – likes/dislikes/preferences in art
    – your experiences of art as a subject at school
    – how much art is part of everyday life

Vocabulary

Idiom/metaphor: preposition collocation (2)

e.g. 'I'd like somewhere completely *off the beaten track*' (*A good holiday* dialogue)

3.7 Exercise

In the sentences below, John uses a preposition phrase. Contradict what he says, to show your understanding of the idiom he used.

e.g. **John:** He certainly spoke <u>at length</u> about his journey.

> **You:** *I thought he was quite brief, considering how much he had experienced.*

1 **John:** I'd love a weekend cottage in the countryside, right <u>off the beaten track</u>.

You: I think you'd be bored. You'd miss ...

2 **John:** There's been no news from the conference room. I guess negotiations are <u>at a standstill</u>.

You: No, I think things ...

3 **John:** We'll never get the job finished. We're already two weeks <u>behind schedule</u>.

You: Oh come on. If everyone works really hard I'm sure we ...

4   **John:** I'd hate to be famous – you're always <u>in the limelight</u>.
      You: Well, if you're rich enough, you can afford …

5   **John:** I gather plans for improving the sports stadium are <u>in the pipeline</u>.
      You: Unfortunately, I've just heard that they …

6   **John:** Phew, it's hot today. I think there's a storm <u>in the offing</u>.
      You: Well actually, the weather forecast said the storm …

7   **John:** I'm sure I was chosen <u>at random</u> to be the workers' spokesman.
      You: No, they chose you …

8   **John:** I bet Phil is <u>on edge</u> about his exam next week.
      You: Surprisingly, when I saw him yesterday he seemed …

9   **John:** Don't you think that table looks <u>out of place</u> in such a modern room?
      You: No, not really. I think it …

10 **John:** It is <u>out of the question</u> for us to accept the offer.
      You: On the contrary, I think …

11 **John:** I feel completely <u>out of touch</u> with modern office technology.
      You: It has changed a lot, but you'll soon …

12 **John:** What a ridiculous decision! He must be <u>round the bend</u>!
      You: He isn't, you know. He's quite …

13 **John:** I've put the medicine on that shelf, <u>out of reach</u> of the children.
      You: Unfortunately, I think they can …

14 **John:** The Minister's remarks on the leadership crisis were <u>off the record</u>,
           and shouldn't have been printed.
      You: That's not true, actually. According to my journalist friend, …

Descriptive verbs: eyes

e.g. 'I'm happy if I can just *gaze* at the sea.' (*A good holiday* dialogue)

3.8 Exercise

Identify the verbs connected with ways of looking which are appropriate to the following situations.
e.g. if you impolitely look at someone for a long time: *stare*

catch a glimpse of   gaze   gape   glare   keep an eye on   blink   glance
stare   peep   wink   stare into space

1   If you come out of a dark room into bright sunlight
2   If you stand open-mouthed looking in disbelief at something
3   If you are looking quickly at your watch to see the time
4   If you are looking through a hole in the fence at your neighbour
5   If you see Niagara Falls for the first time
6   If you are angry with someone
7   If you want to let someone know you're only joking
8   If you ask someone to make sure the baby doesn't get into trouble
9   If you just manage to see the President as she flashes by in her Rolls-Royce
10 If you look blankly through the window at nothing

Check with your teacher that you have 'matched' correctly.
Now try using your eyes in the above ways!

Discuss the definitions of the words and the kinds of situations in which you can use them.

End of vocabulary

CHAPTER 4
Speculations/degrees of certainty

4.1 Exercise: speaking

Look at the following ways of expressing degrees of *certainty*. With your neighbour, take it in turns to finish as many statements as possible. For example, speculate about
– why one of your colleagues is not at school/work/home today
– what was the cause of the very loud noise you have just heard
– why your favourite football/baseball team lost their last game

certain
He/it must (be) ... (present/future situations)
She/it must have (been) ... (past situations)

75% certain
It's quite likely that ...
He/it'll probably ...
There's every chance that .../of her ... -ing
I wouldn't be surprised if ... (+ past or past perfect tense)
He may well (be) ...
I bet/guess ...
I should think/imagine that ...

possible
She/it could/may/might (be) ...
He/it could/may/might have (been) ...
There's a chance that/of ...
There's always a possibility that/of ...

unlikely
I doubt whether/if/that ...
I'll be surprised if ... (+ present tense)
I don't expect ...
There's little chance that/of ...

impossible
He/it can't (be) ...
She/it can't have (been) ...
There's no chance that ...

4.2 Exercise: intensive dialogue practice

 R27

You are going to listen to a short dialogue called *The Christmas present*, which you will then build up as a group.
Your teacher will appoint a secretary whose job it is to write the group's suggestions on the board. The secretary must write only what he or she is told.
Your teacher will be the tape operator and will stop and start the tape according to your instructions, and that is all!
The aim of the exercise is to get *as exact a transcription on the board as possible*. The group decides how this is to be done.
For further practice, when you have a complete dialogue on the board, your teacher (or the secretary) will rub out selected parts (e.g. all the verbs, or large chunks of B's part). Again, you tell the person at the board what, within the category chosen, to rub out. With your neighbour, practise saying the conversation.

4.3 Exercise:
pairwork

With your partner, choose at least two of the following situations and make up a 4–6 line conversation speculating about the following.

1 The weather this weekend (you have a sailing trip planned).
2 What two doctors might be saying. They are trying to work out the problem with a patient who has severe stomach pains, and is an explorer.
3 What two detectives investigating a bank robbery might be saying. They don't know how the thieves got into the bank.
4 Someone at the door. It's midnight.
5 Top scientists discussing a photo of aliens doing strange things.
6 A possible future career for one of you.

4.4 Exercise:
overheard
remarks

R28

Listen to these remarks. Where might they have been made? What might the context be? What could have led up to them?
With your neighbour, discuss the possibilities for some of them, using language from the list on page 143 for some of the statements.

1 He doesn't stand a chance.
2 We never used to be like that.
3 I haven't done that for ages.
4 If that's the case, there's no hope for us.
5 You should never buy just one.
6 I've always said you should think twice before saying 'yes'.
7 It's not a good investment at this stage.
8 It'll work better if you wind it up.
9 I've never known it so bad.
10 They were terribly unlucky.
11 That's something I would never put up with.
12 What rope?

4.5 Further practice:
discussion

In a group, discuss what changes or lack of change there might be in your town or city in the next five years. Consider points such as:
– political actions
– cost of living
– 'fashionable' topics for concern
– rise or fall of industries, people, etc.

4.6 Interview
exercise

Read through the following passages and then be prepared to say where you think they may have been taken from and what they are about (use the language of speculation where appropriate).

1 'Many thanks for the wonderful response we have received for our Christmas Appeal. Even now we are still knee-deep in mail and, although a daunting prospect for our appeals staff, it is a very welcome sight for all of us since it means more funds for us to go on helping blind and partially sighted people.'

2 'What is good for the food industry can be fatally bad for the health of the entire nation. Nothing wrong with junk food once a week, but living on it day in day out is a recipe for disaster.'

3 'Columbus sailed the ocean blue,
In fourteen hundred and ninety-two.
The Spanish Armada met its fate,
In fifteen hundred and eighty-eight.
In sixteen hundred and sixty-six
London burnt like rotten sticks.'

Vocabulary

Idiom/metaphor: clothes

4.7 Exercise

The following items of clothing or parts of clothing need to be added to the sentences below to make the complete idioms.

boots belt shoestring apron sleeve pocket gloves socks shoes

1 If you could <u>put yourself in my</u> ......, you'd realise how I felt.
2 As students with very little money, we travelled around Europe <u>on a</u> ....
3 He's never able to keep money for long. As soon as he has some, it <u>burns a hole in his</u> ....
4 He was told by his boss that his sales figures were not good enough and, unless he <u>pulled his</u> .... <u>up</u>, he'd lose his job.
5 I know you were determined to win the argument, but it was a bit <u>below the</u> .... actually to play him a tape recording of what he said six months ago.
6 Don't reveal all your plans at the first meeting. It's a good idea to <u>have something up your</u> .... to surprise them with later.
7 This steak is terrible, I can't eat it. It's <u>as tough as old</u> ....
8 He's terribly sensitive! You'll have to <u>handle him with kid</u> ....
9 It's time she became independent. She can't stay <u>tied to her mother's</u> .... <u>strings</u> for ever.

With a partner, make up a short (2–4 line) dialogue which illustrates (but doesn't use) one of these phrases. With a bit of luck, your fellow students will say which phrase you are talking about!

e.g. A: *I'm not going to tell him all the facts straightaway.*
B: *Why not?*
A: *It might be better to surprise him with something later.*
(*Other students guess:* You want to keep something up your sleeve.)

Descriptive verbs: holding

e.g. 'Go on, have a *squeeze*.' (*The Christmas Present* dialogue)

4.8 Exercise

cuddle grip snatch grab cling to clench squeeze clutch snuggle hug

What verb of 'holding' would you use if you were:
e.g. holding your money tightly because you were afraid of losing it: *clutch*

1 holding on to a lifebelt to stop yourself sinking
2 putting your arms round someone
3 taking a book quickly and roughly
4 pressing an orange to get the juice out
5 holding a child's hand tightly
6 holding a baby close to you
7 making a fist out of your hand
8 lying comfortably in someone's arms

Now write example sentences of your own to practise the verbs.
(*Note:* some verbs can overlap e.g. **grip, clutch, cling to**)

End of vocabulary

CHAPTER 5 Regrets

5.1 Exercise: listening & speaking

 R29

1 Listen to the dialogue *A death in the family* and say what has happened and why.

2 Listen to the whole dialogue once more and, with a partner, build it up orally from the following key words. Do not write anything, as the aim of the exercise is to reproduce the conversation with all the natural rhythms of speech.

A: Look / mess. / all / fault. / never / left / door open.
B: warn / before / that.
A: know / wish / listened. / more and more forgetful.
B: no point thinking / now. / clear / lot up.
A: OK. I / known / happen / Tim / away too.
B: What / say / gets back?
A: I / tell him / truth. / myself entirely.
B: suppose / cat *was* / following / instincts.
A: OK / rub it in. / really / last straw / yesterday.
B: Why / happened yesterday?
A: sure / want / know?

3 Listen to the conversation again if you have any problems filling in the gaps. Practise saying the dialogue with your neighbour, paying particular attention to the strong and weak parts of phrases like **might have known, should never have left**, etc.

5.2 Exercise: speaking

With a partner or in a small group, read through the following ways of expressing regrets and reacting to them. Take it in turns to express a regret of your own and reactions to that regret.

e.g. **A:** *I might have known I'd be late this morning.*
    B: *Well, I did warn you about the bus strike.*
or **B:** *It can't be helped. You're here now.*

Discuss together, and with your teacher, whether some of the phrases are, for example, 'stronger' than others, or more fatalistic.

regrets	*reactions/responses*
If only/I wish . . . (+ past/past perfect)	I did warn you about . . .
I should (never) have . . .	I did say you should . . .
I can't think why I . . .	It can't be helped.
Whatever made me + inf	What's done is done.
(*Note: no 'to'*)	
Why didn't I . . . when I had the chance?	It's too late to . . .
I might have known . . . would . . .	You can/could always . . .
(= it's typical this should happen to me)	
It's not my fault that . . .	There's no point . . . (+ -ing)
I blame s'one for s'thg	It's no use . . . (+ -ing)
I'm to blame for . . .	It's not worth . . . (+ -ing)

5.3 Exercise: short conversations

What might the following people be saying in these situations?
Make short, 2–4 line, conversations.

5.4 Interview exercise

In a small group, discuss how your life would be affected and what thoughts would go through your head if:
– you lost all your money
– you crashed your/your parents' car
– you got arrested for shop-lifting
Use the language of regrets where appropriate.

Vocabulary

Idiom/metaphor: vegetation

e.g. 'This really is *the last straw* after yesterday.' (*A death in the family* dialogue)

5.5 Exercise

Look at the following idioms, and match them to their definitions.
- to beat about the bush
- to sleep like a log
- to put something in a nutshell
- the last straw
- to turn over a new leaf
- to branch out
- to stem from
- to weed out
- to go against the grain

to summarise or say briefly...
to get rid of what is not wanted...
to change your behaviour to something better...
to sleep very well...
to avoid speaking directly about a subject, not get to the point...
the breaking point after a series of problems...

to expand by doing different things ...
to come from/have its origins in ...
to have difficulty accepting something because it conflicts with your beliefs,
opinions etc. ...

Now put the idioms into the following sentences.

1 She was extremely tired after her long journey and ....
2 Since my last disastrous report on your daughter, I am happy to say she seems to have ....
3 Why is it that you never seem to keep to the point? Stop ....
4 The party was defeated at the last election because of the unpopularity of a new tax they had introduced. They had made many wrong decisions before, but for most people this ....
5 His decision to resign .... his wish to spend more time with his family.
6 I could go on for hours about my reasons for resigning, but ...., I've had enough.
7 We looked at the applications from all 120 applicants and .... the ones which were not suitable.
8 She started off as marketing manager for a chain store but later decided to .... on her own. The results of this decision can now be seen in all major cities.
9 However much it .... to agree with him, you have to admit that for once he has come up with a good plan.

Make a drawing of one of the idioms and see if your partner can recognise it! Your partner will do the same for you.

Special vocabulary: identical pairs

e.g. 'I'm getting *more and more* forgetful.' (*A death in the family* dialogue)

5.6 Exercise

Use one of the following pairs to complete each sentence as imaginatively as possible.

hand in hand   one by one   round and round
over and over (again)   bit by bit   on and on
(to be) on the up and up   step by step   day after day
fewer and fewer   all in all

e.g. Don't try and do it all at once; ...
     Answer: *just do it bit by bit*.

1   If you follow the instructions, ...
2   The ministers left the room ...
3   I've told you ...
4   In prison we had the same food ...
5   You don't have to go ...
6   The lovers strolled ...
7   Let's stop this discussion now – we're just going ...
8   I am glad to say that our business is ...
9   It is a sad fact that the public libraries are used by ...
10 To sum up, I can say that ...

End of vocabulary

CHAPTER 6
Plans and arrangements

6.1 Exercise: brainstorming

As a group with an appointed secretary, brainstorm as many different ways of expressing plans and arrangements as you can think of. Consider the following categories:
– asking about someone's plans
– stating your plans
– stating your changed plans
– agreeing (or not) about time/day/place etc.

6.2 Exercise: speaking / discussing

As you are reading through the following list, discuss with your teacher which phrases would be more suitable in conversation with a) a close friend b) your boss.

stimulus	*response*
What are you doing . . . ?	I'm thinking of going . . .
Have you got any plans for . . . ?	I'm planning to go . . .
Would you like to . . . ?	I've arranged to go . . .
I was wondering if you'd like to . . . ?	I'm supposed to be going . . .
	(indicates reluctance)
	Well, I was going to . . . but . . .
	I was supposed to be going to . . .
	I had planned/arranged to . . .
	I wanted to . . . but . . .
	(the above four indicate a change of plan)
Shall we . . . ?	That's fine with me.
Why don't we . . . if that's all right with you?	That suits me fine.
Let's . . .	That sounds great . . .
We could always . . . (follows on from a previous suggestion)	That'll be . . .
I tell you what . . . (suggestion to follow)	That'd be . . .
Do you fancy/feel like . . . ?	I can't make Saturday I'm afraid.
	Saturday's no good for me.
(I'll) see you later then.	Bye for now.

6.3 Exercise: dialogue

🔊 R30

Your teacher will divide you into two groups, As and Bs. The A group look at page 241, and the B group look at page 242. You will find half of a conversation in which two people are discussing their plans for the forthcoming weekend. As a group, discuss what you could say in your missing half of the conversation so that it 'fits' with the other half, and write it down .

Then, find a partner from the other group. Each of you should read the part that has already been scripted (that is the part that you have *not* just written!). As you are listening to your partner, compare what you hear with what you and your group wrote together.

Go back to your A and B groups and discuss the differences you heard and whether they are important differences – your original suggestions might be just as good! Agree on any changes you need to make and then reform your A/B pairs to try the conversation again.

By now, your dialogue will probably be very close in form to the one on the cassette. Listen to it and compare. Discuss any differences – are they significant differences or just synonymous expressions?

6.4 Exercise: speaking

Skeleton dialogue. Use the following prompts to have a conversation with your neighbour.

A

Enquires about B's plans

Own plans have changed

Responds enthusiastically

B

Tells plans – concert. Enquires about A's plans

Invites A to concert

A & B arrange time & place

6.5 Exercise: speaking

All of you in your group have decided to go out for a meal together one evening next week. Make an arrangement which is suitable for you all!

6.6 Interview exercise

You and your partner are business associates trying to agree a day and a time for a two-hour meeting next week. Draw a diary page in your notebook; your teacher will now dictate, to each of you separately, the appointments you already have for those days.
Now try and fix the appointment with your partner – you may have to be prepared to alter some existing arrangements.

Vocabulary

Idiom/metaphor: shapes

6.7 Exercise

Look at these expressions and use them in the sentences on page 151.

a vicious circle (*a situation without an escape*)
to go round in circles (*to go over the same ground without achieving any progress*)
to be all square (*to be equal when scoring or counting*)
to be in the right frame of mind (*to be mentally in the appropriate state*)
to make ends meet (*to try to balance income and expenditure*)
to be at a (bit of a) loose end (*temporarily, to have nothing to do*)
to go to pieces (*to break down, mentally*)

1 We've been through all these points before – we're just ....
2 It's almost impossible to .... when you've got no job and two children to look after.
3 Everyone says, 'We'd love to employ you but you need some experience first'. You get experience from a job but, to get a job, you need experience! It's ....
4 You lent me £5 but I paid for your train fare so that's OK, isn't it? We ....
5 It's important to be .... when you take an examination. It's no good feeling negative before you start!
6 She stood up to make a speech but, when she saw the sea of faces in front of her, she ....
7 Until my new job starts next month, I'm ......, so would you like me to help you decorate your flat?

Think of a situation when you could use one of these expressions. Describe it to your partner and see if he or she can guess your chosen idiom.

e.g. I can't marry him unless I've got a resident's permit and I can't get a permit unless I'm married to a local. (*It's a vicious circle, isn't it?*)

Verb combinations: 'out of'   *Theme: food*

6.8 Exercise   Complete the following sentences with any words or phrases that make sense.

1 You *promised* to cook this weekend, so you can't .... now.
2 She couldn't make the cake because, when she looked in the cupboard, she realised she .... sugar.
3 When they started shouting and being rude to the other customers, the manager .... the restaurant.
4 The shop had .... parmesan cheese so I got some cheddar instead. Is that all right?
5 There are enough people trying to give their advice about this recipe so, if I were you, I would just ....
6 Oh no. I've just .... eggs, right in the middle of making these pancakes. Could you nip out and get me some?
7 He always manages to .... the boring jobs in the kitchen, like peeling the potatoes. We should make him do them next time.
8 There's no need to be so bad-tempered with everyone, just because your soufflé didn't rise. Why don't you ....!
9 I never learnt to cook. At school I .... cookery and did woodwork instead.
10 When I was trying to diet, I kept having strong desires for large pieces of cake. Fortunately, my workmates managed to .... every time I felt tempted.

Compare what you have written down with a partner. Then look at the following verb combinations and decide which one fits in which sentence. Write a definition for each one.

- to sell out of s'thg ....
- to back out of s'thg ....
- to talk s'one out of s'thg ....
- to snap out of it ....
- to throw s'one out of s'where ....
- to be out of s'thg ....
- to run out of s'thg ....
- to opt out of s'thg ....
- to get out of s'thg ....
- to keep out of s'thg ....

Note: a sell-out

End of vocabulary

CHAPTER 7   Asking questions

Asking the right kind of question depends on many things, e.g. the situation you are in, the reason for the question, who you are talking to and the relationship between speaker and listener. (If you are in an English-speaking environment, make a point of listening to the ways people ask questions, particularly in the area of requests.)

7.1 Exercise: listening & speaking

 R31

Listen to the following questions or beginnings of questions and, in the space provided on the cassette, suggest either a suitable continuation or a suitable response. (You will hear one possibility after the gap on the cassette).

1   Alex, do you mind if I ask you a question?
2   Mary, will you be driving through the city centre tonight?
3   John, I hope you don't mind me asking, but . . . ?
4   Do you happen to know Steve's new address?
5   I know it's none of my business, but . . . ?
6   Shut the door, could you?
7   Would you mind if I opened the window? It's a bit stuffy in here.
8   Do you mind me going out tonight?
9   You haven't got a pen I could borrow, have you?
10 Why on earth did you tell him?
11 Do you mind not playing the violin all night?
12 Would it be all right if I left the class early tonight?

Identify and write down the questions which fulfil the following functions.
1   Three ways of asking personal/delicate questions.
2   One way of indicating a strong emotion like surprise or bewilderment.
3   One way of checking information before making a request.
4   One way of complaining (slightly sarcastic!).
5   One 'open' request, which allows the listener to say 'no' easily.
6   One 'open' question, for information.
7   One quick request for an everyday action.
8   Two fairly formal ways of asking for permission.
9   One way of checking that an action is acceptable.

7.2 Exercise: asking & responding

In pairs, perform the following 'role plays' – one of you asks the question or makes the request, and the other responds. (In situations like these, it is very important to use the right form of words, and what is 'right' in one language may be quite inappropriate in another.)

1   You want to look up a word in a classmate's dictionary.
2   You would like a friend to give you a lift to your house.
3   You'd like to know if someone's hair is naturally blond or dyed.
4   You want to borrow some money from a friend. You're pretty sure, however, that he/she is a bit short at the moment.
5   You're curious to know how big a pay rise a colleague in your office received.
6   You don't understand why your friend lent £200 to someone he/she hardly knew.
7   You didn't understand a teacher's explanation of the rules of spelling in English. Ask her/him to explain again.

8 Ask your boss for a day off (you want to go to the airport to meet an incoming friend).

9 A friend is driving you up the wall by constantly interrupting what you're saying.

10 Your colleague has agreed to work late tonight to cover for you. You want to check that he/she has no objections to this.

11 You and your friend are watching TV. Your friend has got the remote control. You want it!

7.3 Interview exercise: role play

You are one of a group of journalists who have the opportunity to interview a successful or famous person in your country. Decide who is going to play the role of the famous person, and also decide who this famous person is! He/She is known to be a difficult person to interview.

Journalists: prepare some questions to ask on such areas as
– enjoyment/satisfaction of work
– things proud of/biggest mistakes
(During the interview, you must be prepared to vary the style of your questioning in response to the celebrity and the other journalists.)

Famous person: look at the areas you are going to be questioned on and think about your answers.

Vocabulary

Idiom/metaphor: domestic

e.g. 'A friend is *driving you up the wall* by constantly interrupting what you're saying.' (Exercise 7.2 sentence 9)

7.4 Exercise

Put the following explanations into the sentences below, making any necessary changes.
to start the day badly
to take too many unnecessary things
a party to celebrate your new home
to be familiar or to remind you of s'thg
to make s'one very annoyed
to forget about s'thg (for a while), put s'thg out of your mind
to get on with s'one very well
without cost, free
from your own garden
to preside, lead (a meeting)

1 Whenever I go on holiday by car, I always find I ......, which annoys my wife intensely.

2 Would you like to come to our ......? We'd love you to see where we live now.

3 **Mary:** These potatoes taste really good.
   Rudi: That's because they are ....

4 Now we're having a baby, we will have to ...... our plans for a world trip.

5 At the opening of the new Greek restaurant in Cowley Road, the guests had to pay for their food but the drinks were ....

6 Our usual Chairperson is going to be away next week, so I wonder if you could .... the meeting?

7　What's the matter with you today? You've been in a bad mood all morning. Did you ......?

8　I've heard that name before, but I can't remember the circumstances. It certainly ......

9　I never thought those two would like each other, but just look at them. They are getting on ......

10　She has the most irritating habit of sniffing all the time. I don't think she realises that she's doing it, but it ......

Match these idiomatic expressions with the sentences above.

(to be) home-grown	a house-warming party
on the house	to ring a bell
to get out of bed on the wrong side	like a house on fire
to drive s'one up the wall	to shelve
to take everything but the kitchen sink	to chair

Write a sentence illustrating the use of one of these idioms. Don't put the idiom in the sentence, use a synonymous expression instead. Then put a key word from the idiom in brackets after the sentence.

Pass this to your neighbour, who will then rewrite the sentence using the idiom.

e.g. I don't understand why they have split up. They seemed to be getting on really well. (FIRE)

Descriptive verbs: mouth noises

7.5 Exercise

R32

Listen to the noises on the cassette and identify them with the help of the list below.

yawn　sigh　hum　gasp　scream　sneeze　groan　hiccup

Put the verbs, in their correct form, into the sentences.

1　She ...... when she saw a rat in her cupboard.

2　You've been ...... for the past hour! Were you late to bed last night?

3　Why are you ...... so deeply? Life's not *that* bad, is it?

4　Pepper makes me ......

5　If you can't remember the words of the song, just ......

6　He lay on the ground, ... with pain.

7　Did you know that Pope Stephen died from ......? Apparently he suffered from it for three years.

8　She ...... when she opened the beautiful box and saw what was in it.

Choose appropriate verbs from the list above, and any others you can think of, to describe different sorts of noises you might hear people making at:

a football match

the dentist's

during and after a Roman feast

End of vocabulary

CHAPTER 8   Opinions

**8.1 Exercise:
speaking**

With a partner, take it in turns to a) express an opinion and b) react to an opinion.
Use the following propositions for your examples.
Wisdom comes with age.
What's the point of studying history?
Professional sports people are paid too much.
No good pop music has been written since The Beatles.

opinions	*reactions*
Well, personally . . .	
To my mind . . .	
My own feeling is that . . .	That's true to some extent, but . . .
I (honestly, really) believe/think . . .	Up to a point, I agree.
Don't you think that . . . ?	
The thing that worries/strikes me	
is . . .	
It seems to me that . . .	Yes, but don't forget . . .
It's time we + past tense	That's no answer.
	Rubbish! Come off it!
One thing we haven't thought of/	On the other hand . . .
mentioned/taken into	I'm not sure that's true . . .
consideration is . . .	
That's not exactly what I was	Quite; Exactly; Right; Absolutely. (all
meaning/trying to say.	ways of agreeing)
What I'm trying to say is . . .	
What I mean is . . .	

Discuss with your partner, and the teacher, the strength of the reactions. Do you
see any differences in the way this area of language is expressed in English as
opposed to your own language?

**8.2 Exercise:
reading &
listening**

R33

Two people are discussing an article in the newspaper about food. B's responses
are in the wrong order. Reorder them so that they follow on from A's comments,
and then check by listening to the dialogue on tape.

A: Listen to this: 'Would you eat what
you eat if you knew what the thing
you ate had last eaten?'

A: It's this article in the paper talking
about what we eat. It says many of
the incidents of food poisoning in
humans are a result of diseased
food fed to animals.

A: Right. First it was eggs and chicken,
now it's beef. Personally, I'm
thinking of becoming a vegetarian.

A: You mean stop eating all together!

B: Oh, I'm with you now. I agree, it's
horrifying. Soon it won't be safe to
eat anything.

B: That's no answer. Think of all the
chemicals they spray on fruit and
veg. I honestly believe we've got to
be more radical than that.

B: Exactly. In the end, it's a question of
money.

B: Quite. Have an apple.

B: Pardon? What on earth are you
talking about?

A: On the other hand, are we willing to pay more for food produced more naturally and in smaller quantities?

A: It seems to me that the government will have to consider more subsidies to keep the price of food down.

A: No thanks, not after that discussion!

B: No. What I'm trying to say is that we, the consumers, are going to have to think again about what we want. Mass production of food leads to lower prices, but also all these health scare problems too.

8.3 Exercise: controlled discussion

Discuss the following topics with your neighbour, adding any ideas of your own. Try to use phrases from the list on page 155 to express your opinions.

1 Nuclear power to be phased out

Good – it's dangerous (accidents, waste)
start investigating alternative technologies instead

Bad – people lose jobs
electricity will become more expensive
other sources, like coal, bad for the environment too
everything has risks

2 Bus fares to rise by 20 per cent

Good – they should make a profit
as a result, more investment to improve the service

Bad – people will use private cars more
more pollution
elderly and poor will become more isolated
government should subsidise public transport

3 Cigarettes to be made illegal

Good – anti-social
expensive (jobs, medical bills)
passive smokers

Bad – smokers have rights – freedom of the individual
helps you concentrate

8.4 Interview exercise

Discuss your opinions of the following.

1 World-wide ban on Wednesday TV

It has been decided by the International Court that TV should be banned throughout the world on Wednesdays.

2 Is it too late for the tigers?

Conservationists fear that it may be too late for the tigers to be saved.

3 International football: a thing of the past?

In an attempt to stop the riots that have taken place at several internationals, FIFA has put a two-year ban on international games.

Vocabulary

Topic vocabulary: food

Look through the following vocabulary bank and identify the words you cannot explain.

In a group, try and help with each other's problems.

to be spicy	carbohydrates	to bake
hot	fibre	
greasy, oily, fatty	cholesterol	to peel
dry	seasoning	to chop
bland	herbs/spices	to slice
tasteless	nourishing	to grate
rich	to be good for you	to mix
sweet, sour, bitter,		to pour
savoury	to boil	to drain
	to simmer	to stir
a well-balanced diet	to roast	to melt
additives	to fry, to sauté	to heat
vitamins and minerals	to grill	to defrost

8.5 Exercise

Taste

Complete the following sentences.

1   A dish without a sauce can be d ...
2   Chilli makes food h ...
3   Chips can be very g ... or o ...
4   Indian food is s ...
5   Food with no flavour is t ... or b ...
6   Using a lot of cream makes food very r ...
7   Lemons are s ...
8   Foods containing sugar are s ...
9   Foods that are salty or with spices are s ...
10   Some orange marmalade can taste quite b . . .

Contents

1   What does 'seasoning' include?
2   Give some examples of 'spices', e.g. cinammon
3   Give some examples of 'herbs', e.g. mint
4   Name some foods that are rich in vitamins, fibre, carbohydrates, cholesterol.

Actions

Complete the following verbs.

1   to de .... frozen peas
2   to c .... onions
3   to s .... tomatoes
4   to m .... chocolate in a pan
5   to s .... the sauce in the pan to stop it sticking
6   to p .... a peach
7   to g .... the cheese
8   to m .... flour and milk together

8.6 Exercise

Say what you know about Italian, Chinese, Indian and Mexican food.
Write the recipe (including the ingredients) for a typical dish from your country.

Current questions

1 The quality of food is deteriorating. (Everything we eat seems to be full of danger.)
2 We are what we eat.

Idiom/metaphor: food

8.7 Exercise

Read the following text and, together with a partner, work out approximate meanings for the underlined phrases.

Mavis decided to turn her talent for sewing into a money earner. She made ties, belts and bags of exquisite silk which sold, amongst her friends, like hot cakes. She was amazed how easy it was to make money. 'This is a piece of cake,' she thought. 'Soon I'll be the breadwinner of the family; Derek can give up his job and become my financial adviser.'

Things carried on like this for some months. Mavis found her new life very stimulating and was always full of beans, unlike Derek, who seemed to be getting quieter and quieter. One day they decided, or rather Mavis decided, that they should take pot luck and expand into dresses, trousers and jackets. Derek gave up his job to look after the money side of the business, but one problem arose which could not have been foreseen – due to a severe climatic disaster, silk production came to a standstill. This was food for thought. What now? Give up or try another material? Mavis decided to try cotton and, although the new line was not as successful as the silk goods, the company, according to Derek, still made good profits. Derek, who seemed to have found a renewed interest in life, egged Mavis on to invest and expand, which she did.

Then one day she was visited by the tax inspectors who pointed out one or two financial irregularities – irregularities which meant only one thing . . . Derek had been cooking the books and the company was not growing; it was, in fact, bankrupt.

1 to sell like hot cakes ....
2 a piece of cake ....
3 the breadwinner ....
4 to be full of beans ....
5 to take pot luck ....
6 food for thought ....
7 to egg someone on ....
8 to cook the books ....

Write a sentence illustrating the use of one of these idioms. Don't put the idiom in the sentence, use a synonymous expression instead. Then put a key word from the idiom in brackets after the sentence.

Pass this to your neighbour, who will rewrite the sentence using the idiom,

*e.g. The new Fiat has been so well designed, I'm sure it will sell quickly.
(CAKES)*

End of vocabulary

CHAPTER 9
Pessimism and encouragement

**9.1 Exercise:
listening for
specific points**

 R34

1 Listen to the following conversation between two people. The woman has just
come out of an interview and is feeling rather depressed about her chances of
getting the job; the man is trying to be encouraging and supportive.
What problems did the woman think she had?
a) .... thinking straight
b) .... Professor Franks
c) .... nervous
What encouragement did the man give?
d) .... long
e) .... CV and references
f) .... hang on
g) .... illness

2 Listen to the recording a second time. Half the group should listen for any
phrases the woman uses to express her pessimism and the other half should
listen for the ways in which the man tries to encourage her. Tick any phrases
you hear on the list below.

pessimism	*encouragement*
I knew I should(n't) have . . .	Have you ever thought of/about + -ing
I could kick myself for . . .	Try . . . + -ing . . .
	Why don't you . . . ?
I might just as well . . . (go/have gone)	You could always . . .
I don't stand much chance of . . .	You never know (+ positive remark)
The awful thing is . . .	Not necessarily (+ positive remark)
Trust me to . . . (ironic)	It's not *that* bad.
Just my luck to . . . (ironic)	It's not the end of the world.
Let's face it, (+ negative remark)	Don't let it get you down.
	Cheer up.
	If the worst comes to the worst . . .

**9.2 Exercise:
dialogue building**

 R34

Work as a group and fill in the blanks in the conversation. If necessary, ask to hear it
again. When you have finished, listen once more to check you have done it
correctly.

After the Interview
A: I've (1) .... away my chances (2) .... getting that job.
B: Not (3) .... You were (4) .... there for a long time.
A: Only because I (5) .... I (6) .... all the time.
B: Come (7) ...., ... up. I bet it wasn't (8) ....
A: It was, you know. One of the interviewers was Professor Franks. (9) ....
.... to get him.
B: Well, it's not (10) .... of the (11) .... if you don't (12) .... the
job.
A: I know, but it's not (13) .... day you get the opportunity (14) .... work
(15) .... people you like and (16) ....

B: You're still (17) .... a chance. You've got a really (18) .... CV and (19) ....

A: Mmmm. I could (20) .... for having been so nervous. (21) .... me to (22) .... a mess of it.

B: Everyone's nervous at interviews. I'm sure they'll (23) .... that (24) ....
....

A: I (25) .... it. I (26) .... just (27) .... go home. No one in their (28) .... would want to (29) .... me on that (30) ....

B: You (31) .... know. I'd (32) .... on if I (33) ....

A: The (34) .... thing (35) ...., I know I (36) .... be (37) .... the job.

B: Well, don't (38) .... up then. If the (39) .... comes (40) .... the (41) ...., you could (42) .... plead (43) .... and ask for another interview.

A: Now (44) .... a thought!

Practise the dialogue with a partner.

9.3 Exercise: speaking

Work in pairs and practise the conversations that might take place between two people – one is depressed and the other is encouraging. Use the language from above.

1 You've just heard that your holiday cruise has been cancelled because the company has gone bankrupt.
2 You are talking about the weather for the weekend (you have a picnic planned). You feel sure it's going to rain and everything will be ruined.
3 You are waiting for the election result in your country. You're not very optimistic about the chances for your political party.
4 You are in the middle of trying to put up some shelves, and everything seems to be going wrong.
5 You are waiting for the results of your university exams.

9.4 Interview exercise

With a partner, look at the following passages and be prepared to say where you think they may have come from and what they are about.

1 'Razors pain you;
Rivers are damp;
Acids stain you;
And drugs cause cramp.
Guns aren't lawful;
Nooses give;
Gas smells awful;
You might as well live.'

2 'Hello, it's Teresa Crossley from Poole. I just wanted to say that *my* main feeling when it happened was one of bitterness. What had I done wrong? Nothing. It was just my luck to be in the wrong job at the wrong time. The awful thing was, I really enjoyed the work.'

3 'D.S. Harris & Sons regret to announce that as from Friday, March 20th this shop will cease to trade. Customers who have work outstanding should ring 0823-928561. Creditors should contact Lloyds Bank on 0823-724940. We apologise for any inconvenience this may cause to our customers and beg to assure them that this action is being taken very much against our will.'

Vocabulary

Idiom/metaphor: bodies (head)

9.5 Exercise   Look at the underlined expressions in the following sentences. With a partner, write a definition for each expression. If you are working in a group, share your definitions and decide which is the best one.

1   Try as we may to find excuses for his behaviour, we've got to <u>face up to</u> the fact that he's just not a very nice person.
2   She nearly <u>jumped out of her skin</u> when she saw a dim shape in the shadows.
3   Just give me a minute to remember, <u>the answer's on the tip of my tongue.</u>'
4   If you read too much propaganda, you'll find yourself <u>being brainwashed.</u>
5   <u>No one in their right mind</u> believes that life after a nuclear war is possible.
6   It is said that the police often <u>turn a blind eye to</u> speeding because they haven't got enough manpower to deal with the situation.
7   I can't possibly take a holiday this month, I'm afraid. I'm <u>up to my eyes in</u> work.
8   My cat is used to haute cuisine and <u>turns her nose up at</u> tinned food.
9   Can I <u>pick your brains</u> about something? I've got a marketing problem and I would value your advice.
10 He worked for hours on the problem, getting nowhere, and then suddenly he <u>had a brainwave</u> and the solution became clear.

- to face up to s'thg . . . .
- to jump out of your skin . . . .
- on the tip of my tongue . . . .
- to brainwash . . . .
- no one in their right mind . . . .

- to turn a blind eye to s'thg . . . .
- to be up to one's eyes in s'thg . . . .
- to turn your nose up at s'thg . . . .
- to pick s'one's brains . . . .
- to have a brainwave . . . .

Special vocabulary: abbreviations

9.6 Exercise   Answer the following quiz questions, using one of the abbreviations below, and explain what it stands for.

DIY   GMT   IOU   CV   AGM   CD   PTO   PS   c/o   sae

1   What do you see at the bottom of a page, telling you to look at the next page?
2   What can you send with your letter if you very much want to get a reply?
3   What should you write when you have borrowed money from somebody?
4   What kind of shop sells tools and materials to people who want to improve their own homes?
5   What abbreviation (from Latin) describes the summary of your life and work, which accompanies your job application?
6   Which meeting of all the shareholders of a company must take place once a year?
7   What can you put at the end of a letter, after you have signed it, to introduce an afterthought?
8   Which description of the time takes its name from a part of London?
9   What has taken over in popularity from records and tapes?
10 If you are writing to someone who is staying at another person's house, what do you write on the envelope before their host's name?

End of vocabulary

CHAPTER 10 Telephoning

The essentials for successful communication by phone are:
– clear beginnings and endings of the conversation
– the ability to get your message across clearly and concisely
– knowing how to react to what is said to you
– the right 'tone'

10.1 Exercise: speaking/ discussion

Discuss the following with your teacher. What differences are there between how you would talk to someone you know well and how you would talk to someone you had a more formal relationship with?

1 How do you identify yourself on the phone?
2 How do you ask to speak to Mr X?
3 How do you check the identity of the person you're speaking to?
4 How do you make sure you speak to the relevant person, if you don't know who you should be speaking to?!
5 How do you offer to take a message or ask someone to take a message?
6 How do you check when the person wanted will be in?
7 What do you say when you are reconnected with someone after a problem on the line?
8 How do you signal the end of the conversation, or alternatively, what might you hear from the other person that signals the end?

10.2 Exercise: dialogue building

Stuart Hirtenstein works for Aztec Printing and he wants to speak to Howard Long at Longman Publishers about a missing manuscript. The telephonist answers his call first, then passes the call to Howard Long's office, where the secretary answers. In pairs, say what you think the complete conversation should be.

Tel: Longmans. Good morning.
SH: speak/Howard Long please?
Tel: Who/?
SH: Stuart Hirtenstein/Aztec Printing.
Tel: moment please. I/you
   (pause while being connected)
Sec: Hello, Howard Long's office.
SH: Hello/Stuart Hirtenstein. speak/Howard/if/free?
Sec: afraid/not/office/moment. I/help?
SH: Yes. ask him/any news/manuscript/expecting yesterday?
Sec: Yes I/that. I/ask him/call you?
SH: Please. after 4.00/fine.
Sec: I'm sorry, what/you say/your name/?
SH: Stuart Hirtenstein. That's H . . .
Sec: Thank you, and/number?
SH: Bath 729651.
Sec: Fine. I/get/Mr Long/ring you.

10.3 Listening & reconstructing

 R35

Listen to the conversation on the cassette and see how accurate you were. Then sit back to back with your partner and use the prompt words above to practise saying the dialogue once more.

10.4 Exercise: speaking	Sit back to back with a partner and practise some telephone conversations. Look at *either* the part marked 'Caller' on page 241 *or* the part marked 'Recipient' on page 242. Pay particular attention to the beginning and ending of each conversation.

Make sure both of you have had the opportunity to be Caller and Recipient.

10.5 Exercise: mini-role plays	Below are some further remarks which might be said on the phone. In pairs, work out a short conversation around each of them. Decide the context of the conversation and what the relationship is between caller and recipient.

1 'I'll get back to you about that.'
2 'What was it about again?'
3 'He's not answering, I'm afraid.'
4 'Can you tell me what it's about?'
5 'Were you given a reference number?'
6 'I'll have to check that with the Accounts Department.'
7 'Was Mrs Harwood expecting your call?'

10.6 Interview exercise	Take it in turns to be the Caller and Recipient in the following telephone conversations.

CATERING COURSES

Leith's School of Food and Wine offers a wide range of courses for those who want to start a career in a restaurant or catering firm, be it on the culinary or managerial side. Evening classes and holiday courses are also available for aspiring amateur cooks. If you simply want some inspiration for your dinner parties, why not include a half-day cookery demonstration on a trip to London? These are offered once a month on Saturdays, from 9.30am. Very good value at £30 which includes lunch and a glass of wine. For details, contact Leith's School of Food and Wine on 071-229 0177

BANISH THE BLUES

FANCY A CHANGE OF SCENE THIS SPRING? Michael Barry suggests you hop over to the magical island of Herm. The smallest of the Channel Islands, only 1½ miles long, Herm has sandy beaches on one side and a rugged coast on the other. It is family-run with only one hotel, and the number of visitors is restricted, so it's blissfully quiet. For details of one-week breaks, call the White House Hotel on (0481) 722159.

Vocabulary

Topic vocabulary: finance and big business

Look through the following vocabulary bank before completing the exercise.

the economy; economic	interest rates	to go into liquidation
inflation; to be inflationary	to invest; an investor; an investment	(company)
a deficit	a recession	capital
to come under pressure	a wage rise or increase	a profit; to be profitable
to go into the red	————————	a loss
stock market	to go bankrupt	shares
		assets

10.7 Exercise

Complete the missing words, selecting from the list on page 163.

1   The Government's e .... troubles intensified yesterday with the nation's current account going £2.2 billion into the r .... This is the second worst d .... on record. As a result of this bad news, the pound came under p .... and the s .... market fell to its lowest level this year. The Chancellor has ruled out an early increase in interest r .... so the Bank of England has been forced to intervene in the foreign exchanges to defend the pound.

2   Wage r .... should be kept to the level of i ....

3   Mr G Fox, head of Fox Games plc, has gone b .... and his company has gone into l .... Fox Games was a highly p .... company in the early 80's, with thousands of people rushing to buy s .... when it went public. I ....s received an excellent return on their c .... for the first six years but when economic r .... began to bite, profits turned to l .... In an attempt to keep the company going, Mr Fox sold off some of its a ......, but even this was not enough to prevent the inevitable.

Current questions

1   Should information about a person's bank account be kept secret?
2   It is impossible to be both a successful business person and honest about money.

Verb combinations: '(a)round'   *Theme: technology*

10.8 Exercise

Match the verb combinations on the left to their definitions on the right.

● to come round =	to look for the best price
● to get round s'thg =	to explore, to see what's available
● to shop around =	to behave childishly
● to call round =	to find a way to avoid s'thg
● to look around =	to persuade s'one to do s'thg
● to fool around =	to visit
● to talk s'one round =	to recover consciousness

Put the verb combinations in their correct form into the sentences below.

1   Some of the new fax machines are very expensive, so it's a good idea to ....
2   Please don't .... If we lose the programme on that computer, we'll have weeks of work re-programming it.
3   There are strict rules governing the use of data banks, but somehow some direct mailing companies manage to ....
4   The boss was dead against investing in a new computer network for the office, but we succeeded in .... and machines are being delivered next week.
5   If you .... at the showroom, you will be able to see our latest range of cordless phones.
6   She fainted after spending eight hours staring at a VDU. She .... after a few minutes, and decided to stop for the day!
7   The offices are on the 25th floor and are open-plan. The environment is carefully controlled from a central computer, so air temperature, humidity etc. are constant. Why don't you .... by yourselves for a while and then I'll be happy to answer your questions later?

End of vocabulary

Grammar

What is the grammar of any language? It is no other than a collection of general observations methodically digested.

George Campbell,

1776

INTRODUCTION

Many students reach a high level in English and start to worry about something called 'advanced grammar'. Fortunately, it doesn't really exist. What is necessary at this level is consolidation of what is already known or half-known, and an extension of that knowledge in some areas.

The aim of this section is to focus on those structural areas which either cause consistent problems at advanced level or are regularly 'tested' in the Proficiency exam.

The section is *not* a comprehensive grammar and does not necessarily explore all the aspects of a particular grammatical area.

It is strongly recommended that students use a good reference book in order to get a full explanation.

The section begins with a 'Review of tenses' and a 'What's wrong?' exercise. The level of these two exercises is mainly pre-Proficiency, but they are intended to highlight any grammatical areas that need attention.

Many of the exercises in this section also encourage you to discuss and analyse the grammar, and generally to become more aware of the reasons why something is 'right' or 'wrong'.

CHAPTER 1 Review

Tenses

Put the verbs in brackets into the correct tenses.

1 The old clock .... (stop) in 1970 and .... (not work) since.
2 What .... you .... (do) tonight?
3 They made a big mistake. They should .... (not get) married so young.
4 You look so pale. What's the matter? .... you .... (see) a ghost?
5 While David .... (make) some shelves for the sitting room, Paul .... (try) to sleep.
6 If I .... (realise) you .... (go) to London yesterday, I .... (ask) you to bring me back some of my favourite cheese.
7 You .... (might/tell) me you .... (not/want) to go to the theatre. I .... (not need/bother) to queue for tickets yesterday.
8 Where did you get that black eye? .... you .... (fight)?
9 They .... (move) to the country last year so that their children .... (grow up) away from the city traffic.
10 I'm fed up of .... (tell) the neighbours to make less noise. I wish they .... (move)!
11 When he .... (arrive) at the station yesterday morning he .... (realise) he .... (forget) his briefcase.
12 The road through the city centre .... (repair) at the moment so if I .... (be) you, I .... (avoid/go) that way.
13 When she .... (be) younger she .... (not allow/play) with other children.
14 The plants need .... (water).
15 I was really sorry .... (hear) he .... (die) the previous night.
16 He told me later that he .... (wait) over two hours in the freezing cold.
17 I'm sorry, I didn't quite catch that. When .... you .... (say) the train .... (leave)?
18 Let's go for a walk, ... we?
19 You .... (must be) very frightened when the lift stopped between floors.
20 When you .... (listen) to him speaking, you .... (understand) what I mean. He .... (not change) at all since we last .... (meet) him.
21 I .... never .... (know) you were a Capricorn if you .... (not tell) me.

What's wrong?

Discuss the following sentences with a partner, and correct the mistakes. The mistakes may involve structures, prepositions, choice of vocabulary, word order or tenses.

1 She often has been seen playing tennis.
2 What time do you meet Helen this evening?
3 It's a quite hard job.
4 Are you tired after your long travel?
5 It was a lovely evening so Sarah suggested us to go for a swim.
6 I'm looking forward to see you.
7 She's going to look for a new job when she'll return to her country.
8 I wish I wouldn't smoke so much.
9 I'd rather like to go to the cinema than the theatre.
10 Please remember me to post this letter.
11 We had a lot of difficulties to hear what was being said. (*2 mistakes*)
12 I hope the weather is fine for the weekend. I don't want that it rains for our picnic.

13   Those people standing over there probably are American.
14   It rained during three days without stopping.
15   The war films have a negative effect to people.   (*2 mistakes*)
16   Students used to be able to enter into the University without problems.
17   The news are much better today.
18   Nowadays, a large amount of young people are studying languages.
19   This fact has caused that many people disbelieve politicians.
20   What a beautiful weather today.
21   She became very upset; even she asked me to leave the room.
22   The motorist asked him why had he crossed the road at that point.
23   I've forgotten my money at home.
24   She left immediately her home.
25   The greenhouse effect is a very actual problem.
26   Could you explain me how this machine works?
27   He was died in 1976.
28   Continue walking along the street, passed the cinema and it's on the left.
29   Let's have a meeting sometimes next week.
30   I think to go to Spain for my holidays next year.

CHAPTER 2   Futures

'Will you, won't you, will you, won't you, will you join the dance?'

Lewis Carroll: *Alice in Wonderland*

A: What are you doing?
B: Getting ready. I'm going to visit my Mum in hospital.
A: Oh yes. Give her my love.
B: I will. Did you know it's their wedding anniversary next month? They'll have been married for forty years.
A: Good heavens. I hope we last that long. By the way, what time will you be back?
B: About six o'clock. Why?
A: John and Sylvia are coming for dinner tonight, remember?
B: It's OK, I haven't forgotten. Will you be using the car this afternoon?
A: No, I won't.
B: Oh good, I can use it to go to the hospital then.
A: You can't, I'm afraid. It won't start. When I see that mechanic again, I'll kill him!
B: What a nuisance! I must hurry then. The bus leaves in five minutes.
A: I'll come with you to the bus stop.

2.1 Exercise

Look at the dialogue and, with a partner, try to analyse why the particular future forms are used in the underlined parts.

Then, with the aid of your teacher or a grammar book, summarise your thoughts and write example sentences to illustrate the following.

● A use of **going to**. Do you know another use?
● A difference between **going to** and the present continuous as used for a future.
● As many different occasions as possible when **will** is used.
● A use of the future continuous. Do you know another use?
● The function of the future perfect.
● Two uses of the present simple in connection with the future.

2.2 Exercise

Choose one of the future forms to complete the following sentences. In some cases, more than one form is possible.

e.g. I'm *flying*. (fly) to Athens next week for a conference and then the following week I'm *giving*. (give) a lecture in Saloniki.

1 The train .... (leave) at 4.00 so be at the station at ten to.
2 This time next week, I .... (lie) on a beach in the Caribbean.
3 1989–1991 .... (be remembered) as years of sweeping political changes in Eastern Europe.
4 The preparations for the concert have not been completed and most people are sure that it .... (be) a disaster.
5 By the time this century .... (end), we .... probably .... (destroy) most of the tropical rain forests.
6 You look tired. Sit down and I .... (make) you a cup of tea.
7 I doubt if robots .... (replace) factory workers totally in the next ten years.
8 A: I forgot to give Steve his book back.
  B: Don't worry. I .... (see) him later. I .... (give) it back to him.
9 As soon as she .... (leave) college, she .... (look) for a job.
10 I'm afraid I .... (not be able to) cook for you tomorrow evening. I .... (work) all day and .... (not have) time to go shopping.
11 Give me the money or I .... (send) the photos to the newspapers.
12 She's forty-nine now so next birthday she .... (be) fifty.
13 Look at that child leaning over the river bank. He .... (fall) in.
14 Jane .... (leave) the company on Friday after working there for ten years.
15 Do you think you .... (use) the Channel Tunnel when it .... (be) built?
16 I .... (come) and see you before I .... (go). That's a promise.
17 Don't ring me at 6.00 tonight. I .... (cook) dinner then. Ring later.
18 She has promised to write as soon as she .... (arrive) there.
19 When .... (leave) the next coach for Penzance ....? .... (Be) it direct, or I .... (have to) change?
20 Of course you can use my summer house on the coast. But remember, when you .... (get) there next month, that it .... (not clean) since last summer.

CHAPTER 3   Passive I

'Education is what survives when what has been learnt has been forgotten.'

Professor Skinner

General review of the passive form

Because of the form of the passive construction in English, it is sometimes easy to confuse passive and active.

3.1 Exercise

Say whether the following are active or passive.

1 It was moving.
2 It was moved.
3 I'm going to be alone.
4 He's going to be shot.
5 She has been writing all day.
6 He has been seen.
7 You might have been arrested.
8 He likes being tickled.

3.2 Exercise

In order to check that you are happy with the basic passive forms, change the following from active to passive constructions, keeping the same verb tense. At the same time, decide whether, in the passive constructions, it is necessary or useful to indicate who the 'agent' is – study these two examples:

a) *He is said to be a heavy drinker.* (. . . *by people* . . . would be quite superfluous)
b) *The explorer was killed and eaten by cannibals.* (the 'agent' is significant here, and must be shown)

1 Over 350 million people speak English.
2 Lexicographers are constantly adding new words to the dictionaries.
3 The languages of the former British Empire contributed a lot of colloquial vocabulary which people use in English today.
4 People were using English as an international language from the nineteenth century.
5 Some countries have adapted English so it is hardly recognisable as the same language.
6 The Court in London had used French before English became an acceptable language for polite society.
7 The Scots will never allow their language to die.
8 The Welsh will continue to encourage the teaching of Welsh in schools.
9 We ought to have kept the distinction between 'fewer' and 'less'.
10 The Scots, quite understandably, hate people calling them English.
11 It is possible to learn a language by ear without anyone having taught it to you.

(*Note:* it is not normal to have a passive form of the various perfect continuous tenses, nor of the future continuous).

Impersonal constructions

Study these sentences.
a) We do not know if/whether any prisoners escaped. (*active*)
b) It is not known whether any prisoners escaped. (*passive*)
c) Whether any prisoners escaped is not known. (*passive, rather formal*)

d) People believed that he had fallen over the cliff. (*active*)
e) He was believed to have fallen over the cliff. (*passive*)
f) It was believed that he had fallen over the cliff. (*passive*)
g) That he had fallen over the cliff was generally believed. (*passive, formal*)

These constructions, with a variety of introductory verbs, are very commonly used in news reporting. The tenses can vary in both parts of the sentence.

3.3 Exercise

Rewrite the following sentences, practising the above constructions.

1 People say he opened a Swiss bank account for the 'hot' money.
He . . .
2 Everyone believes he is living in the USA.
It . . .
3 People do not know whether the real criminals have been brought to justice.
Whether . . .
4 It is expected that the US Federal Court will find the ex-president guilty.
The US Federal Court is . . .
5 The newly-elected government alleged that widespread corruption had taken place.
It was alleged . . .

6   Nobody knows for sure, but they say the money was taken out of the country in diplomatic bags.
    The money is supposed ...
7   It was claimed that the money was invested for the good of the country, not for the President's personal profit.
    The money was claimed ...
8   They say the man is considering asking for political asylum.
    He is reported ...

CHAPTER 4   Passive 2

(Getting attacked by Sir Geoffrey Howe in the House of Commons) 'is rather like being savaged by a dead sheep.'

Denis Healey, Labour politican, talking about a Conservative politician.

'Get'

Sometimes, especially in spoken English, **get** can be used instead of **be** in a passive construction. It is often used to talk about a sudden, unexpected or accidental action, e.g. *I got knocked over by a wild skier.*

4.1 Exercise

Finish the following sentences imaginatively, using **get** together with the verb in brackets.

1   I'm sorry about your key. It .... (bend) ....
2   My friend has just had ten stitches in his hand. He .... (bite) ....
3   During the gales the man .... (hit) ....
4   A: What was the result of the trial?
    B: He .... (fine) ....
5   A: What happened to your arm?
    B: It .... (break) ....

Needs, wants, requires

Needs/wants (informal); **requires** (formal): meaning 'something should be done'. Study these sentences.

a)   The car needs washing (*or* needs to be washed).
b)   He needs sacking (*or* needs to be sacked).
c)   The garden wants digging.
d)   The situation requires careful handling.

4.2 Exercise

Finish the following sentences, using a verb in the passive.

1   You couldn't see out of the windows. They needed ...
2   Give me some idea of what wants ...
3   The whole question of why people are sent to prison requires ...

Have something done, get something done

Have/get something done: used to express the idea of employing or asking someone to do something for us, e.g. *I want to get some copies made of this photo.*

4.3 Exercise

Convert the following using the above construction.

1 It would have been impossible for the car to have been repaired in time.
   It would have been impossible to …
2 It's no good, it will have to be cut.
   It's no good, you …
3 Am I going to perm your hair this time?
   Are you …
4 The job should have been done by professionals.
   He should …

Modal auxiliaries

e.g. *Why did you take a camera with you? You might have been arrested.*

4.4 Exercise

Finish the following sentences.

1 The government should have published the results of the enquiry.
   The results …
2 You could see the prisoners sitting on the prison roof.
   The prisoners …
3 His family ought never to have left him alone.
   He …
4 Is there any way we could have avoided the problem?
   Couldn't the problem …
5 It was not necessary to interrogate him for so long.
   He …

Participles and gerunds

e.g. *He clearly remembers being taken into a darkened room.*

4.5 Exercise

Complete the following sentences using a passive construction.

1 After the writer was threatened, he went into hiding.
   After …….
2 I can't really say anything if I'm not asked to.
   I can't really say anything without …….
3 I really feel strongly about others who tell me how to run my life.
   I very much resent ……. by others how to run my life.
4 She was really excited about her father taking her to Disneyland.
   She was really looking forward ……. by her father.
5 Was she upset that they refused her?
   Was she upset at …….

CHAPTER 5   Conditionals

If I were mild, and I were sweet,
And laid my heart before your feet
And took my dearest thoughts to you,
And hailed your easy lies as true;
Were I to murmur 'Yes' and then,
'How true, my dear' and 'Yes' again,
And wear my eyes discreetly down,
And tremble whitely at your frown,
And keep my words unquestioning –
My love, you'd run like anything!

Dorothy Parker: *Dilemma*

Study the following groups of conditional sentences.

'Standard' conditionals	*Variations*
Form 1	
If you read the instructions, you'll be able to understand it.	Read the instructions **and** you'll be able to understand it.
If you don't read the instructions, you won't be able to understand it.	Read the instructions **otherwise/or** you won't be able to understand it. **Unless** you read the instructions, you won't be able to understand it.
If by any chance you should (happen to) see him, could you give him a message?	**Should** you (happen to) see him, could you give him a message?
Form 2	
If I had time, I would start again.	**Had I** time, I would start again.
If I became President, my first act would be to ban custard.	**Were I to become** President, my first act would be to ban custard.
Form 3 & 'mixed' conditionals	
If he had listened to her advice, he would still be working here now.	**Had he listened** to her advice, he would still be working here now.
If I hadn't been driving slowly, I might have been involved in the accident.	**Had I not been driving** slowly, I might have been involved in the accident.

There are other words that introduce conditional clauses. Note that the structures in group a) below are not normally used with Form 3 conditionals.

a)   I'll lend you my bike, **provided/providing** you take care of it.
         so/as long as
         on condition that
     (the above have the meaning of 'if, and only if')
b)   **Supposing/Suppose** we left immediately, when would we arrive?
     (the above has the meaning of 'What if' and is often used with questions.)
c)   **Without** their help, I will never succeed. (with all 3 forms of conditional)
d)   **Given** the chance, I would definitely go. (with all 3 forms)
e)   **Not to** have paid would have been illegal. (with 2nd and 3rd forms)
f)   **But for** her bad spelling, she'd be a great teacher. (with 2nd and 3rd forms)
g)   **If it weren't for** you, life would be meaningless. (with 2nd and 3rd forms)

5.1 Exercise

Finish each of the following sentences so that it has the meaning of the sentence before it.

e.g. If we don't get the co-operation of the local authorities, the tax will never be collected.

Without ... *the co-operation of the local authorities, the tax will never be collected.*

1 As you didn't explain the situation to me, I put my foot in it.
   Had ...
2 You can come with us if you promise not to make a nuisance of yourself.
   ... *provided* ...
3 If the President is defeated, there will have to be a new election.
   Should ...
4 If you explained the situation to him, I'm sure he would understand.
   Were ...
5 If you gave up your job, how would you live?
   Supposing ...
6 If it hadn't been for the rain, it would have been a nice picnic.
   But for ...
7 If we hadn't gone, they would have been offended.
   Not to have ... (careful with the second part of the sentence!)
8 We couldn't have bought the house without help from the bank.
   If it ...
9 Assuming there are no problems, the shuttle will blast off on Friday.
   Unless ...
10 If you don't plant the seeds now, the plants will never grow in time for summer.
   ... *otherwise* ...

CHAPTER 6   I wish/if only

I wish I loved the Human Race
I wish I loved its silly face;
I wish I loved the way it walks
I wish I loved the way it talks
And when I'm introduced to one
I wish I thought 'What Jolly Fun!

Walter Raleigh

I wish and **If only** express regret and can only be followed by certain tenses.

6.1 Exercise

Look at the following sentences, paying particular attention to the verb tenses used. In each case, finish each thought that is being expressed.

e.g. I wish I had a car (but *I haven't*).

Regrets + past tense
Expressing dissatisfaction with a present situation.
1 I wish (*or* If only) I didn't like her (but ...
2 If only I could see him every day (but ...
3 He wishes he were lying on a sunny beach somewhere (but ...

Regrets + past perfect

Expressing dissatisfaction with a past situation.

4   I wish I hadn't been standing under the tree when the storm started (but …

5   If only he had concentrated at the right moment (but …

6   If only I could have gone (but …

Regrets + would

Expressing dissatisfaction with a present situation, and a desire for it to improve in the future.

7   I wish you wouldn't keep doing that (but …

8   She wishes he would ask her (but …

9   If only he would be more understanding (but …

(This form is difficult to use: it is important to get the feeling that the person doing the wishing has very little power over the situation and feels frustrated by this. For this reason, 'I wish I/we would' and 'If only I/we would' are not used. Wishes for yourself are usually expressed as '**I wish I could have a holiday next year**'.

6.2 Exercise

Make sentences with either **I wish** or **If only** to express your feelings about the following situations. Write more than one sentence in each case.

e.g. You have to work tonight.

I wish I didn't have to work tonight.

or *If only I had done the work at the weekend, then I could go out tonight.*

or *I wish Mrs Johnson wouldn't keep giving us so much work to do.*

1   It's raining.

2   You're short of money.

3   You're lonely.

4   You can't go to Sue's party on Sunday.

5   You can never remember where you put your keys.

6   It's always you that does the washing up.

7   Your closest friend has just emigrated to America.

8   Your neighbours are extremely noisy.

9   You have to do your military service next year.

10   There's nothing good on the TV tonight.

CHAPTER 7
Negative inversion

'*Never in the field of human conflict was so much owed by so many to so few.*'
Winston Churchill

The general rule for word order in English (subject–verb–object) can be broken by placing certain adverbial words or phrases, at the *beginning* of a sentence: this is done to produce a more dramatic effect, particularly in story-telling, stating strong opinions and the giving of rules.

Look at the following examples.

	'Normal'	*Dramatic inversion*
a)	The result was never in doubt.	**At no time** was the result in doubt.
b)	I have never heard such a terrible lecture.	**Never** have I heard such a terrible lecture.
c)	You can't see such large forests anywhere else.	**Nowhere else** is it possible to see such large forests.
d)	He didn't realise the extent of the damage until he saw it in daylight.	****Not until** he saw the damage in daylight did he realise how bad it was.
e)	I can only relax after I have had a drink.	****Only after** I have had a drink can I relax.
f)	I was not only tired, I was also hungry.	**Not only** was I tired, (but) I was also hungry.
g)	Almost as soon as I got into the house, the telephone rang.	**No sooner** had I got into the house **than** the telephone rang.
h)	The sun rose and almost immediately it began to rain.	**Hardly** had the sun risen **when/before** it began to rain.
i)	A public figure has seldom been more completely humiliated.	**Seldom** has a public figure been more completely humiliated.
j)	He little realised that she had heard every word.	**Little** did he realise that she had heard every word.
k)	It was such a heavy vase that he dropped it.	**Such** was the weight of the vase that he dropped it.
l)	He spoke so quickly that nobody could understand.	**So** quickly did he speak that nobody could understand.
m)	He must not leave the country on any account.	**On no account** must he leave the country.
n)	I wouldn't go back to university under any circumstances.	**Under no circumstances** would I go back to university.
o)	The club will only admit men under exceptional circumstances.	**Only under exceptional circumstances** will the club admit men.

*Notice that **only**, **not until** and **not even** introduce adverbial clauses, and the inversion comes in the *second* part of the sentence.

7.1 Exercise

Make complete sentences from the following, adding articles and changing the verb forms where necessary.

1   Never / I see / such / brilliant acting.
2   Not only / Jon / play / piano / he also / play / clarinet.
3   Hardly / we / leave / building / when it / catch fire.
4   Not until ten years later / they / find out / truth.
5   Only under exceptional circumstances / prisoners / be / allowed to work.
6   Not even after I / explain it three times / he / understand / what I / mean.
7   So thick / fog / be / I / decide / not to go out.
8   Only if both sides agree / settlement / be reached.

7.2 Exercise

Imagine yourself in the world of detective fiction; how could the following sentences be finished?

e.g. Only after he saw the broken window ... *did he realise that a burglar had been in the room.*

1   Not until the ice melted …
2   No sooner had he drunk the wine …
3   Only by patient investigation …
4   Not only was he accused of murdering Lord Lucas, …
5   At no time …
6   Hardly had he opened the safe …

7.3 Exercise

Now imagine yourself as president of a golf club. Make some rules for the members.

1   Under no circumstances …
2   On no account …
3   At no time …
4   Only under exceptional circumstances …

7.4 Exercise

Write a 'normal' sentence containing one of the adverbial words or phrases (see examples in the left-hand column opposite). Pass your sentence to a partner and ask him or her to put the word or phrase at the beginning of your sentence in order to express the same meaning, but in a more dramatic way.

e.g. A: People only appreciated how good Pat was at her job after she had left.

B: Only after she had left did people appreciate how good Pat was at her job.

CHAPTER 8   Reported speech

'They told me you had been to her
And mentioned me to him
She gave me a good character
But said I could not swim'
Lewis Carroll: *Alice in Wonderland*

General review of reported speech

8.1 Exercise

To remind yourself of the 'mechanics' of changing direct speech into indirect speech, complete the following.

1   Tense changes ('backwards one step') e.g. present to past.
    'I've got no idea what time he'll arrive,' Martin said.
    Martin said …
2   Conditionals 2 and 3 and 'I wish' don't change.
    'If John left now, he would arrive on time,' Rebecca pointed out.
    Rebecca pointed out (that) …
3   Pronoun changes.
    'I'll give you a ring later,' said Sue.
    Sue said …
4   Time word changes ('today' becomes 'that day' etc.) and word order changes in questions.
    'Could you pick it up tomorrow?' asked Fred.
    Fred asked …

Introductory and summarising verbs

The *essence* of a message is reported, thus in some way summarising it. Word for word transcription is not usual. The use of introductory verbs is important.

In all cases, it is very important to consult your dictionary to find out how to use the verb – with a preposition, an object, a gerund, an infinitive etc. (see also page 184).

e.g. *to apologise to s'one for doing s'thg*
to compliment s'one on their appearance or on achieving s'thg

a) 'Formal' verbs used in newspapers, articles, reports of interviews etc.

acknowledge	announce
comment	confirm
declare	demand
describe	disclose
enquire	explain
inform	question
say	state
tell	wonder

b) Special verbs that summarise the essence of what has been said.

accuse	admit
advise	agree
apologise	beg
blame	complain
compliment	confess
congratulate	convince
deny	encourage/urge
insist	offer
observe	persuade
promise	remind
suggest	thank
threaten	warn

8.2 Exercise

Complete the following sentences.

e.g. The President congratulated *Switzerland on its 700th birthday*.

1. One of the injured described how ....
2. A spokesman for Ford UK denied ....
3. When questioned about the safety procedure, the captain of the vessel acknowledged ....
4. The unions accused the company ....
5. It was revealed earlier today ....
6. The Prime Minister announced that she .... the following year.
7. Buckingham Palace insisted that if ....
8. The judge enquired whether ....
9. The man was warned not ....
10. On being asked about her feelings, the actress replied that .... and suggested that reporters ....

8.3 Exercise

Transfer the following reported comments into direct speech. Fill out your answers to make them as natural and realistic as possible.

e.g. She complained bitterly about the lack of communication within the department.

> *Nobody knows what's going on in this department. We never get told anything.*

1 The authorities urged the man to give up his protest.
2 She promised faithfully to pass the message on to her sister.
3 The spokesman admitted that the previous year had not been the most successful in the company's history.
4 The judge reminded the witness that he was under oath and was obliged to tell the truth.
5 The salesman persuaded me that the two-year-old car was the best buy for me.
   Salesman: . . .
   Me: . . .
6 The leader of the opposition blamed the government for the rise in the inflation level.
7 The manager questioned the accuracy of the sales figures.

8.4 Exercise

R36

You are going to listen to a woman, Jane, talking about being bullied at school. As you are listening, look at the suggested reporting verbs below which summarise what she says. After listening, write a summary of what she said, using the verbs below to help you. (You may want to use others from the two lists opposite). Begin your summary: Jane started by saying that the bullying began . . .
– she was asked why . . . .
– she explained . . . .
– she then described . . . .
– she admitted . . . .
– she confessed . . . .
– she observed . . . .
– she refused . . . .

CHAPTER 9   Modal auxiliaries I

'You can't be serious.'
John McEnroe

Possibility, probability, certainty

can't   might   could   may   should   must

These words are often used to express 'degrees of probability'. When doing the exercise below, try to establish to your own satisfaction the 'strength' with which each word expresses probability or possibility. (Notice that there are no absolutely clear rules: many native English speakers will disagree about the strength which they attribute to a word like **could**, and this may also depend on the way in which the word is spoken.)

**9.1 Exercise:
present
infinitives –
active and
passive**

Look at the sentences below, and write a further description of the situation as in the examples.

e.g. You must be fed up of waiting!

I'm sure that you are, you've been waiting for six hours.

He can't be hungry already!

He had a huge meal only an hour ago.

1 Ask Ann, she might be able to help.
2 How's your French? You should speak it pretty well by now.
3 They obviously can't be expecting us yet.
4 He may arrive late, of course.
5 You must be feeling pretty tired!
6 Don't worry about the missing £1000 – there should be a perfectly simple explanation.
7 Do you think that man over there could be watching our house?
8 We may be too late to get our entry in.
9 Don't open the car door! They *could* be real policemen.
10 They might still build the bypass, I suppose.
11 Look at that old piano: it can't be played very often.
12 We might be greeted a bit more warmly on our next visit (if we . . .)
13 I realised that he might arrive late.
14 I was sure that the men couldn't be speaking Chinese.

**9.2 Exercise:
past infinitives –
active and
passive**

Do the same with this exercise; this time the infinitives are in the past.

1 Lendl can't have been trying very hard!
2 The news about your sister must have been a great shock for you.
3 I'm afraid Tim may have been delayed.
4 They should have telephoned by now.
5 She must have eaten something that disagreed with her.
6 They can't have got far yet.
7 I suppose she might have been trying to tell us something important.
8 Of course, Jim could have been eaten by cannibals on the way here . . . !
9 He must have been doing at least 120.
10 Gentlemen, we may have taken insufficient account of market forces.

9.3 Exercise

Make at least two responses to the following, using modal constructions with either the present or past infinitives.

1 **A:** Where on earth is my wallet? I've looked everywhere for it.
  B: . . .
2 **A:** So there I was, stuck on the top of Mount Viper in temperatures well below zero, with no sleeping bag.
  B: . . .
3 **A:** I wonder why dinosaurs became extinct?
  B: . . .
4 **A:** Because the police can't trace him, they assume he has left the country.
  B: . . .
5 **A:** Food shortages are becoming a real problem in some countries.
  B: . . .
6 **A:** That's funny. There's no answer, but they said they'd be in.
  B: . . .

7   **A:** I wonder how the team will do this afternoon.
    B: …
8   **A:** What do you think will happen if we leave this plant outside for the winter?
    B: …
9   **A:** I feel really sorry for Michael, losing his job like that.
    B: …

CHAPTER 10
Modal auxiliaries 2

'I ought, therefore I can.'

Lorenzo Dow

Obligation and necessity

Study these sentences.

a)   You | **should(n't)** | go alone.   = good/bad thing to do/to have done
       | **ought(n't) to** |

b)   You | **should(n't)** | **have** gone alone.
       | **ought(n't) to** |

c)   You | **must** | tell the truth.
       | **have to** |

d)   We **will have to** change our attitude to the environment.   = obligation/duty

e)   I **had to** fight to defend myself.

f)   You **mustn't** give him the answers.

g)   You | **needn't** | go.   = it is not necessary to go
       | **don't need to** |
       | **don't have to** |

h)   You | **didn't need to** | go.   = it was not necessary to go (we don't
       | **didn't have to** | know whether you went or not)

i)   You **needn't have** gone.   = you went, but it was not necessary

10.1 Exercise   Fill in what B says, choosing from the above modals.

1   **A:** I know you're short of beds so I've brought my sleeping bag with me.
    B: Oh, I've just bought a new bed so …….
2   **A:** Why didn't you do your homework?
    B: Because Tony said we …….
3   **A:** It's all my fault that the dog escaped.
    B: Yes, you …….
4   **A:** What are my chances of passing my final exams?
    B: Well, you ……. devote more time to studying if you really want a *good* degree.
5   **A:** He made me so angry I couldn't speak.
    B: …….

CHAPTER 11   Gerunds 1

*'Under socialism all will govern in turn and will soon become
accustomed to no-one governing.'*

Lenin: *The State and Revolution*

After the preposition 'to'

Look at the following sentences.

a)   I'm *looking forward to **seeing*** you soon.

b)   She's gradually *getting used to **getting up*** at 6 o'clock.

In the sentence *I'm looking forward to seeing you soon*, 'to' is a preposition, not
part of an infinitive – it is very common to hear the mistake, 'I'm looking forward to
see you.'

If you're not sure whether the 'to' is a preposition or part of an infinitive, try putting
a noun or pronoun after the 'to' e.g. *I'm looking forward to my birthday.*

If it works, then the 'to' is a preposition and any verb that follows it must be in the
-ing form.

11.1 Exercise

Below are the most frequently used 'to' phrases that take a gerund. With the help of
your teacher, or an English–English dictionary, finish each sentence in two ways:
firstly by putting a noun or pronoun after the preposition 'to', and then by
completing the sentence with a verb in the **-ing** form.

e.g. After two years living on his own, he's become accustomed to . . .

   (i) *an independent lifestyle*

   (ii) *being a free agent*

1   I'll never get used to . . .
2   They strongly objected to . . .
3   Having started his criminal career by shoplifting, he later resorted to . . .
4   She reacted very badly to . . .
5   It's impossible for me to give up smoking completely but I try to limit myself
     to . . .
6   Mother Teresa devoted her life to . . .
7   She has signed a contract for a world tour and so is committed to . . .
8   After finishing a long stretch in prison, it is sometimes difficult for ex-inmates
     to adapt to . . .
9   Having missed the last bus home, we had to resign ourselves to . . .
10   The child confessed to . . .
11   I do not take kindly to . . .
12   The Minister was totally opposed to . . .
13   To refuse to pay income tax is tantamount to . . .
14   After working in the fresh air for 20 years as a farmer, he didn't take to . . .
15   The rebels were unsuccessful in the end, but they certainly came close to . . .
16   There was no grass left for the animals to eat, so they were reduced to . . .
17   'Enjoy yourself, smoke, drink,' said 99-year-old Mr Trout. 'This is the key to . . .
18   After the operation, she didn't feel up to . . .

CHAPTER 12   Gerunds 2

'What really flatters a man is that you think him worth flattering.'
G.B. Shaw

Choosing between -ing and the infinitive

Look at the following sentences which illustrate the use of gerunds/infinitives after certain verbs.

a)   We'll have to *postpone **visiting*** my parents until the weather is better.

b)   Please *remind **me to speak*** to John tomorrow morning.

c)   In this monastery we do not *permit **speaking*** during meals; you are, however, *permitted **to discuss*** spiritual matters while working in the fields.

d)   *I mean **to learn*** German during the next year; it's going to *mean **giving up*** at least three evenings a week.

12.1 Exercise

What ideas about the uses of gerunds/infinitives can you deduce from the above? Try to complete the following summary.

'Some verbs, e.g. *postpone*, are followed by (1) ... , and others, e.g. *remind*, (2) ...
In some cases, e.g. with the verb *permit*, (3) ...
However, in other cases, e.g. with the verb *mean*, (4) ... .

12.2 Exercise

In order to do this exercise, you will need to refer to the lists on page 184 to see whether a gerund or an infinitive is appropriate. In some sentences, more than one form of the verb may be possible. Complete the following sentences using the verbs in brackets.

1   The company doesn't allow (smoke) in the office.

2   I would hate you (misunderstand) me.

3   He vaguely remembers (be hit) from behind.

4   The doctor advised her (not/get up).

5   By going into the burning house, he risked (be kill).

6   Try (take) more exercise and see if that makes your knee more flexible.

7   The car is filthy dirty. It wants (wash).

8   If we want (arrive) before 8.00 a.m., it means (get up) at the crack of dawn.

9   The author deeply regretted (cause) offence to any section of the community.

10   More than anything else, I dread (hear) the words, 'Don't call us, we'll call you.'

11   When he saw his key still in the ignition, he realised he had locked himself out of his car. He tried (open) the lock with a piece of wire but couldn't. His wife suggested (phone) the police.

12   I don't mind you (come) late, but how can you expect me (believe) those fantastic excuses?

13   By pretending (be) deaf, he avoided (answer) some difficult questions.

Verbs followed by gerund or infinitive

List 1: verbs which take the gerund
List 2: verbs which take the infinitive
List 3: verbs which can take both and which have similar meanings
List 4: verbs which can take both, but which have different meanings

Note: 'object possible/necessary' means the verb can or must take an object.

a)   I *appreciate living* in a hot climate. (appreciate + gerund)
b)   I *appreciate his/him cooking* dinner for me. (appreciate + object + gerund) (the possessive – 'his' in the above example – is only usable when followed by a gerund. It is correct usage, but rather stylised – most English people would say or even write 'him' here)
c)   He *asked to leave* the room. (ask + infinitive)
d)   He *asked me to leave* the room. (ask + object + infinitive)

List 1 (Verb + gerund)

Admit
Appreciate (object possible)
Avoid
Can't help (object possible)
Can't stand (object possible)
Delay
Deny
Dislike (object possible)
Enjoy (object possible)
Fancy (object possible)

Finish
Keep
Mention (object possible)
Mind (object possible)
Miss (object possible)
Postpone
Practise
Resent (object possible)
Risk (object possible)
Suggest

List 2 (Verb + infinitive)

Afford
Agree
Ask (object possible)
Decide
Expect (object possible)
Fail
Force (object necessary)
Forget
Help (object possible)
Hope
Learn

Manage
Offer
Prepare (object possible)
Pretend
Promise
Refuse
Remind (object necessary)
Seem
Threaten
Wish (object possible)

List 3 (Verb + gerund or infinitive – same meaning)

Advise (object necessary with inf.)
Allow (object necessary with inf.)
Begin
Can't bear (object possible)
Continue
Hate (object possible*)

Intend
Love (object possible*)
Permit (object necessary with inf.)
Recommend (object necessary with inf., possible with gerund)
Start (object possible with gerund)

List 4 (Verb + gerund or infinitive – different meanings)

Consider (object necessary with inf.)
Deserve
Dread
Like (object possible*)
Mean (object possible)
Need (object possible with inf.)
Prefer (object possible*)

Propose
Regret (object possible with ger.)
Remember (object possible with ger.)
Stop (object possible with ger.)
Try
Want (object possible with inf.)

*Note: When 'would' is used with these verbs, only the infinitive is possible.

CHAPTER 13   Participles

'By the time you swear you're his
Shivering and sighing
And he vows his passion is
Infinite, undying
Lady, make a note of this:
One of you is lying.'

Dorothy Parker

Participles are used, mainly in written English, in two ways:
– in -**ing** clauses connected with time or reason
– descriptively, like adjectives

Time and reason clauses

13.1 Exercise

Look at the following sentences which use participles, and discuss how they could be rewritten without using participles.

1 **Listening** to the radio, I heard the voice of my old professor. (Time)
2 **Having left** her native Yugoslavia, Mother Teresa entered a convent in Dublin. (Time)
3 He was killed **climbing** Mount Fuji. (Time)
4 Never **having travelled** to the Far East, I decided this was the year to do it. (Reason)

Notice that the subject must be the same in both parts of the sentence.

13.2 Exercise

Look at the following sentences, say what is wrong, and rewrite them correctly.

1 Being a sunny day, I decided to go for a walk.
2 Not having cooked a soufflé before, the recipe presented a few problems.

13.3 Exercise

Join the following pairs of sentences together using a participle construction.
e.g. The woman sat down by the campfire. She started to ask me questions.
   Having sat down by the campfire, the woman started to ask me questions.

1 I slammed the door. I left the room.
2 She was living in Italy. She met the Pope.
3 They couldn't recognise the exotic bird. They had never seen one like it before.
4 The man died in prison. He protested his innocence until the end.
5 He got wet through. He was caught in a thunderstorm.
6 My work was completed. I turned off the lights and left the office.

Descriptively, like adjectives

Study these sentences.
a) Do you know that man **standing** with his back to us? (who is standing . . .)
b) The plane **boarding** at Gate 12 is the 12.30 flight to Paris. (which is boarding . . .)
c) The river **running** through the park is very polluted. (which runs . . .)
d) The trio **playing** quietly in the background were from Poland. (who were playing . . . /which was playing . . .)

e) The magical sword **stolen** in a long-forgotten battle was returned anonymously. (which was stolen . . .)

f) The child **saved** from the flooded river was in a state of shock. (who was saved . . .).

Notes: The **-ing** form is usable in sentences that say what is or was happening at the time. Sentence c) however, illustrates the **-ing** form being used to describe permanent states.

In sentences e) and f) above, the past participle is used with a passive meaning.

13.4 Exercise

Complete the following sentences with present or past participles.

1 The car .... beyond repair was towed to the local garage.
2 The body .... on the ground was identified as that of Raoul Gomex, a local politician.
3 She has different members of her family .... all over the world.
4 There's a parcel at the post office .... to be picked up.
5 Whose are those keys .... on the hook?
6 She loved Darjeeling, the Himalayan town .... by the huge mountain of Kanchenjunga.
7 Bolivia, ... after its discoverer Simon Bolivar, is rich in minerals.
8 The woman .... throughout the world as the 'Steel Witch' has died.

CHAPTER 14   Relative clauses 1

*'Rock journalism is people
who can't write interviewing
people who can't talk for
people who can't read.'*
Frank Zappa

Defining or identifying

In this type of construction, pronouns like **who, which, whose** etc. introduce information which is essential to the sense of the sentence. Without this information (printed in *italics* below) it would be impossible to know exactly who or what was being referred to.

Who, which, that

Who is for people, **which** is for things and **that** is for either people or things. In some cases, where the pronoun is the object, the **who, which** and **that** can be omitted (see sentences (c) and (d) below).

Study these sentences.
a) He's the man *who/that left the black case for you.*
b) They lived in a house *which/that was built at the turn of the century.*
c) He left the books *he needed* on the bus. ('which' has been omitted)
d) The girl *he fell in love with* left him at the altar. ('The girl with whom he . . . ' – note the two different positions of 'with')
e) The house on the left is the one *in which we were born.* (or 'the one we were born in').

Whose

Whose can refer to people or things and is followed by a noun. It can also be used in 'non-defining clauses' (see Chapter 15).

Study these sentences.
a) I think we should employ someone *whose main experience is in accounts*.
b) I would like to thank all those people *without whose help I would never have succeeded*.
c) This is the college *whose founder was Lord Nuffield*.

Where, when, why

Study these sentences.
a) He lived in the street *where the murder took place*.
b) Midnight is the hour *when strange things happen*.
c) That's the reason *why she never married*.

14.1 Exercise

For each of the following sentences, write two or more clauses defining the words in *italics* using different pronouns. Choose from **who**, **which**, **whose**, **that**, **whom**, **where**, **when**, or no pronoun at all.
e.g. The cinema is being pulled down.

The cinema which is next to my house is being pulled down.

The cinema where I met my wife-to-be is being pulled down.

The cinema I love is being pulled down.

1 *The man* is standing over there.
2 *Anyone* can do it.
3 That's *the book*.
4 We bought *the first house*.
5 I'd much rather go to *a place*.
6 I well remember *the day*.

CHAPTER 15 Relative clauses 2

'Here lies our sovereign Lord the King,
Whose promise none relies on;
Who never said a foolish thing,
Nor ever did a wise one.
The Earl of Rochester about Charles II

Non-defining or non-identifying

Non-defining or non-identifying relative clauses add extra, non-essential information about people or things which are already clearly identified.
A comma must precede the extra information (and must come after it if the information is in the middle of a sentence).
That cannot be used.
This type of construction is most often used in written English.

Study these sentences.

a) Mr Jones, *who was no longer the Chairperson,* said nothing at the meeting.
b) We went for a walk round Blenheim Park, *which was designed by Capability Brown.*
c) Clive Anderson, *whom Jeremy met in Botswana,* has just retired.
d) 'Nodding by the Fire', *with which Helen Ronsard made her name,* is a very evocative book. (or . . . , **which** Helen Ronsard made her name **with** . . .)
e) Can I introduce Desmond, *whose sister works in Marketing?*
f) She lives in Lapland, *where the Chernobyl disaster had catastrophic effects.*
g) She'll arrive at 6.00 p.m., *when the documents will be ready for signing.*

15.1 Exercise

For each of the following sentences, write two non-defining clauses following the words in *italics*. Use **who**, **whom**, **which**, **whose**, **where**, **when** or a preposition construction (see (d) above)

e.g. Glasgow has changed dramatically over the last ten years.

Glasgow, where she was born and brought up, has changed dramatically...

Glasgow, whose poor housing conditions were the shame of Scotland, has...

Remember the need for commas.

1 *London* is becoming more and more crowded.
2 *Agatha Christie* died in 1976.
3 The purpose of *this book* is to help advanced level students to reach proficiency standard.
4 *Napoleon's pen* was put in the national museum.
5 She encouraged *her mother* to restart her career.
6 *Ferrari* are trying to be the number one motor-racing team in the world.
7 *1914* marked the end of an era in world history.

15.2 Exercise

Join the following pairs of sentences together using either defining or non-defining structures. Think carefully about the necessary punctuation.

1 I bought a new bike. I badly needed it.
2 Ronald Reagan became President of the USA in 1981. He started life as an actor.
3 She lived in a village. Nothing exciting seemed to happen there.
4 The World Wide Fund for Nature (WWF) is a conservation organisation. It has helped to save the tiger from extinction.
5 Letitia C. was a politician. Her career suffered from her habit of opening her mouth and putting her foot in it!
6 He is going to work in Manchester. The headquarters of his firm are in Manchester.
7 I met a man yesterday. He couldn't speak a word of English.
8 The life story of Martin Luther King has been made into a musical. His 'dream' has still not come true.
9 Salmon seem to have an amazing in-built homing instinct. They can be seen jumping up their river to spawn every year in the spring.
10 I have just drunk a cup of coffee. It tasted rather bitter and smelt faintly of almonds . . .
11 The Pope spends a lot of time travelling around the world. His home base is the Vatican.

12   The tax on cigarettes is something you pay reluctantly. The government would not be able to finance the health service without it.
13   There was a concert yesterday. Hundreds of fans were arrested there for possessing drugs.
14   Mecca is the place of pilgrimage for Muslims. It gets extremely hot there in summer.
15   Pat lives in Bath. I'm going on holiday with her next month.
16   'That's the man! I saw him attacking the old lady.'

Determiners: how much, how many

... **of whom** and ... **of which** can be used in non-defining clauses to indicate 'how much' or 'how many'; they are preceded by **many** (only for 'countables'), **much** (only for 'uncountables'), **all**, **some**, **both**, **none**, **the majority**, **half**, etc.

15.3 Exercise

Complete these sentences.

1   Six thousand people were questioned, *three-quarters of* ...
2   They arrested five men, *none of* ...
3   The Association tested twelve different washing machines, *some of* ...
4   The rescuers tore at the rubble, *most of* ...

15.4 Exercise

Join the following pairs of sentences together, using **of which** or **of whom**.

1   They've got five cats. They are all females.
2   The quarterly accounts provide plenty of information. Unfortunately, much of it is useless.
3   He owns two houses. One is in the south of France.
4   She lived with her three children. The children were unemployed.

Now continue these sentences.
5   His annual income is £50,000, ...
6   She couldn't stop buying second-hand cars, ...
7   And this is the staff of the Personnel Department, ...

CHAPTER 16   Relative clauses 3

'I wish more people wanted to talk to me for what I am, not what I do.'

Martina Navratilova

The pronouns 'which' and 'what'

These relative pronouns can be used in a different way from that practised in the previous two chapters.

16.1 Exercise: 'which'

Look at how **which** (preceded by a comma) is used in the following two sentences. What does it refer to?

a)   He treated his children very badly, **which** upset everyone who saw it.
b)   They gave me a present, **which** was very nice.

Now continue these sentences.

1 I've never been to Paris, ...
2 She introduced me to the Managing Director, ...
3 They worked flat out from Sunday until Wednesday, ...
4 On her 50th birthday she decided to take up golf, ...
5 If you buy your ticket before 9 o'clock, it'll cost you twice as much, ...
6 They just meet once a year now, ...
7 London Zoo may have to close down, ...
8 I received several phone calls from strangers after winning the lottery, ...

16.2 Exercise: 'what'

What can be used as a relative pronoun. It has the meaning of 'the thing that' or 'the thing which'.
Study these sentences.

a) **What** I meant to say was that I didn't really want to go.
b) **What** she really likes is tucking into large piles of cream cakes.
c) I'll tell you **what** he told me.

Now re-write the following sentences to incorporate **what**.

1 You need a holiday by the sea.
  What ...
2 I came downstairs for something, but my memory is awful these days.
  I can't remember what ...
3 He discovered something. It excited him very much.
  What ...
4 That's the answer I was expecting.
  That's exactly what ...
5 Do you know my opinion?
  Do you know what ...?

CHAPTER 17   Articles

'The sheep and the wolf are not agreed upon a definition of the word liberty.'

Abraham Lincoln

A or **the** or nothing? That is the question. It is amazing how much time can be spent agonising over the uses of these little words. Grammar books contain lots of rules and advice about their use, but it is easy to be overwhelmed.

17.1 Exercise

In the sentences below, there are some examples of more specific usage of **a, an, the** or no article.
First look through the sentences and decide if the use of articles is right or wrong (there are some deliberate mistakes). Where they are wrong, how can you correct them?

1 Go past the hospital and turn left at the prison on the corner.
2 Seventeen people were taken to the hospital after the recent flooding in London.
3 When she left the school, she trained as a teacher. Now she teaches at University of Chicago.

4   The pollution caused by cars in our city centre is unbearable.
5   War should only be contemplated if all other options have failed.
6   The elephants are the heaviest animals in the world.
7   The politics are dominated by men.
8   The moon is worshipped by some tribes.
9   It was an unusual profession for someone with an university education to take up.
10   The deaf are handicapped in many ways.
11   She usually goes to work by the car but, as her boyfriend had borrowed it, she decided to miss the work and stay in the bed.
12   In hot countries, it is normal for people to have the dinner late in the evening.

From the above sentences, discuss with your neighbour and your teacher what conclusions you can come to about some of the uses of articles.
Think about points like:
– categories of words (e.g. 'institutions', means of transport, meals, countries, towns etc.)
– general or specific reference (e.g. *violence* or *the violence*)
– uniqueness (is there only one?)
– abstract words (e.g. *love*)
– countable and uncountable nouns

17.2 Exercise

Complete the following using **a** or **the** or no article.

In (1) .... early part of this century, (2) .... most people in (3) .... Britain went to (4) .... church regularly. (5) .... religion was (6) .... important part of people's lives. It was normal to see (7) .... whole families, wearing their best clothes, on (8) .... way to (9) .... local church, which would be packed for (10) .... morning service. Going to church was (11) .... main activity on Sundays. Everything else was closed – there were no shops open, no sport taking place and certainly no places of public entertainment operating. (12) .... entertainment that existed took place at (13) .... home. Families would read (14) .... books, or one member would play (15) .... piano and (16) .... others would sing. However, since (17) .... 1950s, there has been (18) .... steady decline in (19) .... importance of (20) .... religion. This can be attributed to (21) .... number of different factors, but perhaps (22) .... television is (23) .... most significant one.

CHAPTER 18
Countable/uncountable nouns

'No news is good news.'

anon

An uncountable noun is one that represents mass and cannot be 'counted' e.g. rice, water.
Unlike a countable noun, an uncountable noun cannot be preceded by **a** and it cannot be made plural.

18.1 Exercise

Most of the words in *italics* below are commonly seen as 'mass' nouns, but they can also be used as countable ones. With the aid of your dictionary, fill in the other one of the pair and give a brief definition.

Uncountable use	Countable use
The log fire gave the room *atmosphere*. (it felt special – warm and welcoming)	1 ....
2	He set up *a business* dealing in antiques. (a company/firm)
3	One of the main *difficulties* has been money. (obstacles)
4	The interview was a painful *experience*. (s'thg important that affects you)
Don't spread scandal and *gossip*. (uninformed conversation)	5 ....
6	He has *a knowledge* of history that no-one else has. (knows lots of information about)
7	She has a very passionate *nature*. (character, as shown by behaviour)
It is *success* which makes people big-headed. (achievement)	8 ....
How much *toast* do you want? (pieces of toasted bread)	9 ....
10	She told me all her *troubles*. (problems in life)
11	The *works* of Mozart are being re-recorded. (s'thg produced by an 'artist')

18.2 Exercise

In the following group, all but one of the words can be used with singular or plural verbs, depending on whether they are seen as a singular unit or as individuals comprising a unit.
e.g. *The school is closed for the day for repairs.*
The school are going on a skiing trip to Austria.

Which word is the odd one out and why?

government, team, crowd, army, family, police, staff, committee, crew.

18.3 Exercise

The following words can cause problems. Discuss:
– whether they are countable, uncountable (or both?)
– what their plural forms are, if any

person	scissors	meat	travel
accommodation	information	advice	weather
sheep	news	furniture	measles
fish	research	scenery	mathematics
hair	paper	fruit	luggage

Choose six of the above words which you find interesting and write sentences to illustrate their uses.

CHAPTER 19
Past for present and future

'Had we but world enough, and time,
This coyness, lady, were no crime.'

Andrew Marvell: *To His Coy Mistress*

19.1 Exercise   In the following sentences, past tenses are used, but with either a present or future connection. What is the context that the speaker is operating in? Which sentences express the speaker's feelings strongly?
a) It's time we went.
b) It's high time Susan got down to some serious work.
c) I'd rather/sooner you didn't go away with him.
d) I wish we had a car.
e) If I accepted the offer, where would we live?
f) If I were you, I'd say 'no'.
g) Would you mind if I smoked?
h) Did you want to see me now?
i) I was wondering if you felt like going to the cinema tonight?
j) Was there anything else, madam?

19.2 Exercise: 'I'd rather'   **I'd rather** is 'I *would* rather', and it means 'would prefer'. It never changes to 'should' or 'had' and does not have a past or future form. **I'd sooner** is less common, but has a similar meaning.
a) I'*d rather/sooner walk than wait* here for a bus.
b) **A:** Would you like to go out tonight? **B:** *I'd rather not.*
c) I'*d really/much rather you didn't* drive in the fog. (Two possible meanings: i) I don't want you to drive now, or ii) I dislike your habit of driving in the fog.)
d) I'*d rather you hadn't gone* there.

'It's time'   **It's time** means 'the time has come' and can be strengthened by the addition of 'about' or 'high', especially in non-infinitive constructions.
a) *It's time to say* goodnight.
b) *It's time for us to leave* London and go abroad.
c) *It's time we paid* more attention to her.
d) *It's about time something was done* to improve the facilities in this town.
e) *It's high time she realised* her responsibilities.

Use an 'I'd rather' or an 'It's time' construction in the following situations.
e.g. He keeps asking me to lend him money – it's quite embarrassing.
    I'd rather he didn't ask me for loans.
    We still don't appreciate the dangers of over-exploiting the world's resources.
    It's time we appreciated the way we are over-exploiting the world's resources.
1   If I had the choice, I'd take the blue one. The other colours are not me at all.
2   When the government was elected three years ago, they promised to cut taxes but nothing has happened yet. I'm getting fed up with waiting.
3   You do not think your husband/wife made a wise choice in accepting a job at the company where you work.
4   You don't want your dog to be put in kennels while you go on holiday.
5   A ban on traffic is long overdue, in your opinion.

CHAPTER 20
Word order

'In a hole in the ground there lived a hobbit.'
J R R Tolkein: *The Hobbit*

Word order problems in English depend very much on your mother tongue and how much you directly translate what you want to say or write.

20.1 Exercise

Below are twenty sentences, nineteen of which show mistakes in word order made by students of different nationalities. Together with a partner, identify the errors and rewrite the sentences so that the words are in the right order. Remember that one sentence is correct!

1 I like very much coffee.
2 She would have never suggested that.
3 She had curly blond long hair.
4 I yesterday went to the cinema.
5 They still are living in the same house.
6 Always he stays at the same hotel.
7 It was a quite warm day.
8 Can you tell me what is the time, please?
9 He raised slowly his head.
10 I go often abroad.
11 Never have I seen anything like that.
12 Do you know how is the weather in France?
13 I asked him to not speak so rudely.
14 It was a such big breakfast that nobody could finish it.
15 From where does he come?
16 The cake is enough sweet, don't add any more sugar.
17 The Chinese tall vase was bought for £1000 at the auction.
18 They gave to their father the key.
19 How he is handsome!
20 I have no idea where has he gone.

20.2 Exercise

Look at the following sentences and notice the *inversion* which has taken place. Write a sentence of your own using the same construction.

1 She applied for university, as did most of her friends. (after *as*)
2 She wasn't exhausted after the walk and neither was Jean. (after *neither*, *nor*, *so*)
3 On the chair was sitting a woman dressed entirely in red. (after adverbial expressions of place, but only with intransitive verbs of position or motion – useful for dramatic effect in narrative/descriptive writing)
4 Up jumped the cat. (after prepositions of movement – only usable with a single word verb, *jumped* not *was jumping*)
5 Here comes John. (after *here* or *there*, but not with a pronoun – *There he goes.*)
6 Happy though/as she was, she still couldn't forget the moment last week when Tony had cried. (after certain adjectives describing feelings)

(See Chapter 7 for negative adverbial inversions)

Exam practice

Examinations are formidable even to the best prepared, for the greatest fool may ask more than the wisest man can answer.

Charles Caleb Cotton

Part 1
How to tackle the questions

Paper 1 – Reading comprehension

Section A

'In this section you must choose the word or phrase which best completes each sentence. Give one answer only to each question.'

The format of the paper:
In Section A there are twenty-five separate questions, each with a multiple-choice answer. You make your selection, then transfer your answer to a computer sheet which is given to you in the exam.

What is tested:
– collocation e.g. *provoke an outcry*
– general appropriateness of vocabulary e.g. *glance, glimpse, glare*
– verb combinations e.g. *get over*
– structural words e.g. *if, unless*
– words determined by their prepositions e.g. *consist of, by chance*

> **Hints**
> 1 It is impossible to learn all the items that can be tested in this section. The best preparation is to start reading books, newspapers, magazines etc. as far in advance of the exam as possible. The students who do well on this paper are the ones who develop an eye for the right combinations of words.
> 2 Look at the whole sentence, particularly any prepositions, before filling in the gap.
> 3 Be aware of the pitfalls of this type of testing; for example, words that look similar to ones in your own language should be treated with suspicion!
> 4 Always choose an answer even if you have no idea at all – there is a 25 per cent chance of being right!

Section B

'In this section you will find after each of the passages a number of questions or unfinished statements about the passage, each with four suggested answers or ways of finishing. You must choose the one which you think fits best. Give one answer only to each question. Read each passage right through before choosing your answers.'

The format of the paper:
1 There are usually three separate passages to read with a total of fifteen questions.
2 All the questions have multiple-choice answers.

Hints

How to tackle multiple-choice questions

1   Read the text right through at least once before looking at the questions. The clearer the idea you have of what the writer is saying *before* you look at the questions, the easier you will find them to answer.

2   Look at the first question, but if possible do not look at the four choices. Find the relevant part(s) of the text that deal with the subject matter of the question, and underline it/them.

3   In your mind, decide what the underlined parts are saying, and then try to answer the question in your own words.

4   Look at the question again and the four choices: choose the one which seems most appropriate and closest to the answer you have already thought of. Sometimes, this choice has to be made by process of elimination – it is often easier to identify what is wrong than what is right.

5   (As a training exercise, it is a good idea to imagine how you would justify your choice, if asked).

6   Get as much practice as possible with multiple-choice questions on reading passages. It is important to become familiar with the 'psychology' behind this kind of testing.

7   To make it more fun (!) try to spot the answer that has been put there deliberately to mislead you. In this way, you stand a better chance of not falling into the set traps.

Paper 2 – Composition

'Write **two only** of the following composition exercises. Your answers must follow exactly the instructions given. Write in pen, not pencil. You are allowed to make alterations, but make sure that your work is clear and easy to read.'

The format of the paper:

1   There are five choices, four are general titles and the fifth is based on the set books.

2   A word limit is usually given for each question.

The paper is assessed on organisation and clarity of content, accuracy of grammatical control, fluency and range of expression.

The questions are based on the following styles of writing:

– narrative (telling a story)

– descriptive narrative

– personal (how the topic affects/relates to you)

– discussion

– discursive with opinion/suggestion

– giving instructions/explanations

– a speech

– a letter

– a report or article

– (the questions based on the set books require styles of writing similar to the first five of these)

> **Hints**
> How to choose which compositions to write
> 1 Know your strengths and weaknesses and base your choice on these; for example, most students find story telling and descriptive compositions easier to write than discursive ones.
> 2 Follow your interests: generally speaking, you will write better on a subject that interests you.
> 3 Make sure you understand the question. This is especially important if you have to write your composition using some given information, e.g. a telegram, an advertisement, an article or some statements.
> 4 Watch out for question 4! This question can either seem complicated to understand (see point 3 above) or be easy to understand but tricky to do!
>   e.g. *'Tell someone how to make a ...'*
>   A clear task, but do you know the necessary vocabulary and is your brain organised enough to do this clearly and logically?
>   e.g. *'Write a letter to the authorities to complain about ...'*
>   A letter is somehow a comforting kind of question, because it has a clear format, but for this one you need to get the right 'tone' for your audience – the 'authorities'.
> For 'getting ideas' and 'organisation' look back to the Writing section, particularly Chapters 1 and 5.

General advice

1 In the Proficiency exam you do not usually have time to write your compositions in rough first and then copy them out. So make sure you correct *neatly*.
2 Paragraphing is *essential*: it shows organisation and it makes your composition much easier to read.
3 If you have big writing, consider using alternate lines or/and leaving an extra line space between one paragraph and the next.
4 In some compositions, contracted forms (I'm, haven't etc.) are acceptable, e.g. when you are writing natural, informal language as in a letter to a friend, in some speeches or in narratives. Discussion-type compositions, 'formal' letters etc. should be written using the full form.
5 It is relatively easy to write *one* composition but *two* is more than doubly difficult. You only have two hours for Paper 2, so make sure you don't put all your energy into writing the first composition. Leave enough time for the second one.

Set texts

For each exam there are three set books, which are optional, that is you can choose to read them or not. You can also choose whether to read one, two or three of the books. The books are tested in:

Paper 2 – Composition, where a question for each book is set; however, you can only write one composition based on the texts, the other composition must be a general one.

Paper 5 – Interview, where you can choose to have your interview based on one of the books. The format for the interview remains exactly the same (see page 204)

By reading a set text, you give yourself an extra choice. However, if you do not *enjoy* reading, it might be more beneficial for you to concentrate on other parts of the exam.

Hints
How to tackle a set text
1   Read the book through once for overall 'feel'/understanding/enjoyment.
2   Having finished it, write down your reactions and, if possible, support them by giving an example or reference to some part of the story/play.
3   Read the book again, this time in more detail.
4   Keep a separate notebook, or section of your file, where you can collect information, as you are reading, about:
   – the different people
   – the relationships with each other
   – the events
   – the atmosphere
   – significant scenes
   – the significance of any objects
   – any special techniques the writer uses and the effectiveness of them
5   Ask yourself some general questions:
   – what was the author 'saying' in the book and was he or she successful?
   – what does it tell us about the time and place in which it was set?
   – is the title an appropriate one and why?
   – are the first and last sentences of particular significance?

Paper 3 – Use of English

Section A – *Question 1*

'Fill each of the numbered blanks in the following passage with **one** suitable word.'

This is the instruction for the first exercise on the Use of English paper. Although it is part of the structure paper, it is more a test of reading comprehension and the question does not often require you to supply an item of pure vocabulary.

What items are being tested?

– prepositions (including verb combinations)

– verb tenses and auxiliaries

– relative pronouns (don't forget '**whose**' for things as well as people!)

– linking words (e.g. **whereas**, **since**, **however**)

– words which refer backwards or forwards (e.g. **it**, **this**)

– words used for emphasis, modification, exemplification, comparison (e.g. **at least**, **just as**, **in particular**)

– quantifiers (e.g. **some**, **little**, **few**, **all**, **no**)

– adverbs (e.g. **usually**, **hardly ever**, **well**, **rarely**)

– collocation (e.g. **at a complete loss**)

You will probably need about 15–20 minutes to answer this question.

Hints
1 Read the text once to yourself, making a 'silent noise' to fill the blanks.
2 Ask yourself what it is about; use your own language to answer if you want.
3 Go back to the beginning and start filling in the blanks.
4 If you can't find a word to put in a gap, remember your reading skills:
  – what kind of word is required (verb, preposition, etc.)?
  – look at the surroundings of the word (is there any punctuation to help? does this sentence, or part of sentence, link to what comes before or after? is the gap part of a phrase or collocation?)
5 If the sentence is rather long, find the basic subject, verb, object pattern.
6 Read the text again when you have finished, or done as much as you can.
  – check you haven't made a spelling mistake (e.g. *wich, usualy*!)
  – check for plural/singular nouns
  – check that verbs are in the right tense

Section A – *Question 2*

'Finish each of the following sentences in such a way that it means exactly the same as the sentence printed before it.'
e.g. Immediately after his arrival things went wrong.
  No sooner . . .
  No sooner had he arrived than things went wrong.
  There are usually about eight sentences for you to 'transform'.

What items are being tested? A variety of structures can be tested in this format, but the most popular include:
– negative inversion (like the example above)
– conditionals
– direct/indirect speech
– comparative/superlative
– active/passive
– past tenses with present/future meaning (e.g. **it's time we went**)
– changing form of word (e.g. from adjective to adverb)
– use of modals
– concession clause words (e.g. **However**, **No matter**, **Much as**)

Hints
1 Identify, where possible, what is being tested. It will help you to focus your attention on the specific problem.
2 Keep your answer as close as possible to the original – include all the relevant information.
3 Keep the verb tense the same as the original.
4 Use the original sentence to help you with accuracy.
  e.g. The Prime Minister was determined to remain in office.
    The Prime Minister had no . . .
    The Prime Minister had no intention of leaving the office.
  or *The Prime Minister had no intention of leaving office.*
  Which answer is correct?
5 Get plenty of practice with this kind of question – the more you do, the more familiar you will become with the *types* of sentences that can be tested in this way.

Section A – *Question 3*

'Fill each of the blanks with a suitable word or phrase.'

e.g. Even if I had stood on a chair, . . . reach the light bulb.
*Even if I had stood on a chair, I **wouldn't have been able** to reach the light bulb.*

A wide variety of structures can be tested here. Favourites include:
– verb tenses
– **sooner/rather/prefer** . . . **than/to**
– gerund/infinitive constructions
– **there's no point, it's no use, it's not worth, it's no good**
– **it's ages since**
– **be better, had better**
– conditionals (inc. conditional words other than **if**: inversions)

> **Hints**
> 1 Make sure you understand not just the words, but sometimes the feeling behind what is written (look out for exclamation marks!).
> 2 Is the first word after the blank a preposition? If so, does your word or phrase fit with that preposition?
> 3 As with Question 2, practice is beneficial with this question.

Section A – *Question 4*

'For each of the sentences below, write a new sentence as similar as possible in meaning to the original sentence, but using the word given. The word must not be altered in any way.'

e.g. His arrival was completely unexpected.
TOOK
His arrival took us completely by surprise.

The choice of words given in this question can be almost infinite!

> **Hints**
> 1 Think about the grammatical function of the word you are asked to use.
> 2 Is the word part of a phrase or collocation that you know? e.g. NOTICE – to take notice of someone/something, to give in your notice, etc.
> 3 Good luck!

Section B

'Read the following passage, then answer the questions which follow it.'

There are approximately fourteen open–ended questions, and the last one is a short summary of some aspect of the text.

Hints
1 Read the passage through at least once before you look at the questions.
2 Decide exactly what the question is asking, and how to begin your answer, e.g.
   – 'In what way does the woman tell her husband?' *In what way* usually means *How* and could be answered *By writing him a note and leaving it* on the kitchen table.
   – 'Why does the writer . . . ?' is probably best answered *Because (s)he is trying to make the reader . . .*
   – 'What does the author mean when he says . . . ?' Answer: *He means that . . .*
   – 'What is meant by 'bottle up your feelings'?' Answer: *It means keep your feelings inside you, don't show people how you feel.*
   – 'What does the word 'it' in line 23 refer to?' Answer: *'It' refers to 'the money'*
   – 'What is it that 'does not fulfil our requirements'?' Answer: *the bed.* (This question is usually asking for the 'subject' of the verb.)
   – 'Give another phrase for 'a wildly inaccurate response'. Answer: *a completely wrong answer.* (Make sure you give alternatives for *all* the important parts of the phrase.)
3 Before writing the summary, make sure you understand *exactly* what you are being asked to summarise – it will probably be some particular part of the story, not the whole thing. Read the question carefully: if it asks for the disadvantages of something, don't write the disadvantages and the advantages – you will lose marks. (For techniques of summary writing, see the Writing section, page 95.) Keep as closely as possible to the suggested word limit. Don't copy whole sentences, or even groups of phrases – use your own words as much as possible.

You will probably need a good hour to answer Section B properly.

Paper 4 – Listening

The format of the paper:
1 There are three or four different passages to listen to on cassette and questions will follow each one. The passages are normally heard twice.
2 You will hear a voice on the cassette saying, for example, 'You are going to hear a radio programme about new books. For questions 1–6 you will have to fill in the information required in the boxes. You will hear the piece twice.' You then have approximately 15 seconds to look at the questions before you hear the passage for the first time.
3 At the end, you will be given time to transfer your answers to a special computer marksheet.

Hints

Before you hear the passage

1   Check that you can identify on the question paper which questions relate to the passage you're going to hear. Do the questions go over the page, for example?

2   Look at the question type – multiple-choice, true/false, filling in pieces of information, identifying a picture or set of pictures, re-ordering information etc. Make sure you know what you are expected to do.

First listening

3   In the ideal world the first listening should be used in order to get a good overall understanding without worrying about the questions. However, exam listening is not ideal!

4   If the questions are long and/or complicated, e.g. multiple-choice, true/false, it is probably better, as far as possible, to listen and follow the sequence of the questions. You will probably find you can answer a few, leaving the trickier ones for the second listening.

5   If the questions require you to fill in some gaps or to identify a picture from the description, then you can probably do the task at the same time as listening.

Between listenings

6   You have approximately 15 seconds before the second listening, during which time answer anything you can and also *identify the questions that are causing you problems.* Is there anything you must listen for specifically next time?

Second listening

7   Now you must complete all your answers. You have about 15 seconds at the end of the passage to check through before you go on to the second passage.

8   Make sure you've answered *all* the questions. For example, with multiple-choice or true/false, *put something, even if you have no idea of the answer.* Statistically, you have a good chance of being right!

Do's and don'ts

1   *Don't panic:* easier said than done – listening comprehension in an exam format is a stressful activity. However, work out your strategy well before the exam (following the suggestions and tips above) and establish a pattern for yourself. Plenty of practice will enable you to become familiar with it.

2   *Do read quickly:* you need to get used to skimming questions and not stopping if there's a word you don't understand.

3   *Do follow the instructions:* if you're asked to choose *one* answer, A, B, C or D, then *one* answer is what they want. Make sure you understand what is required – to tick, cross, circle, fill in etc. If you change your mind, make sure your correction is clear.

    When you hear the voice say, 'That is the end of the first part of the test. Second part.', stop working on the first part. If you are still trying to answer a question, do it immediately and then clear your brain ready for the second part. If you don't, you will be unable to follow what is about to happen.

4   *Do be prepared,* as in the Reading Comprehension section, *for the techniques and psychology behind multiple-choice questions.* One such technique is the use of a key word from the passage in one of the suggested answers – quite

possibly one of the wrong ones:

e.g. Sheila is an artist talking about her mother's attitude to her (Sheila's) profession.

Sheila: Well, we didn't have a row or anything. No, it's just that she didn't like the idea, that's all.

Inter: How did she see your career, then?

Sheila: Well, she wanted me to get some qualifications at university and then go into banking or something like that.

Inter: And she'd been to university herself?

Sheila: No, she hadn't, actually. She worked for an engineering firm after leaving school. She has tremendous general knowledge though, and I think she'd have liked to go on to higher education but . . .

Inter: So she wanted you to?

Sheila: Yes, I guess so.

Inter: So you're saying your mother didn't want you to do what she's done but she didn't want you to be an artist either? And you never felt tempted just to follow her wishes?

Sheila: No, never.

Question: Sheila's mother hoped her daughter would

      A achieve more than she had herself.

      B become a successful engineer.

      C follow the same course as she had.

      D go to the same university.

It is easy to see how wrong answers could be chosen – the words 'engineering' and 'university' are both used in the extract, and 'C' could have been chosen on a false understanding of the underlined section. 'A' is the correct answer.

Also be suspicious of 'absolutes' (like **never**, **always**) in multiple-choice or true/false answers. Very often the *correct* answer is not as 'strong'.

Paper 5 – Interview

You can take the interview – individually (12–15 minutes)

                                      – in pairs (20 minutes)

                                      – in groups of three (25–27 minutes)

The format of the paper:

1 Introduction and one or two 'social' questions.

2 Description/discussion of one or more photographs.

3 Skimming through one or more short reading passages and then discussion, relating it/them to the photograph(s)/general theme.

4 Communication activity – you are briefed on a task to perform. This may be:

    – a statement to discuss or express opinions on

    – a list of criteria which you have to prioritise, and then justify

    – diagrams, leaflets or adverts etc. to comment on

    – a role play

The three main parts of the interview (2–4 above) are linked to one theme, e.g. city life, technology.

(If you are doing the interview based on one of the set books, the format is the same – photograph(s) in some way connected to the book, short extracts from the book to comment on and relate to the story, and finally a question or statement given by the examiner to discuss.)

The interview is assessed on six scales: fluency; grammatical accuracy; pronunciation (sentences); pronunciation (individual sounds); interactive communication; vocabulary resource.

Photographs: hints

1 Don't get bogged down in detailed description of everything you can see. Apart from a brief factual description, express your personal thoughts or interpretations about where it might be, who the people are, their relationships or roles, the activity, the atmosphere, etc.
   Use language like: **appear/seem; looks; looks as if; could be/might be**, etc.

2 You may be asked to find similarities or differences between two photographs. If so, try to find interesting things to say:
   e.g. not – *They've both got people in.*
         but – *They both show people working with their hands, creating something.*

3 If you don't know/can't remember the name of an object in a photo, either avoid mentioning it or find another way of identifying it:
   e.g. *That thing (that looks like a . . .)*
         The thing you use for opening bottles with/to open bottles with.

Passages: hints

1 If you are asked: 'Where does this extract come from?' the answer is not 'Britain' but, for example, 'a magazine article on beauty hints'.

2 You may well be asked to relate a passage to a photograph; however, the connection is not always obvious so you have to search for a more 'abstract' connection.
   e.g. *This passage is about the difficulties of being a newspaper reporter and I think it relates to the first picture in some way, because that picture could very well be a scene in a newspaper office.*

Communication activity: hints

1 Keep talking (relevantly!). Back up your opinions with reasons, examples, illustrations etc.

2 If you are working in a pair or group, interact with the other(s) – ask questions, for example.

General advice

1 If you are asked something and you don't know the answer, say so.
   e.g. *I've no idea, I'm afraid. It could be . . .*

2 If you don't understand something the examiner says, say so.
   e.g. *I'm sorry, I don't quite understand. Do you mean/want me to . . . ?*
         Could you say that again please, I got lost in the middle.

3 Be aware that at Proficiency Level you should be able to extend your talking into more 'abstract' topics. The examiner will ask you questions relating to the theme which will give you the opportunity to get away from the 'concrete' – for example with the photographs, where the conversation is directed away from the specific on to the more general.

4 At the end of the interview, don't ask the examiner 'How did I do?' or 'Was that all right?' The examiner is not allowed to tell you!

Part 2
Test Papers

PAPER 1   READING COMPREHENSION   1 hour

Section A

In this section you must choose the word or phrase which best completes each sentence.

1   The process by which all applications are examined is well under . . . .
    A review   **B** way   **C** going   **D** schedule

2   . . . . hearing the news, she burst out laughing.
    A When   **B** Once   **C** By   **D** On

3   Members of the jury are chosen . . . . random from the electoral register.
    A by   **B** on   **C** in   **D** at

4   The Frankfurt- . . . . flight took off with the hijackers on board.
    A direction   **B** bound   **C** going   **D** destination

5   We could hear thunder . . . . in the distance and knew we had to hurry.
    A rattling   **B** shaking   **C** rumbling   **D** sounding

6   . . . . to popular opinion, education standards in this country are rising.
    A Contrary   **B** In contrast   **C** Comparing   **D** Compared

7   She felt much happier in the company of . . . . people.
    A same-thinking   **B** like-minded   **C** like-thinking   **D** same-minded

8   The whole evening was a disaster from start to . . . .
    A end   **B** stop   **C** finish   **D** conclusion

9   When I saw him on TV, I thought he . . . . as a warm and sensitive person.
    A came across   **B** came through   **C** came away   **D** came up

10 His statement is not . . . . with yours. In fact, there are major differences.
    A compared   **B** similar   **C** agreed   **D** consistent

11 His . . . . for work is amazing. He never seems to need or take holidays.
    A ability   **B** capacity   **C** capability   **D** possibility

12 Put your hand up . . . . you can't hear at the back.
    A provided   **B** as long as   **C** in case   **D** if

13 Her clothes were . . . . but she could not afford to buy any new ones.
    A dilapidated   **B** decrepit   **C** shabby   **D** run-down

14 Her parents no longer seem to . . . . any influence over her.
    A put   **B** have   **C** take   **D** place

15 They paid their staff a bonus at Christmas, as a goodwill . . . .
    A gesture   **B** mark   **C** sign   **D** signal

16 My job is stressful enough; I don't want to . . . . any more responsibility.
    A take over   **B** take in   **C** take up   **D** take on

17 The new rule . . . . into effect at the beginning of next month.
    A takes   **B** makes   **C** comes   **D** assumes

18 The Parliament . . . . 650 members, 620 of whom were men.
    A comprised   **B** consisted   **C** composed   **D** concerned

19 The newly-painted door was stuck so she gave the handle a sharp . . . . and it opened.
    A grab   **B** drag   **C** grip   **D** tug

20 The champion . . . . defeat when her opponent took her queen.
    A agreed   **B** said   **C** conceded   **D** relinquished

21 When assessing his progress, you must . . . . in mind that this is his first term in office.
    A take   **B** think   **C** bear   **D** consider

22 His trip abroad was cut . . . . because of his sudden illness.
    A down   **B** short   **C** back   **D** up

23 . . . . of the appalling weather, Saturday's match has been cancelled.
    A Owing   **B** Due   **C** In view   **D** Resulting

24 I don't . . . . rule give interviews, but on this occasion I will agree to it.
    A as a   **B** on the   **C** in a   **D** by the

25 Everybody should be treated equally. I don't see why they should . . . . an exception just for you.
    A make   **B** do   **C** have   **D** put

Section B

In this section you will find after each of the passages a number of questions or unfinished statements about the passage, each with four suggested answers or ways of finishing. You must choose the one which you think fits best. Give **one answer only** *to each question. Read each passage right through before choosing your answers.*

FIRST PASSAGE

Everyone who reads the traditional type of detective story, whether casually or addictively, will be familiar with the sort of objection to Agatha Christie and her kind voiced by Edmund Wilson, Bernard Levin and others, for they are only rehearsing the kind of argument heard over and over from people who do not respond to the appeal of the mystery story and are bewildered or irritated by their immunity. Most enthusiasts are somewhat at a loss as to how to counter such arguments: on the one hand, they sense how difficult it is to defend Christie and her contemporaries on their accusers' grounds; on the other, they have a vague sense that, however reasonable the grounds may sound, these accusers are somehow missing the point, and that the sort of appeal these writers have for an enormous and devoted public rests on quite different foundations.

This latter feeling is healthy and right. The attackers do miss the point, and they miss it very often because they bring to Christie all the preconceptions about what a novel should be which accumulate in the minds of those whose reading is mainly in the great eighteenth and nineteenth-century classics of fiction. What they are saying is that *as novels* these works are beneath contempt: they look for solidly realised character drawing, for psychological depth, for evocative descriptions of settings; they look, even, for some 'criticism of life', some statement about the human condition. And when inevitably they come back empty-handed from their search they come to the conclusion that life is too short to fritter away their time on such a trivial, feeble-minded means of wasting time.

But in fact they are like a man who prospects for gold in a coal field. The first thing to get clear is that by approaching Christie and her fellows as novelists and by looking for the same sort of qualities one may hope to find in novels, these critics are making a mistake which prejudices the issue right from the start. Crime writers are not trying to write *Crime and Punishment*. Agatha Christie is a teller of popular tales, and should be judged by criteria appropriate to such a genre.

It is never very sensible to act as an evangelist for the detective story: if someone says, 'I've never been able to acquire a taste for crime fiction – who do you recommend I try?' the sensible answer probably is, 'Don't bother. If you have tried and you haven't responded, then probably the response isn't in you.' But it is a pity to have become so sophisticated in one's reading that one can no longer thrill to a line like 'Mr Holmes, it was the footprint of a gigantic hound!' or even 'With a happy sigh she melted into his arms.' Because to have lost the power to make these basic responses is to have lost the elementary response to fiction as *story*.

26 According to the writer, those critics who object to Agatha Christie

    A find it difficult to defend their arguments.

    B respond positively to the appeal of her mystery stories.

    C are applying the wrong standards to her work.

    D are bewildered and irritated by her work.

27 Those who have read mainly classical fiction

    A are right and healthy in their feelings about Christie's work.

    B do not approach Christie's fiction with an open mind.

    C are contemptuous of novels with vivid descriptions.

    D criticise Agatha Christie's statements about the human condition.

28 Who comes back 'empty handed'?

    A Novelists.

    B Critics.

    C Crime writers.

    D The public.

29 How should Agatha Christie be judged?

    A As a story teller.

    B As a novelist.

    C As an evangelist.

    D As a critic.

30 Those who ask for advice about what crime fiction to read

    A have lost the capacity for basic responses.

    B should simply not try to respond to it.

    C may be unlikely to respond to it.

    D are probably not sophisticated enough to respond to it.

SECOND PASSAGE

Mr Gibbs' Preparatory School for Boys occupied a house in Sloane Street in London, 134 to be precise. Whereas other British schoolboys wore caps which fitted fairly tightly to the head, and which boasted a multiplicity of colours, with coats of arms or monograms in evidence, the boys of Mr Gibbs' wore caps curiously like the shape of that favoured by Lenin, and what is more, cherry red without any heraldic symbol. Mr Gibbs himself was a fairly burly old gentleman, who was extremely cordial, and also extremely absent-minded. He seemed to have some difficulty shaving, since, apart from his immaculate white military moustache, his jaw was often decorated with tufts of bloody cotton-wool. He also sang a great deal, as though the cherished privacy of his bathroom travelled with him. What he sang were not so much recognisable tunes, as a kind of personal parlando set to melodies very much his own, reminiscent of Schoenberg, by negligence rather than design, for he was not very musical. He imparted news in this manner, both pleasant and unpleasant, rather like the town-crier in his own little city.

I learned at Mr Gibbs' how to survive by emphasising the clumsy and comic aspects of my character, and to hide my secret ambitions for fear of challenging those better equipped by nature too openly. For instance, I was often encouraged to play in goal during football matches, partly because I was not the fastest of runners with the ball, and partly because I was large, and therefore occupied more of the goal-mouth than a slender boy, the theory being that there would be a greater chance for me to deflect the ball unwittingly simply by being hit by it.

During the summer I was introduced to the game of cricket, and felt my inherent foreignness for the first time. The ball is far too hard for my taste, a lethal projectile left over from some long-forgotten battle. (I have always imagined cricket as a game invented by roughnecks in a moment of idleness by casually throwing an unexploded bomb at one another. This game was observed by some officer with a twisted and ingenious mind who devoted his life to inventing impossible rules for it.) The genius of the British lends itself not so much to the winning of games as to their invention. An astonishing number of international games were invented by the British, who, whenever they are surpassed by other nations, coolly invent another one which they can dominate for a while by being the only ones to know the rules. Whoever thought up cricket deserves a special commendation, since here is a game so doggedly peculiar and dangerous that no foreign nations, apart from those of relatively recent independence, subjected to an English type of education, have ever adopted it.

31 Mr Gibbs sang

    A only in the privacy of his bathroom.

    B Schoenberg music.

    C totally unrecognisably.

    D compositions unique to him.

32 Most British schoolboys wore caps

    A without badges.

    B like Lenin's.

    C that were too small.

    D that were of more than one colour.

33 While at Mr Gibbs', the author

    A had an open character.

    B was ambitious.

    C was very careless.

    D didn't push himself forward.

34 In sporting terms, the author

    A was probably a very fast runner.

    B was probably rather keen on cricket.

    C was probably a good goal keeper.

    D was probably a clumsy performer.

35 The author says that cricket

    A is an especially good game for the British.

    B can only be played by the English.

    C was first played by soldiers.

    D was invented by a genius.

THIRD PASSAGE

Do you ever feel as though you spend all your time in meetings? It's a cry you hear all too often from harassed people at work. In large organisations, managers spend 22% of their time at their desks, 6% on the telephone, 3% on other activities (including time spent in the toilet), but a whopping 69% in meetings. That means that most managers spend more of their waking hours from Monday to Friday in meetings at work than with their families at home.

There is a widely-held but mistaken belief that meetings are for 'solving problems' and 'making decisions'. For a start, the number of people attending a meeting tends to be inversely proportional to their collective ability to reach conclusions and make decisions. As anyone who spends time in meetings can testify, these are the least important elements.

Instead hours are devoted to side issues, playing elaborate games with one another, and getting involved in a wide variety of red herrings. It seems, therefore, that meetings serve some purpose other than just making decisions.

All meetings have one thing in common: role-playing. The most formal role is that of chairman. He (and it is usually a he) is in a position to set the agenda, and a good chairman will keep the meeting running on time and to the point. Sadly, chairing a meeting well is an art that many chairmen lack. Sadly, because the other, informal, role-players are then able to gain the upper hand. Chief is the 'constant talker', who just loves to hear his or her voice. It is often a man whose criteria of success are determined by the percentage of total conversation he can dominate. Another key role is what Freud would have called the 'anal retentive' type. This is the 'dot the i and cross the t' type, the kind of person who bores everybody present, with the exception of fellow anal retentives.

Then there are the 'can't do' types, the people who always find reasons why something can't be done, usually based on some minor technical problem. These people are cunning, wanting to maintain the status quo. Since they have often been in the organisation for a long time, they frequently quote historical experience as a ploy to block change. A more subtle version of the 'can't do' type, the 'yes, but . . . ', has emerged recently. They have learnt about the need to sound positive, but they still can't bear to have things change.

Another whole sub-set of characters are the 'red herrings' types. These are people who love meetings and want them to continue until 5.30 p.m. or beyond. Irrelevant issues are their speciality. They are also relatively cunning, and *need* to call or attend meetings, either to avoid work, or to justify their lack of performance, or simply because they do not have enough to do. One character present in all groups is the 'silent' type. Most other members of the group project on to them lofty motives or objectives, such as, 'they are above this juvenile exercise' or 'they will only speak if they have something significant to say'. Usually the silent type is just shy, insecure or plain bored.

Because so many meetings end in confusion, and without a decision, another more communal game is played at the end of meetings, called reaching a false consensus. Since it is important for the chairman to appear successful in problem-solving and making a decision, the group reaches a false consensus. It couches its so-called decision in such a vague way that a number of interpretations are possible. Everyone is happy, having spent their time productively. The reality is that the decision is so ambiguous that it is never acted upon, or, if it is, there is continuing internecine conflict, for which another meeting is necessary, to the absolute delight of the red herring types and the regular attenders.

In the end, meetings provide the opportunity for social intercourse, to engage in battle in front of our bosses, to avoid unpleasant or unsatisfying work, to highlight our social status and identity. They are, in fact, a necessary, though not necessarily productive, psychological side-show. Perhaps it is our civilised way of moderating, if not preventing, change.

36   A large number of people at a meeting

    A   is usually efficient.

    B   is important for making decisions.

    C   means problems are solved more quickly.

    D   doesn't help with reaching conclusions.

37   Many chairmen

    A   are not good in their roles.

    B   run meetings well.

    C   keep good control of the other participants.

    D   talk a lot of the time.

38   Which role-player would be most concerned about the record of a meeting being absolutely accurate?

    A   The red-herring type.

    B   The can't do type.

    C   The anal retentive type.

    D   The yes-but type.

39   The most important purpose of meetings seems to be

    A   to give people an opportunity to make suggestions.

    B   to provide an outlet for people's emotional needs.

    C   to change things.

    D   to make decisions.

40   Which word best describes the author's view of meetings?

    A   Social.

    B   Vague.

    C   Productive.

    D   Necessary.

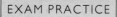

PAPER 2   COMPOSITION   2 hours

*Write **two only** of the composition exercises. Your answers must follow exactly the instructions given. Write in pen, not pencil. You are allowed to make alterations, but make sure that your work is clear and easy to read.*

1   Write a story which begins or ends as follows: 'Just at that moment he heard the clock strike twelve.' (About 350 words)

2   The individual can do nothing to stop environmental problems. It is the responsibility of governments. Discuss. (About 350 words)

3   In two separate paragraphs (up to 200 words each) describe the kind of person you think would make

     a) a good politician
     b) a good teacher
     Give your reasons in each case.

4   Use two of the following headlines and write the articles. (About 150 words each)

     Unemployment up 10%
     Prime Minister resigns
     Information on military bases leaked by civil servant
     The end for smokers?

5   Basing your answer on your reading of the prescribed text concerned, answer **one** of the following. (About 350 words)

     a) Why is the book called '. . . . . . . '?
     b) Describe the relationship between the two main characters.
     c) What events were significant in the book?

     [Please adapt these questions to suit the particular book you have read]

PAPER 3   USE OF ENGLISH   2 hours

Answer **all** *the questions.*
Your answers must be written in ink in the booklet provided in the exam.

SECTION A

1 *Fill each of the numbered blanks in the following passage with* **one** *suitable word.*

Every female child born (1) . . . . this earth within recorded history has had to absorb
(2) . . . . fact: she is a member of that half of the human (3) . . . . considered
inferior to the (4) . . . . half. From the moment of her (5) . . . . , she is marked
off from her brother and receives the stamp of sub-standard. (6) . . . . the circumstances of
her arrival into this world, a long shadow falls across her, the shadow of the second sex. However
(7) . . . . she struggles, however she succeeds, that shadow must touch some part of her and
deform. Men, (8) . . . . , are distorted by virtue of the role set for their sex,
(9) . . . . because they belong to the dominant sex they have more room (10) . . . .
manoeuvre, more ways in (11) . . . . to push their own individuality through the restrictions
of that role. Whatever their handicaps, efforts to break out of the mould are considered at
(12) . . . . respectable, if (13) . . . . necessarily rewarded. Women, on the
(14) . . . . hand, are historically penalised (15) . . . . the same efforts and their
rewards come only from remaining (and (16) . . . . looking) as much (17) . . . .
the stereotype as possible. In a very general way, the female sex has been forced away
(18) . . . . the main pull of evolution – diversity – and pushed into (19) . . . .
The loss, so far, to humanity as a (20) . . . . , is incalculable.

2 *Finish each of the following sentences in such a way that it is as similar as possible in meaning to the*
sentence printed before it.

EXAMPLE: Immediately after his arrival, things went wrong.
ANSWER: *No sooner* had he arrived than things went wrong.

(a) He didn't see the bear until he walked into the room.
Not until . . . .

(b) If we don't leave now, we won't catch the beginning of the film.
It's high time . . . .

(c) Although she is happily married, she feels bored sometimes.
Despite . . . .

(d) It is believed that the actor walked out because of the director.
The actor . . . .

(e) Without your help, I would never have succeeded.
Had ....

(f) The unemployment rate has risen slowly over the last six months.
There ....

(g) It is unusual for the weather to be so warm at this time of the year.
The weather ....

(h) There is no one I like more than you!
You ....

(i) Even if she earned a lot of money, she would still want more.
No matter ....

(j) 'I would recommend that you wrote to all the schools,' said my teacher.
My teacher's ....

3 *Fill each of the blanks with a suitable word or phrase.*

EXAMPLE: He doesn't mind one way or the other; it makes *no difference to* him.

(a) The new film is awful. It's .... seeing.

(b) I'm fed up with rain every day. I wish .... shine for a change.

(c) In three weeks' time the space capsule .... returned to earth.

(d) Your door has been broken for weeks. Don't you think you .... seen to?

(e) There's nothing I enjoy .... lying in the sun.

(f) As he was driving along, a dog dashed out in front of his car; fortunately he .... stop in time.

(g) John .... , otherwise he'd have replied before now.

4 *For each of the sentences below, write a new sentence* **as similar as possible in meaning to the original sentence, but using the word given.** *This word* **must not be altered in any way.**

    EXAMPLE: Not many people attended the meeting.
                turnout
    ANSWER: *There was a poor turnout for the meeting.*

(a) I forbid you to go out tonight.
    question

    ....

(b) It was almost impossible for me to hear a word she said.
    hardly

    ....

(c) There is no similarity between your problem and mine.
    bears

    ....

(d) After he lost his job, the only way he could support his family was by stealing.
    resorted

    ....

(e) He told us we were not obliged to buy any of his products.
    obligation

    ....

(f)   The leaflet explains how you will be affected by the new tax.
    applies

    ....

(g) Everyone was happy with the proposals.
    opposition

    ....

(h) You have to take into account the number of latecomers.
    provision

    ....

SECTION B

5 *Read the following passage, then answer the questions which follow it.*

I had been afraid of Russia ever since I could remember. When I was a boy its mass dominated the map which covered the classroom wall; it was tinted a wan green, I recall, and was distorted by Mercator's projection so that its tundras suffocated half the world. Where other nations – Japan, Brazil, India – clamoured with imagined scents and colours, Russia gave out only silence, and was somehow incomplete. I grew up in its shadow, just as my parents had grown up in the shadow of Germany.

Journeys rarely begin where we think they do. Mine, perhaps, started in that classroom, where the green-tinted mystery hypnotised me during maths lessons. Already questions rose in the child's mind: why did this country seem stranger, less explicit, than others? Why was it untranslated into any precise human expression? The questions were half-formed, of course, but the fear was already there.

Even now I was unsure what drew me into this country I feared. I belonged to a generation too young to romanticise about Soviet Communism. Yet nothing in the intervening years had dispelled my childhood estrangement and ignorance. My mind was filled with confused pictures: paradox, cliché. 'Russia,' wrote the Marquis de Custine in 1839, 'is a country where everyone is part of a conspiracy to mystify the foreigner.' Propaganda still hangs like a ground-mist over the already complicated truth. Newspapers, until you know how to read them, are organs of disinformation. The arts are conservative or silent. Even in novels, which so often paint the ordinary nature of things, the visionaries and drunks who inhabit the pages of nineteenth-century fiction have shrivelled to the poor wooden heroes of modern socialist realism. It is as if a great lamp had been turned down.

As for me, I was entering the country too impatiently to be well equipped. I spoke a hesitant Russian, but had read very little. And I was deeply prejudiced. Nobody from the West enters the Soviet Union without prejudice. I took in with me, as naturally as the clothes I wore, a legacy of individualism profoundly different from anything east of Vistula.

But I think I wanted to know and embrace this enemy I had inherited. I felt myself, at least a little, to be on his side. Communism at once attracted and repelled me. Nothing could be more alluring to the puritan idealist whose tatters (I suppose) hung about me as I took the road to Minsk; nothing more disquieting to the solitary. All my motives, when I thought about them, filled up with ambiguity. Even my method of travel was odd. The Russians favour transient groups and delegations, which are supervised in grandiose hotels. But I was going alone, in my own car, staying at campsites, and planned to cover ten thousand miles along almost every road permitted to me (and a few which were not) between the Baltic and the Caucasus. My head was swimming in contradictory expectations.

(a) Why was the writer afraid of Russia as a boy?

....

(b) Why did Russia seem so big on the map in his classroom?

....

(c) What does 'clamoured with imagined scents and colours' mean in this context? (line 4)

....

....

(d) In what way were his questions 'half-formed'? (line 9)

....

(e) Give an alternative phrase for 'drew me into'. (line 10)

....

(f) According to the writer, what do novels often do?

....

(g) Why are the heroes described as 'wooden'? (line 17)

....

(h) What is implied about society in Russia by the phrase 'a legacy of individualism profoundly different from anything east of Vistula?' (lines 21–22)

....

....

(i) What does 'his' (line 24) refer to?

....

(j) What does 'at once' mean? (line 24)

....

....

(k) In what ways was he 'attracted and repelled' by Communism? (line 24)

....

....

....

(l) Why would the Russians find his travel arrangements strange?

....

....

(m) 'A few which were not' (line 29). Explain the phrase more fully.

....

....

(n) In a paragraph of 70–90 words, describe the author's feelings about Russia and the possible reasons for these feelings.

....

....

....

PAPER 4   LISTENING COMPREHENSION   Approx. 30 minutes

FIRST PART  R37

You will hear an interview with a man who has invented three objects. For questions 1–10 complete the text below using information from the piece you have just listened to.

The chain invention prevents (1) . . . . from catching fire.

What has the dog meat got underneath it? (2) . . . .

The dog has to (3) . . . . the meat before it can eat it.

The bowl contains (4) . . . .

            (5) . . . .

The machine has been built to (6) . . . . larks and to (7) . . . . herons.

How did the inventor feel when Newcastle Breweries bought the object? (8) . . . .

The object is going to be placed in (9) . . . .

What do you think a 'loo' is? (10) . . . .

SECOND PART 🖭 R38

You will hear a description of some ancient wedding customs.
For each of the questions 11–18 tick (✓) one box to show whether the statement is true or false.

		True	False
11	The garter ceremony took place in the 18th century.		
12	The bride would help the groomsmen take off her garter.		
13	Clergymen stopped the garter custom completely.		
14	Confetti was first thrown in the early 1900s.		
15	Rice was thrown originally; wheat came later.		
16	Throwing something is an ancient custom.		
17	The bridesmaids and groomsmen did not stand facing the couple in bed.		
18	The bridesmaids had to hit the bridegroom with the stocking.		

THIRD PART R39

You will hear an interview about mosquitoes. For questions 19 to 23 tick (✓) one of the boxes A, B, C or D to show the correct answer.

19 The mosquitoes on Chris's hand

    A cannot carry malaria.

    B will probably give him malaria.

    C will probably bite him.

    D cannot produce eggs.

A	
B	
C	
D	

20 What does Chris say about mosquito nets?

    A They are useless unless impregnated with insecticide.

    B They are most effective when impregnated with insecticide.

    C Mosquitoes cannot get through them.

    D Mosquitoes get through them easily.

A	
B	
C	
D	

21 Which repellents work best against mosquitoes?

    A The ones which do not contain Deet.

    B The ones which do not get rubbed off.

    C Those which are in the form of a cream.

    D They all work more or less equally well.

A	
B	
C	
D	

22 Anklets are effective because

    A 85% of mosquitoes come from Tanzania.

    B mosquitoes seem to prefer biting you further up the body.

    C they impregnate your ankles with Deet.

    D they result in about 85% fewer bites.

A	
B	
C	
D	

23 What does Chris think about the heated tablets?

    A Their fumes can endanger people's health.

    B Their vapour gets blown away overnight.

    C They seem to kill mosquitoes quickly.

    D They only work in small draughty rooms.

A	
B	
C	
D	

PAPER 5   INTERVIEW

<u>Aggression</u>

<u>Photographs</u>

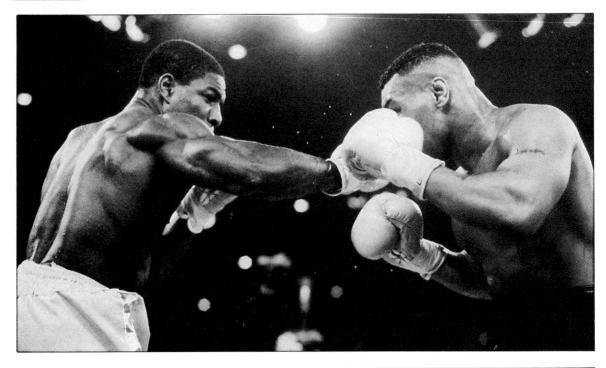

(a) Describe/compare – the people
– the setting
– the possible circumstances leading up to the situation

(b) Discuss – whether violence/aggression is something you are aware of
– the increase in violence in towns and cities today
– whether certain sports encourage aggression

Passages

1. The organisation is a worldwide movement which is independent of any government, political grouping, ideology, economic interest or religious creed. It plays a specific role within the overall spectrum of human rights work. The activities of the organisation focus strictly on prisoners:
It seeks the *release* of men, women and children, detained anywhere for their beliefs, colour, sex, ethnic origin, language or religion, provided they have not used or advocated violence. These are termed '*prisoners of conscience*'.
It advocates *fair and early trials for all political prisoners* and works on behalf of such persons detained without charge or without trial. It opposes the *death penalty* and *torture* or other cruel, inhuman or degrading treatment or punishment of *all prisoners* without reservation.

2. If I should die, think only this of me:
   That there's some corner of a foreign field
   That is for ever England. There shall be
   In that rich earth a richer dust concealed.

3. Responding to the impatient cries of his following, Meanix advanced several inches with a simultaneous heel-toe movement of both feet, rather as a fencer progresses. Then Meanix closed, butting his head hard into his man's chest and wrapping his arms around the torso. With a swift lunge forward of his right leg and a simultaneous jerk he swung the Negro against the bridge made by his thigh and toppled him. To a warm ovation the first round was over.

Tasks

1. Discussion
   What can be done to make cities safer?

   Suggested prompts: more policing
   stronger punishments for those caught
   encourage ordinary people to be more aware
   (e.g. neighbourhood schemes)
   better facilities (more street lighting, more places for young people to go other than on the streets)

2. Discussion
   Aggression is a natural human instinct. What arguments can you think of to either support or attack this statement?

Yes	No
we are animals	we shouldn't let it dominate
always fought/always will	easy excuse for violence
leads to healthy competition	unlike the animals, we have a brain
many aspects of life would be underdeveloped, e.g. sport, business	other instincts are more important

3. Ranking activity
   How would you order these crimes with regard to their seriousness? Justify your choice.

   – robbery with violence
   – physical violence against women or children
   – alcohol-induced crimes
   – arson (i.e. setting fire to a building deliberately)
   – murder of a policeman or policewoman
   – murder of a family member
   – insider trading (i.e. using privileged knowledge for one's own advantage)

Tapescripts

Listening: Chapter 1

Recording 1

Sounds of English

1 She'll be leaving here in six weeks' time.
2 Ask for the bell, please.
3 It's perfectly possible to write with a pin.
4 We passed the men on the way to town.
5 He spent many hours wondering about the city.
6 There's a paddle in the boat.
7 Some parts are more interesting when visited for a second time.
8 I've worn this medal and now I'm going to retire.
9 He was old and had knotty fingers.
10 Did you know she was training to be a belly dancer?
11 The collar is wrong, I'm afraid.
12 We need to test the product before we sell it.
13 You'll have to walk faster if you want to finish.
14 Water was escaping from the leak.
15 Three cheers please for the Kennedys.
16 The mice ran through the hall and escaped into a cupboard.
17 We phoned John last night after supper.
18 He batted the ball across the net.
19 We need new drains. The system cannot cope.
20 My ankle is much better, thank you.
21 If you touch me, I'll sink.
22 This plant stings when you get near it.
23 The ban surprised everyone.
24 Could you collect the homework for me?
25 The farmer had to rescue the ram from the river.
26 First of all, you must heat the chocolate.
27 Don't go too close to the edge.
28 The children laughed at the tin man.
29 The mountain pass was used by the refugees.
30 The cause of the war can only be clearly seen in retrospect.
31 The price was better than expected.
32 Can I take this seat, or is someone using it?
33 Our cat is almost a Persian.
34 I'm interested in real live documentaries on TV.
35 Please take a photograph off the pile of things on my desk.
36 Gosh you are lucky! It's a vast car.
37 The ban started first thing this morning.
38 Genghis Khan's last fort was dedicated to his wife.
39 Her shin hit the table as she fell from the ladder.
40 I watched him in the bath.
41 He was choking because he had just eaten some sheep's eyes.
42 The fans jeered their team at the end of the game.
43 The vine is a very fine one and should be kept.
44 Oh dear! We can't use that yolk, it's a bad one.
45 He breezed in.
46 It seems worth doing it slowly.

Recording 2

1 What's the answer to number ten? (*whisper*)
2 Good heavens, the price of bread nowadays is ridiculous. (*mutter*)
3 I ddddon't really like him. (*stammer*)
4 So I said 'What about Anne then?' but he wasn't going to tell me. (*chat*)
5 Shut up! (*yell*)
6 I'm sorry darling, I forgot it was our anniversary today. (*tease*)
7 Very kind of you – wasn't necessary, you know. (*mumble*)
8 I hope you can all hear me today. (*croak*)
9 I know the answer – it was in 1923. (*blurt out*)
10 Well, I don't know, I'll have to think about it. (*hesitate*)

Listening: Chapter 2

Recording 3

Joe and Paul went to town.
Joseph and Paula went to town.
Jonathan and Christopher went to town.
Antonia and Emmanual went to town.

Recording 4

1 It's going to be difficult to do.
2 I don't care.
3 I was working as little as possible.

4 What are you doing?
5 Where do you live?
6 I can come later.
7 The men are leaving now.
8 The film starts at nine o'clock.
9 Where does the oil come from?
10 He bought it for his sister.
11 I borrowed it from the library.
12 Her attitude disappointed her teacher.
13 Go and tell him.
14 He gave them some water.
15 It's colder than I expected.
16 What was the answer?
17 Where were you last night?

Recording 5

1 What'll you do?
2 That'd be great.
3 It'll be expensive.
4 We could've gone later.
5 He should never've said that.
6 What shall I say?
7 That'll take ages.
8 It'd've been a disaster.
9 I must've been mad.

Listening: Chapter 3

Recording 6

The liner QE2, on her way to the Norwegian fiords, was called in yesterday to help rescue forty-nine oil workers who were trapped on an oil platform in the North Sea. The platform, which had been damaged in gale-force winds, was in danger of breaking up. None of the men was injured.

Recording 7

Here is the six o'clock news.
Richard Bleasdale has been jailed for ten years in Oxford Crown Court on charges of selling arms to terrorists. He was said to have organised the illegal exportation of guns to contacts in North Africa. It is not known how the arms were smuggled out of the country and many of Bleasdale's couriers are still being questioned by the police.
Details of an accident in 1968 at the Hellabeach nuclear power station were disclosed yesterday. The accident, which was not made public at the time, was caused when a pipe burst under pressure and radio-active steam escaped into the plant. The quick action of the station supervisor prevented what could have been a major disaster. Questions about current safety standards at Hellabeach are to be raised in Parliament today.
Britain is in danger of becoming one of the least advanced nations, according to a senior scientist. The scientist went on to say that the country's education system no longer matched those in continental Europe and Japan and, unless the government was prepared to put more money into education, we could expect to see a further steady decline in the coming years.
Because of the recent heavy rain, flooding is causing problems in low-lying areas and residents are being advised to leave their homes as soon as possible.

Recording 8

A letter home from Vietnam

Dear Red
Anyone over here who walks more than fifty feet through elephant grass / should automatically get a purple heart. / Try to imagine grass possessing razor-sharp edges, eight to fifteen feet high / so thick as to cut visibility to one yard. / Then try to imagine walking through it / while all around you are men possessing the latest automatic weapons, who desperately want to kill you. / You'd be amazed at how much a man can age on one patrol. / We're all scared. / One can easily see this emotion in the eyes of each individual; / one might hide it with his mouth, while another might hide it with his actions, / but there is no way around it – we are all scared.

Listening: Chapter 4

Recording 9

1 <u>Kate</u> bought a black skirt. (*not Carol*)
2 Kate <u>bought</u> a black skirt. (*she didn't make it*)
3 Kate bought a <u>black</u> skirt. (*not blue*)
4 Kate bought a <u>black</u> <u>skirt</u>. (*not a shirt*)

Recording 10

1 I'd no idea <u>she</u> was such an impatient person.
2 No, it's double <u>3</u> 9602.
3 I painted the walls <u>white</u>.
4 The Industrial Revolution started in the <u>19th</u> century.
5 He's a very <u>kind</u> person.
6 We were <u>supposed</u> to be going to the cinema.
7 I'm not <u>flying</u> to Edinburgh.

8 They <u>might</u> 've called.
9 They might 've <u>called</u>.
10 I <u>thought</u> it was going to rain.
11 I thought it was going to <u>rain</u>.
12 I <u>hoped</u> you'd understand.
13 I hoped you'd <u>understand</u>.
14 John: We were both on time surely!
Mary: <u>You</u> were.
15 Dick: But you promised me some!
Anna: That's <u>true</u>.
16 Fred: Did you find your gloves?
Joan: My <u>umbrella</u>.

Recording 11

1 You order a steak in a restaurant. You want it rare but it comes well done.
2 'You are lucky having two holidays in two months.'
3 'Who's got my dictionary?'
4 Your friend has to choose between a red and a blue car. You know she likes red so it's no surprise when she chooses that one.
5 'So that's ten thirty outside the bus station, OK?'
6 'Paul comes from Florida, I gather.'
7 'Fancy seeing you – I thought you were away.'
8 'Fancy buying him flowers, and you know she's on a diet!'
9 'What did you two spend your money on today then?'
10 You are commenting disapprovingly about your son who watched you prepare the dinner, lay the table and do the washing up.

Listening: Chapter 5

Recording 12

1 She came to see me because . . . she was worried.
2 Many people regard the monarchy as an out-of-date institution. However . . .
3 It is important not only to look at the instructions . . .
4 They left early in order to . . .
5 At first sight, the town appears very uninteresting . . .
6 There are two reasons for the unpopularity of this government: . . .
7 A: I think most people are against the re-introduction of capital punishment.
B: Actually . . .
8 Should we go to Canada this year, . . . ?

9 I'd never have known . . .
10 We got up at four o'clock in the morning despite . . .
11 For some people it's important to study a language through the grammar, . . .
12 In theory, there is no reason why anyone in the world today should starve, . . .
13 The ground was so dry that when it did eventually rain . . .
14 The good image that ex-President Reagan had was less to do with his actual policies and . . .
15 I wanted to go to his lecture not because . . .
16 Never having lived abroad before, . . .
17 Given the choice, . . .
18 It seems to me the more successful a person is, . . .
19 She can neither see, speak nor . . .
20 He never realised how much he loved her until . . .
21 There are many things to do in this town, like . .
22 There's one thing you have to remember about picking mushrooms: . . .
23 A: They seem to have had some difficulty reading the map.
B: In other words, they . . .
24 If we don't leave now, . . .

Recording 13

Richard is an actor who has AIDS. The disease was diagnosed last November while he was away on a tour. He's been given three years to live. He talked on Woman's Hour this week to Ann Taylor, not so much about facing up to death as a young man, / but facing up to the life he has left to lead. She asked him how he reacted at the time when he first heard the diagnosis.

R: I suppose I was in a state of shock, though I wasn't aware of it at the time. I thought I was going to be able to cope absolutely magnificently, and be wonderful and all that, and erm, against the doctor's advice I actually went back to do the show that evening – it was the only evening show of the whole tour and I wanted to do it. And I felt fine, and the next day I did the first show and I felt fine, and then / the second show I didn't feel so fine and then as the day progressed I started feeling terrible.

I: Was that physically or mentally?

R: It was mentally and in fact we were – I was having dinner in a kind of hamburger restaurant with three members of the company and I just got an incredible attack of panic, and none of them really knew I was – you know, I was crying into my hamburger, and, and nobody really knew what to do and I phoned the local Samaritans who were marvellous and calmed me down and really enabled me to make the decision that I should go back to London and leave the show which I did the next day. I just, I just wanted to be home, you know with it, and try and, well, just sort out what my life was going to be like. Erm, I think I was aware right from the beginning that the problem wasn't going to be about dying,/ it was going to be about how, how was I going to live and what was I going to do with whatever the rest of my life was or is.

I: What about reactions from other people outside your immediate friends, have you been treated in any sort of hostile way?

R: Erm, mostly I've been treated with great kindness. / There are still lots of irrational fears about it. I mean, there is one actress friend of ours that – I think it took her about six months before she dared come and visit, visit the house. I mean, as it happens I wasn't home, but she didn't know that when she came.

I: How has the disease affected you physically?

R: It's the lack of energy that really gets me down the most, I mean / simple things that one had once just taken for granted like going down and doing the shopping. I can't actually guarantee now that I can get back / from doing the shopping and, and I've got a series of, of walls that I'm able to sit on to have a rest before I, sort of, sort of slowly trudge home. And sometimes I need help to climb the stairs. One never knows when the energy's going to go. I was asked, for instance, / to do a play-reading at a fringe theatre and I got there at twelve fifteen and I was really looking forward to it and at half past three my energy had gone and I was feeling really ill and the only thing I wanted to do was / go, go home and go to bed, which I, which I did. I, I was quite amused because there was one actress there who, who came up to me and she said 'Oh are you ill?' and I said 'yes' and she said, erm 'What, what, what is it – some bug?' and I said 'It's the one that kills you – it's AIDS'. And she said, 'Oh what a shame and you were giving such an interesting reading . . . ' which I thought was a very good actorish res, response.

Listening: Chapter 6

Recording 14

Another couple who've won a large amount of money, they're David and Sue from Gloucestershire. Now Dave won over a third of a million pounds back in 1985. It's changed their life radically because neither of them now work and they can live off their investments like a lot of Pools winners can. They are still in the house they owned before the Pools win as well. Dave's keeping himself busy building a, a garage and a, and a snooker room, but Sue says she's getting a little bit bored now.

S: Well, I think there was four of us that used to go out, and we used to always say, well, talk about winning the pools, and in which case we now don't talk about it, erm, but Dave always said he, he'd like to win a lot, so he'd never have to work again, erm, and I always said I didn't want a lot, erm, and I suppose that's what he's done, he just doesn't work.

I: So what have you ended up – have you ended up with the ideal amount, do you think, Dave?

D: Yes, I think so, yeh. A million pounds is a bit too much. It's unmanageable, er, really, for somebody who hasn't, who's never had any money before. It'd be frightening really. It doesn't really dawn on you for days and days, the amount, I don't think, you know, what you can do with it.

S: If you've earned money, then you feel you're entitled to it. And I felt that it, it's almost like Monopoly money, because it's just something that you weren't going to have. And I think if it had been *my* money, I would have given more away or would have perhaps done sillier things, because I felt that it wasn't money that we would have had anyway.

I: So you, you might've taken on the 'spend, spend, spend' idea?

S: Perhaps 'give, give, give'.

I: But if anybody is sitting there now, about to be given a similar amount to you, I mean, what would you warn them about?

S: I think you'll find that you will find it lonely. I think you'll be very lucky if your true friends are still glad for you after the first shock. Because I think it's human nature to be a little bit jealous. I think you lose the enjoyment of being able to boast about things. I mean you can't boast about little things you've bought, or what you're going to do, because the attitude seems to be, 'Well, you can, can't you?' Our real friends, we haven't lost, but I think it's . . . I, I would just hope that if I hadn't won it and somebody else had, I could be glad for them.

I: Do you still do the Pools?

D: No, I haven't done them since I've won, but I've been thinking about it again, actually. I thought I might have another go but er, it's just a once-in-a-lifetime thing, really, to win.

I: Would you say it has changed your life?

S: Of course it has. We've always been hard up. We've always made ends meet, and we've never borrowed from anybody, but we've had, we've had a hard married life and of course it's changed that.

I: But are you, are you three hundred and eighty thousand happier, would you say?

S: I don't think it makes you happier if you weren't happy before. I don't think you are necessarily unhappy if you're hard up, and you're not necessarily happier if you've got money. I think you feel, you feel you ought to be!

I: But is it still a dream come true?

S: Well, it's not a nightmare!

Listening: Chapter 7

Recording 15

The Maldives

The traditional Maldivian heat smacks you a warm greeting as you step from the plane, welcoming you to the islands in the Indian Ocean that make up the Maldives.

The Portuguese ruled here briefly in the seventeenth century, and the islands were a British protectorate for about seventy years before regaining sovereignty in 1965. Racially, the people are mixed, reflecting the migrations of Arabs, north and south Indians and Africans.

Tourism is a growing industry, with most visitors coming from Europe seeking sun and water sports.

In his quest for economic emancipation, the President has made education a priority and is boosting the country's commercial potential. The new airport gives swifter access for tourists and the former airbase on the southern island of Gan has been converted into an industrial and commercial complex. Aid has come from the Japanese and Saudis among others and this has helped improve communications, water supply and sanitation and boost the fishing industry, which employs about half the workforce.

But the Maldives has had its share of knocks, both climatic and man-made. A gradual rise in the sea level threatens to engulf the archipelago within the next thirty years, and drinking water is in danger of drying up. Freak tidal waves hit the airport in 1987 and left a trail of destruction on several islands.

And then, late in 1988, a force of Tamil-speaking mercenaries landed by boat, stormed the Presidential palace and tried to seize control of Male, the capital. In response to President Gayoom's call for help, India dispatched paratroopers and ships, which finally overwhelmed the ill-equipped Tamils and crushed the coup.

Today, the Maldives seem politically stable, with good economic growth and a programme of social improvement including a literacy drive. The image of the Maldives as a coral necklace of islands basking in the sun belies its iron commitment to peace, refusing foreign military facilities and backing the declaration of the Indian Ocean as a peace zone. Putting principles into action, in the late 1970s the country turned down Moscow's attractive offer to lease Gan island for one million US dollars a year – not an easy decision for a country so dependent on foreign exchange for imports.

Recording 16

Bhutan

Bhutan calls itself Druk Yul, the dragon kingdom. Snuggling on the eastern end of the Himalayan range, between India and China, it's relatively inaccessible. Government policy has been to use that inaccessibility to the country's advantage. No more than three thousand foreign tourists are admitted in one year for fear of foreign influences taking a hold on the way of life of the country's mountain people, whose language, Buddhist religion and culture are all closely related to those of the people of Tibet.

The tourists spend about 1.8 million U.S. dollars a year, providing an important contribution to the national exchequer, and the ambitious Sixth Development Plan. The plan makes the preservation and promotion of Bhutan's rich cultural heritage one of its main objectives.

An important aspect of that heritage is the monarchy. The King sits on the Dragon throne, from where he rules his people as both head of state and head of government, but he doesn't enjoy absolute power. Since the constitution was amended in 1969, the king has been accountable to the people through the National Assembly, which can vote for his dismissal. In practice, the people seem to look with favour on their Western-educated monarch.

The king has shown a remarkable ability to attract foreign aid to his remote and undeveloped land. As well as diversifying from an overwhelmingly agricultural economy by encouraging small-scale industry, the current development plan emphasises the need to raise the below twenty per cent literacy level and to bring down the high rate of infant mortality. Bhutan is highly dependent on aid from abroad, the bulk of it coming from India, which has a sort of protector status.

It's sometimes said that the only things Bhutan produces in sufficient quantities for its own needs are liquor and postage stamps, both of which it exports. But even that's an exaggeration, since the highly coloured stamps which have made the country well-known to stamp collectors are produced abroad. Their value as a collector's item, however, gives a not-inconsiderable boost to the country's economy.

Djibouti

Djibouti was the French toe-hold on the Red Sea, a vital stopping place for her ships passing through to the Indian Ocean. Although independent since 1977, the French influence lingers on. In the harbour the aircraft-carrier Clemenceau lies at anchor and sailors frequent the cafés. French aid supports the government's persistent budget deficit and a garrison of about two thousand troops guarantees Djibouti's independence against its larger neighbours, Somalia and Ethiopia. The French presence is not popular but Djibouti is in no position to sever the links, for its economy is precarious.

The country is effectively a city state, with half the population living in the capital. Most of the land is semi-arid scrub, and agriculture is almost non-existent. As a result, food has to be imported at great expense. There are no mineral resources.

The port on the Red Sea, the railway to the Ethiopian capital Addis Ababa, and associated services account for nearly half Djibouti's national income. This leaves the country at the mercy of its combative neighbours, Ethiopia and Somalia. Aside from the port and railway, Djibouti's other largest source of income comes, ironically, from the unwelcome French garrison. They spend their pay in the cafés and hotels, many of which double as brothels, attracting not only French troops but

visitors from the Gulf.

Many Djiboutians cannot find work, probably as many as forty per cent. The large well-paid expatriate community means high prices for food, so most local people live at subsistence level or below. Internal political feuding between two main groups, the Afars, who make up about half the population and the Issa clan, has caused even greater problems, with protests turning to violence.

The President has so far survived without support from the French troops – they are bound by treaty not to intervene in local politics. What happens when the elderly President dies remains to be seen.

Listening: Chapter 8

Recording 17

Jay

Jay is the only one of these women who is British. She is a self-confident, twenty-year-old woman, whose role in the drugs trade was to meet an incoming courier at Heathrow.

'I'd just had my baby and was squatting after moving out of home. I wanted nice furniture, the works. I knew I couldn't live on social security. Well, I had this cousin in America who'd been selling drugs. She told me she wanted to send someone to England. I was petrified, but the first time it was exciting. She gave me five hundred pounds. I had to pick the person up at the airport and get the tickets for the return journey. I was just the go-between.

'The second time, the excitement wears off. I got a phone call one Saturday evening. My cousin said she was desperate. She said she'd sent someone in with some stuff and she needed me to go to the airport. She persuaded me because it was family. I felt obligated, though I didn't want to do it.

'I was tense and nervous. At the airport I missed the man. I rang my cousin and she said the man I was meant to meet was elderly with a heart condition and no money. She said if I didn't meet him at an address she gave me, she would lose all her money. I went to the house. There were eight customs men. I walked right into it. They took me back to Terminal Four. After about three hours, I admitted I knew it was drugs.'

The courier had been carrying two and a half kilos of cocaine. Jay was charged with being 'knowingly concerned with a fraudulent evasion of control on drugs, class A'. She pleaded guilty and also admitted the earlier crime. 'The Judge told me: "I understand that you are the meeter and greeter. You're not the person we want. But I must make an example of you, and I am going to give you two seven-year sentences to run concurrently".'

Rosa

In a way, Rosa was lucky. Unlike the other women, she brought the drugs in by sea. She had one of the biggest loads: three kilos of cocaine strapped to her back, but her sentence was six years. She attributes this to the fact that her trial did not take place in the court at Isleworth, which is the one nearest Heathrow.

Rosa is a well-built woman of forty-three with two grown-up children. She comes from the island of Aruba, the former Dutch colony off the northern coast of Venezuela, but moved some years ago to Holland to find work. She wanted money to return to Aruba to visit her sick mother and agreed to the proposition made by a friend of her brother.

Her size was important for camouflage purposes. On the day of the trip, her brother's friend strapped the packet of drugs to her back. With two jumpers on top, the load worth five hundred thousand pounds could not be detected.

They took the boat from the Hook of Holland to Harwich. 'At Customs I started going the wrong way. The officer called me back and told me to take everything out of my case. He took two biscuit tins out of my case off to the X-ray. I thought I was all right because they were just sweet biscuits. But they came back and said it was cannabis. My brother's friend must have thrown them in for good measure. They asked me if I had any drugs inside me and I said not. Two female officers said I should tell them if I had any more drugs. I knew I had to show them. I took off my jumpers. They couldn't believe their eyes.'

Rosa was told she would get a lighter sentence if she named her co-conspirator. He got nine years.

Sandra

Sandra was well aware that the packets she stuffed into her bra contained half a kilo of cocaine. So why did this twenty-seven-year-old Jamaican infant-school teacher run the risk of the flight to England which ended in a seven-year prison sentence?

'I knew of this woman and she has been dealing in drugs for a long time. I was introduced and she asked me if I would like to take some drugs to England for her. I told her yes. I knew it was wrong. But, you know, you need the money. That's why I did this. We don't have cocaine where I come from.

We have cannabis. I thought the cocaine would be easy to conceal so they would not catch me.

'I knew what I was doing in one sense. But they don't tell you the consequences. People who come here with drugs don't know the length of the sentences they could get. Maybe if they had known, they would not have accepted the offer. The main problem is being away from your family.'

Sandra has two children in Jamaica, aged twelve and seven. Her husband is looking after them, but works shifts and some nights has to leave them alone. 'I live in a violent country and if I inform on the people who got me into this, I am certain I would go back home and never see my family. I am certain they would kill them.'

Faith

Faith, serving eight years, says she made her mistake when she accepted charity from one of the leading lights of her local Gospel Church in Nigeria.

She is quiet-spoken, with a good command of English and gently greying hair. At the age of fifty, she is one of the oldest of the drug couriers in Holloway.

'I'd heard about heroin on television, but I didn't know what it looked like. I never dreamt I would end up carrying any. There was this woman. She was a member of our church and she was rich. She gave big donations to the church so people would respect her. She knew my business was not good. And she knew I was dying to come to England to see my older children.'

Faith's son, a twenty-six year-old chemical engineer working in Britain, was planning an engagement party and Faith wanted to come. The rich woman offered to buy her ticket. Faith knew she could afford it and accepted. 'Don't tell anybody,' the rich woman said. 'I will get my reward from God.'

Two days before Faith was due to fly, the rich woman asked a favour. She had some shoes she wanted to get to a customer in London. She would lend Faith a larger suitcase and send her driver to run her to the airport. On the day of the flight, the driver took Faith to the rich woman's shop where four pairs of sandals were already packed in a nylon bag. They put the bag in the suitcase. Then the rich woman gave Faith a hundred pounds and made sure she had her son's letter of invitation ready for Gatwick immigration control.

Faith says she had no idea she was carrying a package of drugs worth nine hundred thousand pounds. As far as she was concerned, she was dealing with a respected member of her church. When Gatwick Customs officers asked if anyone had given her a parcel, she identified the sandals.

She starts crying about the two younger children she has left behind in Nigeria and the shame she has brought on herself and her family. She told the British authorities the name of the rich woman and the address of her shop, but thinks they did nothing about it. At the end of Faith's sentence she will be deported back to Nigeria. She says: 'When I get back home, then I can confront her'.

Listening: Chapter 9

Recording 18

1 The pregnant woman and the oranges
When I was expecting one of my children, I had an enormous craving for huge amounts of oranges. Ate about ten a day. Everyone used to say 'Ah, you'll have a baby with ginger hair.' And I said, 'Well, not possible, you know, I've got two daughters with fair hair, I'm not going to have a child with ginger hair now.' And I carried on eating oranges. And the biggest shock for me was that the first thing I saw was a baby's head with a mass of bright ginger hair, which was totally unexpected!

2 The magpies
I started exercising somebody's horse, er, and every morning, as I walked down the farm track, there was a single magpie sitting in a tree at the bottom of the lane and I used to think as I went past ohh – the friend I'd got who was terribly superstitious about magpies would be horrified by this, and I never thought anything about it. And at the end of the week, the horse came down on the road, as unfortunately they sometimes do, but they tend to get over their bumps and bruises. However this one took cattle gangrene which the vet said he hadn't seen in a horse in forty years and dropped dead. Which slightly made me wonder about my magpie which I had laughed at sitting at the end of the road. And the next magpie I saw was sitting on the back of a sheep, rather like one of these tick birds on the back of the rhinoceros. I looked at this and thought, 'I wonder what that is all about.' Er, and fairly soon after that discovered that a pet sheep, which friends were keeping for me who kept a sheep farm, it had taken peritonitis after lambing and died. And since then I have looked on magpies with a very wary eye

indeed. Which isn't to say that magpies aren't sometimes wonderful, because I saw five magpies the day I sold my flat in Glasgow, er, and five magpies is, is supposed to be silver – it's not quite gold, gold is six. Er, but in fact I sold the flat for something like four thousand more than I was looking for, so I was quite enchanted. So although I would have said I wasn't superstitious, I now tend to look at these things and think 'I wonder what that means', and then, when something happens, it gives you a funny little shudder and you think 'oh'.

Recording 19
Frederick Forsyth was once a BBC reporter who had a novel that did the rounds of several publishers without success. That novel was *The Day of The Jackal*, which eventually was sold and put Frederick Forsyth on the road to a fortune.

I: People like sticking labels on, on, er, people like you – *millionaire*'s one that sits quite comfortably with you, I think, doesn't it?

FF: It's realistic, yes.

I: Yes, well, what about all the other, the, the guesswork that, er, you see appearing in the press from time to time about how much you're really worth, and how much you're making out of your books, I mean the millions seem to fly around rather carelessly. I mean how, how rich are you really?

FF: Oh Lord. Erm, I suppose if it, if it was all put together, between about four and four and a half million.

I: So you have, what, what the Americans I believe call your 'drop dead' money which is, er, . . .

FF: (*laugh*) That's not a phrase I'd heard.

I: Oh yes, well no, it's er, it's, they call it that so that you must have enough money so that you can say to anybody, any employer, or anybody that upsets you, 'drop dead'.

FF: Oh, it's that, yeah.

I: Freedom, you see.

FF: Oh, I er, yes, I've never heard that phrase. I, I, er, I use another one which is to say there are really three kinds of money – there's getting by money, there's doing nicely money and there's 'up yours' money. And erm, the 'drop dead' money, or the 'up yours' money, is in fact where you can say, er, 'I don't wish to work with that person, I don't wish to undertake that contract, that commission does not interest me and I'm,

I'm not, I'm not doing it.'

I: Is that what money actually does mean to you – freedom?

FF: Yes, it's the most important of all the things that money acquires as far as I'm concerned – independence, freedom, independence, call it what you will.

I: Well, it's easy for you now, of course, because you've got money to live on while you do all this research and the writing, but did you have that period, er, of, of real struggle?

FF: Not really. The first novel I wrote was *The Day of the Jackal* and I wrote that really when I already had a job – wasn't a particularly lucrative job but it was a job, called journalism. And er, I wrote this really, I thought, as a one-off. I never, I never had in mind a dozen novels or even half a dozen – it was a one-off. When I'd done that I was then contracted to write the next one, *The Odessa File*, and I was given the wherewithal to live – fairly modestly but, er, to live at any rate while I did it. And then I was contracted to write the third one, *The Dogs of War* and then I was given even more money to live while I was doing it. So I never actually had to starve in a garret.

I: People in your position, self-employed actors, writers, where there's no guaranteed income often have this sort of deep-seated insecurity, a feeling of insecurity that drives them on and on.

FF: Well, I don't have that. Er, the, the period where, when I was impoverished actually was when, when I was a journalist, particularly when I was a freelance journalist and hadn't got two pennies to rub together, but I never minded it because I enjoyed the job so much, and I didn't have have, particularly extravagant tastes and I never actually went hungry. So I I've never really been fussed about money, it's never seemed to be something that you actually have to, er, lay down your life for, or I'd be prepared to . . .

I: Yes but many people would say that having made as much as you have, why the hell do you go on and on making more, why are you so obsessed or apparently obsessed with the idea of making more money out of books?

FF: Well, no, I'm not obsessed with it – just the contrary; in fact if I were, I would write and write and write. The reality is that I wrote, erm, the last of the original three, *The Dogs of War*, in 1973, I then waited five years to write the next one, 1978 *The Devil's Alternative*, and

another five years, 1983, to write the, the fifth. So five novels, and certainly the last two over a decade isn't, I would have thought, the action of a profit-obsessed writer.

The money that came from the novels was invested, but by professionals – anyway, you'd understand them better than I, having been a, a sort of city chap most of your life. But, er, they talk, er, about, er, debentures and stock and issue and whatever and it, it flies completely over my head. I can't understand, I don't know what they're talking about. All I know is that they present me with some figures now and again and they all look extremely healthy. But that's their professionalism, not mine. That's making money, if you like, by letting other people do it for you. I've never really made any money, except by novel writing.

I: It's extraordinary, isn't it, that, with your fascination with detail, which everybody reads your books knows all about, that you haven't ever been fascinated by the details of the business world, or the money world.

FF: No I'm not. It's a, it's a, a subject that leaves me absolutely cold. I've got no interest whatever.

I: You don't have any feeling of guilt about being enormously rich?

FF: No I don't. I think it was fairly earned. Erm, I didn't cheat or, or strip some assets or put hundreds of men out of work, or wreck a factory, or crush a rival, or drive somebody to jump off a ten-storey building. I just simply sat down and wrote books and perchance they happened to sell and perchance on the royalty basis you will make more money if you sell more books than you will make if you sell less books.

Listening: Chapter 10

Recording 20

Jim, it's arrived. Did you hear the plop as it landed? Are you going or shall I? I don't think I can bear to look. It's been such a long wait for him, and us, – what is it, about two months now since he did them? I don't think they should make people wait that long. Oh, I know you think I worry unnecessarily but it's so important these days – you can't get in anywhere if you don't get the right grades. I'm not surprised he went off to Greece on holiday instead of hanging around here, waiting. The suspense would be too much. He and Michael are going to ring us later this morning to find out, so we've got to phone Michael's mother first and find out his, too. Well, it's no good lying here any longer, one of us has got to go and I suppose it'll have to be me, as usual . . .

Jim!

Recording 21

We've been here for ages and it doesn't seem to be getting any better, does it? I wonder what they're doing down there, or up there, maybe. It doesn't usually take this long to sort out. Do you remember last week, the same thing happened two or three times but never for more than five minutes at a time. I knew we shouldn't have come today – I said there'd be problems, always are when it's this strong. At least we're not alone. The people in the next cabin look worried too. Have you got anything to drink? I need something to take my mind off things. Thanks. You know, I hate heights. I wish I'd put more layers on this morning – it's getting quite cold. No, I can't do that – you're not supposed to move about too much in these things – mind you, it's swaying about quite a bit anyway. Hold my sticks a minute, could you? I want to try and warm up my hands . . . Ahh, that's better. What was that? Did you feel something? Oh thank goodness, we're off!

Recording 22

Tick, slam, roar, creak, snap, whistle, sizzle, rattle, squeak, pop, rumble.

Speaking: Chapter 1

Recording 23

Socialising

1 How do you do?
2 Nice to meet you.
3 How nice to see you.
4 Hello, how are you?
5 How are things?
6 How are you getting on?
7 It seems ages since we last met.
8 What are you doing these days?
9 You're looking great!
10 Terrible weather for January, isn't it?
11 Have you heard about John?
12 I was sorry to hear that Mary lost her job.
13 Hope to see you again.
14 Nice to have met you.
15 I must be off.
16 Remember me to Steve.

Recording 24

Hello and goodbye

A: Hello Anna. It's ages since I've seen you. How are you doing?
B: Not so bad. Busy as usual with exams. And you?
A: Oh, still at the same place you know, but enjoying it.
B: Do you see anything of Jane these days?
A: Haven't you heard? She's gone off to live in California.
B: Oh, lucky her! I could do with a bit of Californian sunshine instead of these grey skies.
A: Yes, so could I. Incidentally, she went on her own, without Geoff.
B: Oh, I'm sorry to hear that. I thought they were very well-suited.
A: Apparently he didn't want to go. Anyway, I must be off – I've got a meeting in ten minutes.
B: Good to see you again, Sarah. Remember me to your Mum.
A: I will. 'Bye for now.

Speaking: Chapter 2

Recording 25

Diversions

A: Did I tell you about the time I nearly got arrested in China?
B: No, you didn't. Incidentally, don't forget you've got to meet Tom in five minutes.
A: No, well, as I was saying. I was in China for a three-week sales conference with . . .
B: Talking of China, we went for a Chinese meal last night. It was delicious. We had . . .
A: Jim, stop interrupting. Now, where was I? Oh yes, well I was walking along the street when I suddenly saw this man pointing at me . . .
B: Oh Mark, before I forget, did you know they were closing our street to traffic this weekend, as an experiment?
A: No I didn't know. How interesting.
B: By the way, it's ten thirty. What time did you say you wanted to leave?
A: Now!

Speaking: Chapter 3

Recording 26

A good holiday

A: What's your idea of a really good holiday?

B: Given a free choice, I'd say somewhere completely off the beaten track, like a small island in the middle of the Pacific Ocean.

A: That doesn't sound like my scene at all – far too lonely.

B: Not at all. I'm not particularly keen on crowded places. In fact, I find it quite amazing that people want to be sociable on holiday.

A: Really? I much prefer having holidays in a town where there's plenty of opportunity to do and see things.

B: I'm happy if I can just gaze at the sea. There's nothing I enjoy more than lazing on the beach with a good book, then having a leisurely lunch before going back to the beach again.

A: That doesn't appeal to me one bit. I'd probably die of boredom.

B: Fortunately we never go on holidays together, so we'll never have to fight about it!

Speaking: Chapter 4

Recording 27

The Christmas present

A: What do you think this is from your mother to both of us?

B: I've no idea. Open it.

A: Not yet. Guess what it is. Go on, have a squeeze.

B: Whatever it is, I don't imagine it's anything very exciting.

A: I bet it's something for the kitchen, a new gadget or something.

B: No, it's too soft for that. It could be something to wear.

A: Yes, you may well be right. She was criticising my shirts last time she visited us.

B: I wouldn't be surprised if she'd given each of us a shirt. She doesn't think much of my taste either.

A: I'll open it.

  B: Go on then.

  A: Da, da. Two identical shirts. You were right.

  B: She must have run out of ideas, sending us the same shirts.

Recording 28

Overheard remarks

   1 He doesn't stand a chance.
   2 We never used to be like that.
   3 I haven't done that for ages.
   4 If that's the case, there's no hope for us.
   5 You should never buy just one.
   6 I've always said you should think twice before saying 'yes'.
   7 It's not a good investment at this stage.
   8 It'll work better if you wind it up.
   9 I've never known it so bad.
  10 They were terribly unlucky.
  11 That's something I would never put up with.
  12 What rope?

Speaking: Chapter 5

Recording 29

A death in the family

A: Look at the mess. It's all my fault. I should never have left the door open.

B: Well, I did warn you before about that.

A: I know, I wish I'd listened. I'm getting more and more forgetful.

B: Well, there's no point thinking about it now. Let's clear this lot up.

A: Yes, OK. I might have known it would happen when Tim was away too.

B: What are you going to say when he gets back?

A: I'll have to tell him the truth. I blame myself entirely.

B: Mmmm. I suppose the cat *was* just following its natural instincts.

A: OK, don't rub it in! This really is the last straw after yesterday.

B: Why, what happened yesterday?

A: Are you sure you want to know?

Speaking: Chapter 6

Recording 30

The weekend

A: Have you got any plans for the weekend?

B: Yes, I've arranged to meet my sister at a Japanese restaurant in London on Saturday. How about you?

A: Well, I was supposed to be going to Brighton for a conference but it's been cancelled.

B: So you'll be at a bit of a loose end, then.

A: Yes, unfortunately.

B: I tell you what, why don't you come to London with me?

A: That'd be great. Are you sure you don't mind me coming along?

B: Course not, as long as you're happy with Japanese food.

A: I've never tried it, but it sounds interesting.

B: Well, I'm leaving Oxford at about eleven on Saturday morning, if that's all right with you.

A: That suits me fine. Thanks a lot.

Speaking: Chapter 7

Recording 31

Asking questions

1 A: Alex, do you mind if I ask you a question? /
   B: No, what?
   A: What do you think my chances are of promotion?

2 A: Mary, will you be driving through the city centre tonight? /
   B: Yes, probably.
   A: You couldn't give me a lift, could you?
   B: Sure, no problem.

3 A: John, I hope you don't mind me asking, but /
   why did you marry her?
   B: I don't know now. I'm beginning to regret it.

4 A: Do you happen to know Steve's new address? /
   B: Sorry, I haven't got it on me.

5 A: I know it's none of my business but / where were you last night?
   B: Working late at the office.

6 A: Shut the door, could you? /
   B: OK.

7 A: Would you mind if I opened the window? It's a bit stuffy in here. /
   B: No, do.

8 A: Do you mind me going out tonight? /
   B: No, of course not. You enjoy yourself.

9 A: You haven't got a pen I could borrow, have you? /
   B: Yes sure, here you are.

10 A: Why on earth did you tell him? /
   B: I didn't see any reason why not.

11 A: Do you mind not playing the violin all night? /
   B: Sorry.

12 A: Would it be all right if I left the class early tonight? /
   B: Yes, of course. Have you got a problem?

Recording 32

gasp, groan, hiccup, hum, scream, sigh, sneeze, yawn.

Speaking: Chapter 8

Recording 33

Food

A: Listen to this: 'Would you eat what you eat if you knew what the thing you ate had last eaten?'

B: Pardon? What on earth are you talking about?

A: It's this article in the paper talking about what we eat. It says many of the incidents of food poisoning in humans are a result of diseased food fed to animals.

B: Oh, I'm with you now. I agree, it's horrifying. Soon it won't be safe to eat anything.

A: Right. First it was eggs and chicken, now it's beef. Personally, I'm thinking of becoming a vegetarian.

B: That's no answer. Think of all the chemicals they spray on fruit and veg. I honestly believe we've got to be more radical than that.

A: You mean stop eating altogether!

B: No. What I'm trying to say is that we, the consumers, are going to have to think again about what we want. Mass production of food leads to lower prices, but also all these health scare problems too.

A: On the other hand, are we willing to pay more for food produced more naturally and in smaller quantities?

B: Exactly. In the end, it's a question of money.

A: It seems to me that the government will have to consider more subsidies to keep the price of food down.

B: Quite. Have an apple.

A: No thanks, not after that discussion!

Speaking: Chapter 9

Recording 34

After the interview

A: I've thrown away my chances of getting that job.

B: Not necessarily. You were in there for a long time.

A: Only because I wasn't thinking straight. I waffled all the time.

B: Come on, cheer up. I bet it wasn't *that* bad.

A: It was, you know. One of the interviewers was Professor Franks. Just my luck to get him.

B: Well, it's not the end of the world if you don't get the job.

A: I know, but it's not every day you get the opportunity to work with people you like and respect.

B: You're still in with a chance. You've got a really impressive C.V. and references.

A: Mmmm. I could kick myself for having been so nervous. Trust me to make a mess of it.

B: Everyone's nervous at interviews. I'm sure they'll take that into account.

A: I doubt it. I might just as well go home. No-one in their right mind would want to employ me on that performance.

B: You never know. I'd hang on if I were you.

A: The awful thing is, I know I would be brilliant at the job.

B: Well, don't give up then. If the worst comes to the worst, you could always plead illness and ask for another interview.

A: Now there's a thought . . .

Speaking: Chapter 10

Recording 35

Telephoning

Tel: Longmans. Good morning.

SH: Could I speak to Howard Long please?

Tel: Who's calling?

SH: Stuart Hirtenstein from Aztec Printing.

Tel: One moment please. I'll put you through.

Sec: Hello, Howard Long's office.

SH: Hello, this is Stuart Hirtenstein. Could I speak to Howard if he's free?

Sec: I'm afraid he's not in the office at the moment. Can I help?

SH: Yes. Could you ask him if he has any news of the manuscript we were expecting yesterday?

Sec: Yes, I'll do that. Shall I ask him to call you?

SH: Please. After four would be fine.

Sec: I'm sorry, what did you say your name was?

SH: Stuart Hirtenstein. That's H i r t e n s t e i n.

Sec: Thank you, and your number?

SH: Bath seven two nine six five one.

Sec: Fine. I'll get Mr Long to ring you.

Grammar: Chapter 8

Recording 36

Bullying

I: Can you tell me something about when all this began?

Jane: It began when I was about 7 years old, but it wasn't called bullying then. Erm, bullying, at that time, I think, meant something physical, really.

I: And have you any idea why it happened to you?

Jane: I think it was because I was different. When I was seven, we moved to another area and people said that I had a different accent, and so on. And then, when I went to secondary school, they said that I was very posh, and this was a non-posh area. And I wore rather old-fashioned clothes, my hair style was old-fashioned and my shoes were very old-fashioned, and people made fun of me.

I: What sort of things happened? What sort of incidents?

Jane: One of the most memorable incidents was after a PE lesson when I looked for my school uniform to change back into and I couldn't find it, and some girls in the class had hidden my school uniform. Eventually, I found it and I was very late for a maths lesson afterwards with a very strict teacher, and the teacher said "Why are you late?", of course, and I tried to explain but, er, she just grew impatient and she was very angry with me, and the rest of the class thought that this was very funny, and I didn't, of course.

I: Did you ever feel that you were able to talk to your teachers about what was happening?

Jane: No, not my teachers. At that time, teachers were not people that you confided in. Erm, I told my parents, and they were very kind and supportive, but it really didn't help because I still had to face the grim reality of going into school every day.

I: Did you find a way of facing it? Did you find that there was any action you could take?

Jane: My action was really passive action. I remember on one occasion I felt sick at school, and I went home at lunch time. When I got home, I ate lunch, so I wasn't actually sick, and it was because the, the unhappiness that I was experiencing at school made me feel sick.

I: Have you had any similar kind of experiences as those you had at school, erm, in your later life in, in . . . while you have been working?

Jane: Yes, I have had experiences of what I would call bullying at work, certainly, on more than one occasion, yes. I think that once you've been bullied, in a way you're scarred for life and perhaps you almost invite a bullying attitude from other people.

I: Can you talk about any of those experiences?

Jane: School days are far enough away for me to feel comfortable about talking about my experiences there, but work is not far enough away, work is here and now, and I really don't feel happy at all about discussing any of the incidents – no.

Examination Practice

Recording 37

Passage 1

BJ: You've got a lady's shoe with a chain hanging out, rather like you have at the back of a car sometimes, a chain·trailing on the ground.

WML: Well, it's a similar idea you see. Since the advent of nylon stockings, la, ladies have been in considerable danger from the nylon stockings rubbing together. This creates static electricity which can set fire to their underwear, and this little chain sort of earths the electricity away so they're perfectly safe.

BJ: Have you ever met a lady whose underwear caught fire?

WML: Well, no because most of them wear these.

BJ: You've got, got a bit of dog-meat there. It appears to have some feet underneath it.

WML: Well this, this is dog-meat for fat dogs, particularly labradors you see and, er, you wind it up and you put it on the floor, and it runs across the floor like that and the dog's got to chase it, thus slimming the dog down.

BJ: I should think that's good. Just let's come

over to the middle of the room because you've got your masterpiece here. Er, it's an amazing contraption, it's about ten feet high (Yes.) and at the top there's the cloud, (Yes.) then there's the sun and then there are a whole lot of wheels which go round joined by strings and at the bottom there's a big bowl of water with some fish in and what looks like a submarine with paddle wheels.

WML: Yes.

BJ: Erm, what is this all meant to do, because underneath . . .

WML: Well, I'll switch it on so you can see, right. (Right.) Well you see, it's a heron scarer and a lark lure.

BJ: A heron scarer and a lark lurer, right.

WML: Well the lark lure part of it you see is that the lark flies along and it wonders to itself 'What's that cloud and sun doing down there?' So it flies down, (Right.) also when the thing works, as you can see, mirrored balls spin round. This flashes in the sun, this also attracts the larks. So you can have this in your garden and lots of larks flying around. Also it frightens away herons which can attack your fish. Right? (Yes.) The submarine helps to frighten the herons away and the faces going up and down in the water, they're, they're very effective at frightening herons as well. But they don't frighten the larks. The other thing that's absolutely fool-proof with this is that if a heron, you know, totally ignores all these things going on, all the fish are in actual fact stuffed.

BJ: Well, there, there's water pouring out of the cloud, and going through the, the sun, coming out of its mouth, it's going down into a sort of cone-like thing . . .

WML: The cone goes down . . .

BJ: And that pulls the wheels round . . .

WML: Turns the wheels round which flash, empties at the bottom, and then the whole thing repeats itself.

BJ: And pumps the water up again. And was it ordered as it was, or did you invent it, or is it for somebody?

WML: It's for Newcastle Breweries. I designed the thing and I've now got to make it work. I never believed they'd buy the thing.

BJ: Where, where are they going to put it?

WML: In a pub.

BJ: But there are not many larks to lure in a pub,

are there?

WML: No, but it has another, another thing which it sort of affects you – have you noticed? It makes you want to go to the loo. The more often you go to the loo obviously the more beer you buy!

Recording 38

Passage 2

KW: There would be a rather rowdy ceremony prior to the eighteenth century which was the pulling off of the bride's garter in the church immediately after the taking of the vows. This was usually on the part of the, the groomsmen who would rush at the bride and, erm, compete with one another to see who could remove her garter. The garter was usually a loosely tied ribbon just below the knee and the bride would help things by raising her skirts to that, er, height to enable them to get it off quickly and easily. Now, this was a, er, obviously a rather rumbustious custom which was largely stamped out by clergymen who disliked this kind of thing happening er, within the church. Sometimes, er it would simply take place outside the church, if the, if the clergymen wouldn't er, er permit it to happen within the church.

FG: To get outside the church couples sometimes had to pay for the door to be richly unbarred. Our newly-weds only have to run the gauntlet of photographers and confetti throwers.

KW: Confetti's been thrown since the early twentieth century at least but it is the descendant of a much much older custom which goes back to the middle ages which was originally, erm, to scatter wheat over the bride and groom, sometimes within the church itself, more commonly when they came out. That has some pretty obvious overtones of fertility symbolism. Wheat gave way to rice later – rice was known in the nineteenth century and then gradually to confetti. But the throwing certainly goes back to the middle ages at least.

FG: As a groomsman or bridesmaid you could also improve your marriage chances by attending when the couple was officially put to bed.

KW: The bride was undressed and prepared for bed by her maids, er, the groom was undressed by the groomsmen and prepared for bed and then they would be formally put in bed together by the, er, bridesmaids and the groomsmen. Following that, it was customary for the maids and the groomsmen to go to the bottom of the bed, turn their back upon the couple and then throw the couple's stockings over their shoulders. The maids, erm, threw the man's stockings and the groomsmen threw the bride's stockings, and if they succeeded in hitting the couple on the head with the stockings this was regarded as being, er, a sign that whoever had succeeded in doing that would be the next one to be married.

Recording 39

Passage 3

I: Chris, you appear to be doing a very dangerous thing – you're putting your hand in a cage of mosquitoes. Now, presumably these aren't the kind that carry dangerous diseases.

Chris: Er, well it's a kind that can carry malaria, Anopheles Gambi from Africa, but these ones haven't fed on anyone, anyone with malaria and therefore they're perfectly safe.

I: But they're certainly excited by your hand being in there. (Yes.) They're hovering around like vultures.

Chris: Yes, these are female mosquitoes that are coming on me. They want blood in order to produce eggs, and they're they're quite hungry, they haven't been fed for a few days.

I: You'd better get your hand out now. You test dozens of different mosquito repellents here. Which do you find are the most effective?

Chris: Well, I would strongly recommend the use of a mosquito net when you're in bed. And, er, there's a lot of interest now in the use of nets like this which are impregnated with safe, modern insecticides, such as permethrin. In this room here, we can release mosquitoes and we sit under this net that you see hanging here, and er, sit there for, for half an hour generally. Fifty mosquitoes are released outside the net and we just see how many get in and how many bite. And if you don't treat the net with the chemical then probably about half of them get through in half an hour.

I: If you're just going on two weeks' holiday to a place which is infested by mosquitoes, what's the best thing to do then?

Chris: You can, of course, use, er, any of the common repellents that you can buy in any chemist's. They mostly have something called Deet, or Diethyltolmalide in them. There are various brands and they can, you can either have them as a stick or a, a lotion or a cream, and all of them in our experience are pretty good, but you do have to put them on again every few hours because they do get rubbed off. These are anklets, they're bands of cotton that you put round your ankles, impregnated with that compound Deet, and because mosquitoes try and bite your ankles mainly when you're sitting on a chair.

I: But don't the mosquitoes just move further up the body?

Chris: Well, not in our experience. Our tests in Tanzania say that you get about eighty-five per cent reduction in total biting.

I: Very often when you're abroad, you're offered for sale little heating devices that heat up tablets. Are those any good?

Chris: Yes, they're very good in our experience. We've done tests in this little room here and er, within half a minute of er, releasing mosquitoes you, you hear them falling to the ground – only of course providing that there's not too much draught, otherwise the vapour will get blown away. The, the tablets that you put on the heater, er, last for about ten hours so they will last overnight.

I: Are we in danger from some of the fumes that it obviously gives off?

Chris: Er, well this compound, er, in it is called bioalletherin and it has been cleared by the Health and Safety Executive as being safe for use in this way. So as far as we can tell, it is perfectly safe.

Pair work material

Reading: Chapter 4

4.4 Practice exercise: two stories of childhood (page 19)

Text B: Childhood memories
(Check you know the meaning of 'pier' before you start reading.)

With my friends I used to dawdle on half-holidays along the bent and Devon-facing sea-shore, hoping for gold watches or the skull of a sheep or a message in a bottle to be washed up with the tide; we used to wander whistling
5 through the packed streets, stale as station sandwiches, round the impressive gas-works and the slaughter-house, past by the blackened monuments and the museum that should have been in a museum. Or we scratched at a kind of cricket on the bald and cindery surface of the recreation
10 ground, or we took a tram that shook like an iron jelly down to the gaunt pier, there to clamber under the pier, hanging perilously on to its skeleton legs or to run along to the end where patient men with the sea-ward eyes of the dockside unemployed capped and mufflered, dangling
15 from their mouths pipes that had long gone out, angled over the edge for unpleasant tasting fish.

Speaking: Chapter 3

3.3 Exercise:
intensive
dialogue
practice
(page 140)

A good holiday (Version 1 – Student A)

A: What's your .... a .... good holday?

B: Given a free choice, I'd say somewhere completely off the beaten track, like a small island in the middle of the Pacific Ocean.

A: That doesn't .... like .... at ...., ... too lonely.

B: Not at all. I'm not particularly keen on crowded places. In fact, I find it quite amazing that people want to be sociable on holiday.

A: Really? I .... having holidays in a town .... there's plenty .... opportunity .... and see things.

B: I'm happy if I can just gaze at the sea. There's nothing I enjoy more than lazing on the beach with a good book. Then having a leisurely lunch before going back to the beach again.

A: That doesn't .... me .... bit. I'd probably .... of ....

B: Fortunately we never go on holiday together, so we'll never have to fight about it!

Speaking: Chapter 6

6.1 Exercise:
dialogue
(page 150)

Group A

A: ....

B: Yes, I've arranged to meet my sister at a Japanese restaurant in London on Saturday. How about you?

A: ....

B: So you'll be at a bit of a loose end, then.

A: ....

B: I tell you what, why don't you come to London with me?

A: ....

B: Course not, as long as you're happy with Japanese food.

A: ....

B: Well, I'm leaving Oxford at about 11.00 on Saturday morning, if that's all right with you.

A: ....

Speaking: Chapter 10

10.3 Exercise:
speaking
(page 163)

Caller (Student A)

1 Phone to speak to your friend. You want to arrange a game of tennis over the weekend.

2 Ring to speak to John. You can't meet him tonight as arranged.

3 Phone to make an appointment as soon as possible with the doctor. You speak to the receptionist.

4 You are a salesperson, selling insurance. Phone a local business to introduce yourself and your product.

5 Phone to book a table for dinner at Luigi's.

6 Ring Cambridge Information Centre to get some information about hotels in the medium price range in Cambridge in July.

7 Ring Southern Electric Co. (again!). You are still waiting for someone to come and repair your electric cooker.

Speaking: Chapter 3

3.3 Exercise:
intensive dialogue
practice
(page 140)

A good holiday (Version 2 – Student B)

A: What's your idea of a really good holiday?

B: .... a .... choice, I' .... somewhere completely .... the .... , like a small island in the middle of the Pacific Ocean.

A: That doesn't sound like my scene at all, far too lonely.

B: Not at .... I'm not .... on crowded places. In fact, I .... it .... amazir that people want to be .... on holiday.

A: Really? I much prefer having holidays in a town where there's plenty of opportunity to do and see things.

B: I'm happy .... I can .... gaze .... the sea. There's .... I enjoy .... lazing on the beach with a good book. Then .... a .... lunch before .... back to the beach again.

A: That doesn't appeal to me one bit. I'd probably die of boredom.

B: .... we never go on holiday ...., so we'll never have to fight about it!

Speaking: Chapter 6

6.1 Exercise:
dialogue
(page 150)

Group B

A: Have you got any plans for the weekend?

B: ....

A: Well, I was supposed to be going to Brighton for a conference, but it's been cancelled.

B: ....

A: Yes, unfortunately.

B: ....

A: That'd be great. Are you sure you don't mind me coming along?

B: ....

A: I've never tried it, but it sounds interesting.

B: ....

A: That suits me fine.

Speaking: Chapter 10

10.3 Exercise:
speaking
(page 163)

Recipient (Student B)

1 A friend will ring you about fixing up some tennis at the wekend. You'd like to, but your weekend is full.

2 Someone rings to speak to John. He's out. Take a message.

3 You work in a doctor's surgery. Someone phones to make an appointment. Agree a day and time.

4 A person selling insurance calls. You're not interested. Be firm but polite.

5 You work at Luigi's Italian restaurant.

6 You work for Cambridge Information Centre.

7 Ms/Mr Martin rings (again!) to ask why someone has not been to repair their cooker. Be ready with a good excuse!

INDEX

R = Reading section; W = Writing section; L = Listening section;
S = Speaking section; G = Grammar section; E = Examination section

tv = topic vocabulary; vc = verb combinations; i/m = idiom/metaphor
sv = special vocabulary; dv = descriptive verbs

Titles of 'texts' are shown in *italics*